W9-BBN-445

EMIL F. SMIDAK

JOSEPH BOULOGNE

called

CHEVALIER
DE SAINT-GEORGES

My book "Pater Noster" I dedicated to all the mothers, who, ever since life began on this earth, are to bear the burdens of life.

This book I dedicated to the mother of Chevalier Saint-Georges.

© Copyright 1996 by
Avenira Foundation for
Research of Human Society
Haldenstrasse 22
CH-6006 Lucerne
Switzerland
Tel. ++41 41 410 95 80
Fax ++41 41 410 95 81

ISBN Nr. 3-905112-07-8

This English edition was translated from the original French edition
by Dr. John M. Mitchell, Redhill, England

JOSEPH BOULOGNE
called
CHEVALIER DE SAINT-GEORGES

Contents

LIST OF ILLUSTRATIONS

From the prologue of Emil F. Smidak, page 7 in this book:

The Knight of Saint-George is unique in the history of European music, first for his origins and then for the diversity of his talents and the manifold facets of his achievement. His life constitutes the central theme of this book.

We shall not be so much concerned with music. Talking about music is rather like picking the petals off a rose. Music is made to be listen to, and for the appreciation of his music we refer the reader to the works he has left behind.

For this reason Avenira Foundation is producing following CD's with the compositions of Chevalier de Saint-George:

CD I: Two Orchestral Symphonies and two Violin
           Concertos
CD II: Four Symphonies Concertante

CD's with other Violin Concertos of Chevalier de Saint-George will follow.

For more information regarding CD's with music from Chevalier de Saint-George please contact
AVENIRA FOUNDATION
Haldenstrasse 22
CH-6006 Luzern - Switzerland
Tel: ++41 41 410 95 80
Fax: ++41 41 410 95 81

INTRODUCTION

This book on Joseph Boulogne Chevalier de Saint-George is the story of a remarkable man. It is also the story of the black races who suffered under the scourge of slavery and the evil trade that sustained that slavery. But, more than that, it is a story of the human spirit and its triumph over suffering. This makes the book a source of inspiration for all men and women, whatever their colour or origin. What we find here is an affirmation of our common humanity.

Joseph Boulogne Chevalier de Saint-George was the child of a French nobleman and a black slave woman. He spanned two worlds. One of the remarkable aspects of his life is that he crossed the frontier that divided those worlds.

His father took him from the French West Indian colony of his birth to live in Paris, when France was the dominant country in Europe. The young boy became a Frenchman. But he took with him in his blood and in his appearance the hallmarks of his colonial and African origin.

He showed quite extraordinary talent. He became a champion swordsman, an equestrian of grace and accomplishment, a man whose company was sought after by the noblest French families at a time when there were severe legal restrictions on the rights of black people. But the essence of this biography is Joseph Boulogne Chevalier de Saint-George's musical genius, as a violinist, conductor and composer. He crossed not only the frontier between races but also the frontier between cultures.

This in itself would make his life story fascinating to read. But there is more. Joseph Boulogne Chevalier de St-George's life not only spanned two worlds geographically and racially. It spanned two epochs, two periods of history divided by some of the most violent turmoil the world has ever seen. He lived through, and played a significant part in, the French Revolution. Men blessed, or cursed, by being born in stirring times are thrown into heroic relief by great events. So it was with Joseph Boulogne Chevalier de Saint-George. The revolutionary background and its wars cast his figure in the heroic mould. Using his skill in arms and the military training he already possessed, he became a senior officer in the French revolutionary army and even formed his own regiment of black soldiers.

His worst sufferings were connected not only with his mixed race but also with the excesses of the Revolution and the cruelties of the Terror. He was unjustly relieved of his command and imprisoned.

Although he was eventually rehabilitated he was not allowed to return to army life. Perhaps his greatest disappointment was his experience on returning to the colony of his birth. He expected to find the liberated slaves of his childhood, but he found discord and strife. He who had crossed the frontier between two worlds could not cross that hidden frontier that divides us from our past. His death was advanced by disillusion.

The book sets this remarkable man in the context of the African culture of which he would have possessed little awareness. Only recently has the knowledge of African civilisations become available to the ordinary reader and it is one of this book's distinctions that it quotes from African sources. Our knowledge takes away the surprise we might otherwise feel at the achievements of this child of Africa and child of France.

To read this book is to admire its central character, and to salute in him the great gifts he bore and realised on behalf of posterity. We owe him a debt that we can at least repay by learning about his life. The pages of the book open in invitation.

Dr. John M. Mitchell
(Author of the book International Cultural Relations.
He translated this English Edition from the original French Edition of
Joseph Boulogne Chevalier de Saint-Georges)

The Chevalier de Saint-George (engraving), Cabinet des Estampes,
Bibl. Nationale, Paris

PROLOGUE

On 26 February 1777 the Concert des Amateurs in the Hôtel de Soubise in Paris was the scene of a remarkable event, as recorded by the capital's press. The orchestra was playing a symphony by Simon Leduc, his third to be precise, in memory of the composer who had just died at the age of only 33. A large audience had gathered to pay tribute to Leduc's reputation as a man of both musical gifts and moral qualities that endeared him to all who knew him. But the audience was not to hear Simon Leduc's symphony to the end. Halfway through the adagio the conductor, moved by the sentiment of the work and remembering that his friend was no more, dropped his bow and broke into tears. The orchestra was caught up in his emotion and the performance had to be interrupted.

The conductor was not only a man of sensibility but also feared as a crack shot. And he was one of the best fencers in the Europe of those days, as masterly in his handling of the sword and foil as in that of the violin bow. Furthermore, he was an accomplished horeseman and huntsman, a champion swimmer and skater, a wonderful dancer and more besides. A contemporary poet dedicated these lines to him:

> "Dans les armes, jamais on ne vit son égal.
> Musicien charmant, compositeur, habile
> à la nage, au patin, à la chasse, à cheval,
> tout exercice enfin lui semble facile,
> et dans tous, il découvre un mode original.
> Si joindre à ces talents autant de modestie
> est le nec plus ultra de l'Hercule français,
> c'est que son esprit exempt de jalousie
> n'a trouvé de bonheur en cette courte vie
> que dans les vrais amis que son coeur s'était fait."

Or, in English translation:

> "He has no equal in the handling of arms.
> He is a charming musician and composer; expert
> at swimming, skating, hunting and riding,
> he takes easily to every kind of exercise,
> and in all of them he finds an original style.
> Like a French Hercules he manages to match
> these talents with the same degree of modesty,
> showing that his nature is free of jealousy
> and has found no happiness in this short life
> but in the true friends his heart had won."

"A French Hercules", the poet says; "a veritable Mars", said another; "the rival of Apollo", a third. There was no shortage of praise for this man who stands out as one of the most extraordinary figures of the eighteenth century and one of the greatest composers of pre-revolutionary France.

Please read what is said in *The Works of John Adams, Second President of the United States*, edited by his grandson Ch F. Adams, Vol. III, Boston, 1851, Diary from John Adams, p. 205:

"17 May 1779 - Landais gave us an account of St-George at Paris, - a mulatto man, son of a former governor of Guadeloupe, by a negro woman. St-George has a sister married to a farmer-general. He is the most accomplished man in Europe, in riding, running, shooting, fencing, dancing, music. He will hit the button, - any button on the coat or waistcoat of the greatest masters. He will hit a crown-piece in the air with a pistol-ball."

So who was this man? His name was Joseph de Bologne, called Knight of Saint George or, in the records of his time simply "the famous Monsieur de Saint-Georges". And when the reader learns what kind of man this was then the full miracle of his life is revealed: *this man was black!*

A black man in the eighteenth century was not considered a human being but an object - a "moveable object", as the laws of the time said, which could be acquired, bought, resold or destroyed at will. A moving object indeed, but not human in the full sense of possessing a human soul. In other words, a being without humanity, so much a piece of merchandise that its value was reckoned in tons.

This man was then black in colour, actually very black although he was a mulatto. He was born of a tragic encounter, an impossible alliance, between a subjugated, dehumanised, suffering Africa and a usurping, morally corrupt but materially all-powerful Europe.

His mother was an African slave and his father a white nobleman. He seemed to be marked out for an early death or the fate of humiliation and degradation common among negroes. Nothing in his beginnings suggested the flowering of a life of such richness or of a genius so comprehensive as was to fall to his lot. Yet the miracle happened: he survived in spite of all the odds against him.

The Knight of Saint George is unique in the history of European music, first for his origins and then for the diversity of his talents and the manifold facets of his achievement. His life constitutes the central theme of this book. Talking about music is rather like picking the petals off a rose. Music is made to be listened to, and for the appreciation of his music we refer the reader to the works he has left behind. What mainly interests us is his music origin. There is a primal source of music, which is hidden and about which nothing much can be said, and there is the manifest source in the individual who gives it expression. This individual is the subject of this book.

Saint-Georges wrote no memoirs. He left no account of the incredible vicissitudes of his life. Others have left their records of him, and some of the principal facts of his career are documented in the archives. But as for the basic facts of his existence, how he lived as a coloured man born of slavery in a world where negroes and slaves were considered sub-human, these sources tell us nothing. We can only try to recapture his experiences by reading between the lines, by putting ourselves in his shoes and imagining how we ourselves would have felt and behaved in the same circumstances. The reader is therefore invited to share in this search for the living human being with all his feelings, fears, joys and agonies.

Seen against the background of the years 1760-1790, the career of the Chevalier de Saint-Georges seems to belong to fairy story. It is at once fascinating and challenging. For it is almost inconceivable that a man of such refinement and with such divers gifts should emerge as if from thin air, from a continent apparently without history and an apparently barbarous race of almost animal savagery, and that this should happen at a time when this race was subjected to the most extreme cruelties known to history, the slave trade. We feel it just does not add up and that there must be part of the picture missing. Such a vast talent does not spring from nothing. It is the fruit of a long ripening process extending over generations, indeed over centuries.

We have tried to identify these generations and centuries, to trace this man's development, his roots and origins. And we have made some amazing discoveries. We have opened forgotten books buried at the bottom of our cultural memory, and read the terrible cruelty they record and the sins of its perpetrators. We have surveyed the full horror of what historians lightly call the discovery and colonisation of America and Africa. We have penetrated the underworld of slavery where abuse, dispossession, torture and death reigned supreme.

We could find nothing there to explain the miracle of Saint-Georges. All the same, there is an explanation. But to find it we have to go back further into the past of Africa itself.

The personal history of the Chevalier of Saint-Georges's mother is probably lost for ever. From the little we know, she probably came from Senegal. Her life is written in the collective drama of those African slaves who remain unrecorded and anonymous. All that remains is the history of the Great Black Mother, Africa, a history that is undeniable even if it had to wait till today to be written after a long period of oblivion. Now at last, beyond the barriers of prejudice and in the light of recent research, we can perceive an immense tract of history teeming with people, life and detail. Ancient and amazing civilisations take shape, with refined artistic expression and great sensibility, and founded upon a sense of brotherhood that seems to be the characteristic of ancient Africa.

In the Americas of today, after these centuries of oblivion, what should parents of African origin tell their children about their ancestors? They are bound to tell them of the terrible depredations suffered by Africa and the Africans. But they should also tell them about what went before, the ancient kingdoms and empires and the greatness that preceded their downfall. They will tell the story of Soundjata, the Lion of Mali, or of King Alfonso who in the sixteenth century brought Christianity to the Congo, and of whom it is said that if he had not been black he would undoubtedly have been canonised. Then there is his son Henry, who in 1513, when he was only 18, gave an address in Latin before the Pope and the assembled cardinals in Rome.

And finally they can tell their children that all the horrors of slavery in the Americas could not suppress men like Saint-Georges and Toussaint Louverture, the hero of the Haitian revolution, who by virtue of his spiritual power dared - although he was "just an old nigger", a former slave - to defy Napoleon. We shall see at the end of this book, where we tell Toussaint's story in detail, that this man was entirely devoted to the cause of raising his people from the degradation in which slavery had plunged them. He so well embodied this historic mission that posterity placed him among the ranks of legendary heroes and Lamartine said of him: "This man is a nation."

Toussaint had a rather sickly appearance and his contemporaries found him ugly, but he possessed a fervent disposition and lively intelligence. He was born in 1743 in a village near Le Cap in St-Domingue, now Haiti. According to tradition he was descended from a Guinean prince, but however that might be his status was that of a slave from the date of his birth. He first served as a stable boy. His white master singled him out and bestowed on him one of the highest functions in the slave hierarchy, that of coachman. After the age of 40 he conceived a burning desire for education. His teacher was an old negro, his godfather Pierre Baptiste. Toussaint had been baptised and remained a faithful Christian throughout his life. After learning to read and write, he is said to have become an assiduous reader of the philosophical and humanitarian works of the Abbé Raynal, and of classical authors such as Herodotus and Caesar. Then he withdrew to the mountains of the Spanish part of Haiti and became the leader of a band of fugitive slaves which he turned into an army. It was with this force that in 1794 he came to the help of revolutionary France against the threat of an English invasion of Haiti. He succeeded in repelling the invaders and, having gained control of the whole island, in 1801 promulgated a constitution precluding for all time the return of slavery and racism to this territory, even though Napoleon was preparing the reintroduction of the slave system in the French colonies. The black general was to be destroyed by Napoleon, but his work survived and led to the creation in 1803 of the first independent black state in the New World.

Like Toussaint, Saint-Georges was a symbol of rebirth. In the eighteenth century, when the black races were at their lowest ebb, these two men appeared as harbingers of their resurrection and the victory of human dignity over barbarity. Both of them seemed chosen by destiny to prove to the world the vanity of racial prejudice; what the one accomplished by his artistic genius the other achieved by his military and political genius. They were both distinguished by the moral quality of a brave and simple heart, and it is this quality that made it possible for them to bear the burden of a colour that was held in contempt.

We must then look for Saint-Georges's roots above all in Africa. The first part of the book is devoted to African history, from its origins to the turning point when the Europeans arrived and the transatlantic slave trade was operating. In the second part we shall try to elucidate St-Georges's paternal antecedents, for these obviously have an importance too. Then finally in the third part we shall retrace the life of the Chevalier de Saint-Georges, observing the historical context of which it was a part. He actually lived through one of the most intense periods of European history, that of the French Revolution, and not as a passive spectator but as an active participant. His personal history would remain unintelligible if we were to omit the events that so much affected it.

In conclusion we must emphasise that this book is not a biography in the ordinary sense and could not be. The personality of the Chevalier de Saint-Georges and the circumstances of his life raise questions and call for a documentation that exceed a purely biographical account. This book is therefore also a historical panorama, and as far as possible we have tried to use personal testimony so as to give the historical events the dimension of living experience.

                                                      Emil F. Smidak

FIRST PART - MOTHER AFRICA

In the history of European classical music, the Chevalier de Saint-Georges is undoubtedly the only composer born a slave, with an African mother shipped to the Americas in the slave trade. We must also take account of Saint-Georges's father, who was white. But if in this book we allocate so much space to the maternal African origins of the Chevalier de Saint-Georges it is for two reasons.

The first is that society has always regarded those born of mixed parentage as blacks or mulattos, and treated them accordingly. In other words, society has always given more importance to the black than to the white parent. Is there any reason to change the rating in considering someone with Saint-Georges's achievements? Should we downgrade the black parent so as to credit his white half with these achievements, and say, "It was not due to his black mother that Saint-Georges was as he was but to his white father"? This argument is gainsaid by the fact that his father also had a legitimate daughter with a white mother and that she was not distinguished by any of the brilliant qualities of her mulatto half-brother.

The miracle of Saint-Georges remains incomprehensible unless we try to understand Africa. One can of course study a composer through a musicological analysis of his works, and such an approach clearly has a value in the context of musical history. But what do we as human beings gain from analyses of this kind? How do they help us to enter into communion with the composer as a fellow human being? In a concert when we savour a fine piece of music our joy does not come only from the harmony of sounds. The musician, the being who produced this harmony, counts for something too. I believe that music is more than a certain structure of notes. In its essence it is a message, a message from one soul to another. And what we have searched for in turning towards Africa is the profound origin of Saint-Georges's message.

The second reason inducing us to lend priority to the maternal origins of the Chevalier de Saint-Georges is the predominant role played by women in society, a much more important role than is generally admitted. I have said this already in my book "PATER NOSTER", dedicated to all the mothers who since life began have borne the burden of existence on this earth. For centuries woman has fought for her emancipation, but even now we have failed to grasp the true importance of her struggle. Not until this question has found its solution, by the combined efforts of men and women, will life on our planet be really capable of positive change.

Saint-Georges's mother, as we have said in the Prologue, remains practically unknown to us, and her personal story is lost in the anonymous drama of African slaves. Well, in the following pages we shall trace the main lines of the history of Africa as the Great Black Mother. What is Africa? Most people when they think of Africa have a picture in their minds of savannahs, tropical forests, giraffes, rhinoceroses , elephants with big ears, gorillas and so forth. That is certainly Africa too. But Africa is above all the millions of human beings, the millions of mothers who have lived on this continent since the dawn of time. It is of these men and women that we must think in reading the following pages.

Our first realisation when we think of Africa's past is that in the annals of mankind there is scarcely anything to equal the extreme exploitation of man by man that was suffered by the Africans. The exploitation of the black man lasted for centuries, on a continental and then an intercontinental scale. It assumed the dimensions of physical, cultural and moral genocide, so that Friedrich Hegel was capable of writing in 1830: "Africa is not a historical continent; it offers no evolution and the events that were produced in it, that is in its northern part, belong to the world of Asia and Europe..."[1] The famous German philosopher is not the only one, nor the last, to express ignorance and contempt concerning Africa. A hundred years after him, in 1928, an English historian stated: "One can say that until David Livingstone Africa itself had no history. From time immemorial the majority of its inhabitants lived in profound barbarism. That was, it seems, the decree of nature. Their lives were stationary, without progressing or regressing."[2]

More recently still, some historians have actually denied African man his place in human history, for instance, the French scholar who wrote in 1957: "These peoples have given nothing to mankind, and there must be something in them that has prevented this. They have produced nothing, neither Euclid, nor Aristotle, nor Galileo, nor Lavoisier, nor Pasteur. No Homer has sung their epics."[3] Others again held Africa to be in debt for everything to the world outside: "One may well ask what Africa cultivated

[1] F. Hegel, *Vorlesungen über die Philosophie der Geschichte*, 1830.

[2] Coupland, *History of East Africa*, 1928.

[3] P. Gaxotte in *La Revue de Paris*, October 1957.

and ate before Christopher Columbus..." and "Nigeria is what it is because it was once, so to say, a mediterranean colony."[4]

How should we reply to all this in the light of the historical facts that open-minded research has now put at our disposal? It may suffice to reply that not only in Africa but in all countries they colonised the Europeans have, in different degrees and ways, denied the validity of the cultural expression of subjugated peoples and elevated their own culture as the only standard. In fact, every human community yields its own special aptitudes which find their expression in their particular context and which pour forth that variety that is the real treasure of mankind. Africa's contribution to human culture has therefore always existed, but it is only today, when a large part of the African heritage has been destroyed, that the West is at last prepared to recognise it.

The greater part of the African past is buried under the earth, and the excavations of the last few decades have yielded only a small portion of its secrets. Competent historians insist that, in spite of the spectacular results already achieved, African historiography has to remain provisional, for new discoveries could supervene at any moment to change it or even revolutionise it.

But whatever modifications might come, one fact remains - the incredible bleeding of Africa by colonialism. How would Africa have developed if the whites had never come - if, instead of enriching the whites, the raw materials, natural products and the toil of the Africans had been applied to their own benefit? That is a question to be asked today when there is so much talk of aid given in the form of credits by rich countries to the Third World and of the enormous indebtedness resulting. For is this not a reversal of the truth? Are not we, the rich countries, profoundly indebted towards the Third World? - for the millions of human beings transported as slaves, for the raw materials which for centuries we took without paying - in other words stole? And would not the recognition of this state of affairs in the end bring genuine aid, not just to the Third World but to the rich countries themselves?

---

[4] E.F. Gauthier, *L'Afrique Noire Occidentale*, Paris, Ed. Larose, 1963, p. 90 and p. 127.

Finally, I would invite the reader to look at the illustration by Robert Hooper of South Africa in my book "Pater Noster" and to read the artist's comment: "The soldier is a symbol for all the rich countries making war on the weak and poorer countries, which are represented in the boy liberated by death." This testimony does not date from past centuries but from today. Has our modern society, so proud of its scientific progress, technical inventions and unparalleled methods of organisation, no other solution to offer the Third World and Africa than that of the old slave-traders?

I. FROM THE FIRST MAN TO THE PHARAOHS

Darwin said: "It is more likely that our first parents lived in Africa than anywhere else." And Father Teilhard de Chardin stated that, "It is at the heart of Africa that man must have made his appearance"[5] Even if this opinion is not shared by all scholars, it is only on the African continent that one finds all the links of the evolutionary chain leading to modern man, and witnesses the accomplished fact of man's birth over the 20 million years of human evolution.

A prehistory 3000 years in advance of Europe
During the long prehistoric period, the human population of Africa was the most numerous and the most inventive. That is why it is said that Africa constitutes the greatest prehistoric museum, because of its wealth of tools of all kinds, easily superior to other parts of the globe in quality and diversity, and of its works of art with all their originality. The rock carvings and polychrome paintings in all the mountainous regions of Africa outnumber those in all the rest of the world, and in their expressiveness and the elegance of their lines constitute one of the greatest treasures of human culture.
The development of agriculture and stock-breeding, that revolution of the Neolithic age, began at about the same time in Africa as in Asia, 7,000 years before Christ, that is to say about 3,000 years earlier than in Europe. Pottery, so important for domestic economy, made its first appearance on the high plateaux of East Africa, and spread to the Sahara and Egypt, and thence to the East. It was one of the most important technical contributions that Africa made to Neolithic civilisation.

Neolithic Sahara - cradle of the Bantus
One of the main centres of civilisation in Africa at this time was the region that now constitutes the Sahara. This vast region was then blessed with a much wetter climate and possessed an abundance of water-courses and lakes. Its inhabitants tended to live in villages and engaged in fishing, hunting and the keeping of livestock. They cultivated wheat, barley and

---

[5] P.Teilhard de Chardin, *L'Apparition de l'homme*, Seuil, 1956, p. 279

textile plants such as flax, while further south, in the upper Niger valley, the main crops were sorghum, millet, rice and sesame. According to recent studies, these plants were cultivated in the Niger valley six to five thousand years B.C. and were an independent achievement of the Africans of the savannahs.

The populations of the Neolithic Sahara, who created the admirable Saharan rock carvings and paintings, were mainly black. In fact, the Sahara seems to have been the initial homeland of the Bantu peoples; when it began to turn to desert 4,000 B.C. they emigrated in increasing waves in two directions - eastwards towards the valley of the Nile, and southwards into the vast continent's interior, where they were to encounter the short hunting race of the Khoï-San.

The Nok civilisation

In their slow advance southwards, which after several centuries was to bring them to the southern tip of Africa, the Bantu produced civilisations of which one of the first was that of Nok in the North of what is now Nigeria. This lasted for 1,400 years, from 900 B.C. to 500 A.D. From 600 B.C. it had mastered bronze and from 300 B.C. iron. The mastery of iron was an important factor in the expansion of the Bantu peoples. As smiths, farmers and hunters these tall black people left many memorials in African legend, where they are described as prodigious giants who could block water-courses with one hand and call to one another from town to town. They often erected fortified townships, of which traces may be seen notably in Chad and Cameroon. Numerous traces of an ancient iron civilisation may still be found on the Katanga plateau and south of Lake Tanganyika (first century A.D.) and in Zimbabwe (third century).

Metal technology brought with it a new social organisation, complex and hierarchical, which was distinguished by the predominant role of the smith as the guardian of the secrets of minerals and fire. The first African chiefs were the smith-kings, and it was from their clan-based fiefs that the great kingdoms and then empires were to develop.

Egypt

The first great African kingdoms were those of the Nile valley, foremost among which was the one the Greeks later called Egypt. The Egyptians called themselves by the name "Khem", which means black. This seems natural enough when one looks at the images of Egyptian art, especially the effigies of the pharaohs, among whom some have decidedly African features, such as Zeser, Khephren, Toutmosis, Tutankhamen and Rameses III. From the time of its birth in the fourth millenium B.C. in the central and southern parts of the Nile valley, which were inhabited by black tribes and replenished by Bantu immigration from the Sahara, Egyptian civilisation had essentially African roots. The inventions of civilisation came from the South, which was traditionally black, and kingship itself seems to have come from the Badarians. Badari saw the first use of copper (about 5,000 B.C.); and the Amratians were black metal-smiths, who built dams, canals and temples for ancestor worship along the course of the Nile right down to the Delta.

For the Egyptians of the Dynastic period, the South was the abode of the gods, and the pharaohs' bodies were usually transported to this mother earth for burial in the holy cities of the Thebaïd. According to Diodoros of Sicily, a Greek historian writing in the first century B.C., the Nubians were considered the ancestors of the Egyptians, and it was from them that Egypt derived most of its laws. And from them too the Egyptians learned to honour their kings as divine incarnations. The same author, writing about hellenised Egypt, also said: "The blacks are thought to have invented all the cults whereby the gods are worshipped. That is why the prayers and sacrifices offered by black people are considered the most acceptable to the immortals."[6] And even up to the high Hellenistic period the priest who burned incense before the king of Egypt was a black man, clothed in a lion-skin.

The Kingdom of Kush

In the North the African character of the civilisation of the Nile valley was modified by contact with other peoples, but it remained intact in the South, in Nubia. Here there evolved from the second millenium B.C. a great black kingdom, that of Kush, also known as Meroe, the "Ethiopia" of ancient authors. This kingdom had a flourishing and original civilisation for over a thousand years. Hieroglyphics borrowed from the Egyptians were used, but the language itself was different and has yet to be deciphered.

---

[6] Diodoros of Sicily, Book III, quoted by J. Ki-Zerbo in *Histoire de l'Afrique noire*, D'hier à demain, Paris, Editions Hatier, 1978, p. 78.

The kings were chosen by oracle, at least in the early period, and as in the rest of Africa the queen-mother played an important part. Kush possessed a well-organised army and its archers were feared as far abroad as Asia. At the end of the 8th century B.C. the king Shabaka conquered all the Nile valley and founded the 25th Egyptian dynasty, known as the "Ethiopian". When Egypt became an Assyrian province during the 7th century B.C., and was defeated successively by the Persians, the Greeks and the Romans, Nubia remained independent and developed differently from Egypt.

From the 7th century B.C. this country, already renowned in ancient times for its gold, developed an iron industry so successful that modern historians have called Nubia "the Birmingham of antiquity". The Kingdom of Kush played an important part in the diffusion of metal techniques in the African continent, and its fame survives in many accounts, especially so far as West Africa is concerned. In the final centuries B.C. Nubia was governed by powerful queens, the Candaces. One of the most famous was Amanirenas "with the glance and stature of a man", who negotiated with the Romans in 23 B.C. and about whom Pliny and Strabo both left historical accounts.

II. CHRISTIAN KINGDOMS, PRIEST-KINGS, AND ISLAM
(1st - 12th Centuries)

African Christians in the very beginning

The Christian message spread through Africa from the first century, starting from Egypt. The anchorites of the Egyptian desert were to play an important part in early Christian spirituality. One of them, Pakum, a peasant in the ancient Thebaïd in the central part of Egypt, founded numerous monasteries there, and it was his disciples who bore the torch into Nubia in the fourth century. About the same time, Christianity was introduced further south, in modern Ethiopia, by monks from Syria. Thus several great African Christian kingdoms were born in the east of the continent; their civilisation and spirituality developed independently and spread right into the heart of the Sahara.

Igbo-Ikwu

Numerous kingdoms developed in other parts of Africa at this time, and modern archaeological research continually reveals new finds. The best known are those from the Niger and Senegal valleys in West Africa, as well as those from Monomotapa, (Zimbabwe) in southern Africa. Their common feature is the figure of the priest-king, derived from the tradition of the smith-king. The most interesting evidence of this figure is found at Igbo-Ikwu in Nigeria in the form of bronze artefacts of great beauty and technical refinement. Igbo-Ikwu must have been the religious capital of a large and powerful kingdom, which was to reach its height in the ninth century and which had its cultural roots in the Nok civilisation mentioned in the previous chapter.

The new era - Mohammed the Prophet

In the seventh century A.D. the great event in the world at large as well as in Africa was the advent and expansion of Islam. In 642 Arab armies conquered Egypt and then pushed on to Nubia. But the black archers of the upper Nile valley, already famous in antiquity, resisted victoriously. In 745 Nubia dispatched its army to Cairo to protest against the imprisonment of the Patriarch of Alexandria, and would not withdraw until the Moslems had set free this Christian religious leader. Thereafter Nubia was to be the

I was really impressed by this prayer "Pater Noster". Before I went into my work, I repeated this prayer again and again until at last I learnt it by heart. I am a religious man, a devout Muslim and as a matter of fact this document touched me deeply. I based my work on the last two sentences. In the illustration I tried to portray the joyless life in our times. Youth indulging in immorality, drugs and other wrongdoings. Personally I view the project of "Pater Noster" as a great cultural work worth your efforts. I am eager to see the fruits of "Pater Noster" and the different ideas and perceptions of your multi-national contributors.

Adbirahman Haji Adan Karie 1980 Somalia / Afrika

PATER NOSTER

Adowgayo

Eebbow awooddaa...
Amranaanta magacaa...
Ifka aanu joogniyo...
Aakhiro idaylkood...
Aduu noogu roonoow,
Noogu yeel mid aayo leh.
Noogu deeg arsaaq badan...
Naga dhaaf denbigayaga...
Xumaantoo dhan naga dhawr.

From E. F. Smidak's book "Pater Noster"

recognised protector of the patriarchate of Alexandria, and its Christian civilisation attained its greatest expansion in the tenth century.

If Nubia remained Christian by force of arms, Ethiopia did so by virtue of its wisdom. Its first relations with Islam were in fact very cordial. One tradition recounts that of all the kings to whom Mohammed proclaimed his mission only Ethiopia's responded positively, and in 615 some of the prophet's companions, persecuted by the Mecca aristocracy, found asylum in Ethiopia where Mohammed himself had sent them. The prophet is also credited with the saying that the Ethiopians "had been allotted nine tenths of mankind's courage". It is interesting to note that one of Mohammed's closest disciples was black - Bilal by name. He was the slave of a Mecca aristocrat, was bought back by the prophet and became Islam's first muezzin. Although Ethiopia subsequently opposed Islamic expansion this was done so courteously that the followers of the prophet agreed not to conduct a holy war against the Ethiopians in spite of their refusing Islam.

Elsewhere however it took only a few decades for the Mohammedan armies to subjugate the whole of northern Africa up to the Atlantic coast. But they did not penetrate very far into the interior of the continent, and south of the Sahara conversion to Islam was achieved less by war than by slow commercial infiltration, and by the ministrations of Arab scholars attached to royal courts, where the conversion of one king usually precipitated that of others.

A magnificent Kingdom - Ghana

That is what happened with the King of Ghana, who reigned over a vast kingdom embracing the Senegal valley and the upper Niger valley. The Kingdom of Ghana was founded before 700 and was rich and well organised. The Arab historian Yacoubi wrote in 872: "The King of Ghana is a great king. In his territory there are gold mines and he has a large number of kingdoms under his sway."[1] Indeed, because of his gold, which funded trans-Saharan commerce, the King of Ghana was regarded as the richest ruler in the world. His court shone in splendour, and his palace was decorated with sculptures and paintings and even had glazed windows.

---

[1] Quoted in J. Ki-Zerbo, *Histoire de l'Afrique noire,* D'hier à demain, Paris, Editions Hatier, 1978, p. 108.

His capital was called Koumbi Saleh by Arab authors, and covered a considerable area. It consisted of two cities. of which the one was Moslem, inhabited by merchants, legal advisers and distinguished scholars attached to the royal court. The other was the royal city proper, surrounded by a large sacred wood where there were snakes associated with the cult of the king, and where the royal tombs were situated. In 1040 the King of Ghana converted to Islam.

Nothing remains of the magnificence of Koumbi Saleh. Even today, no trace has ever been found of the ancient residence of the Ghanaian kings. There is simply an empty landscape, dunes with tufts of grass, and thorny shrubs. But for the Arabic texts it might be concluded that the tales in the African oral tradition were pure legend. The kingdom of Ghana reached its culmination during the ninth and tenth centuries, at the same time as the Carolingian empire in Europe. In spite of its army of 200,000 men, containing 40,000 archers and an impressive cavalry, the kingdom was defeated and sacked in 1076 by the Almoravides from Morocco. The drying-up of the wells did the rest and the population, following their age-old flight before an encroaching desert, emigrated towards the mountains of Guinea in the south and the central region of the Niger valley. Here new kingdoms were to flourish in due course.

III. THE GREAT CENTURIES

The glory of Mali - The marvels of Benin - The mysteries of Zimbabwe

The four centuries from the 13th to the 16th constitute one of the great periods of African history, marked by a general upsurge throughout the continent. In western and central Africa, in the forested region of Guinea and south of the Zambesi - to confine ourselves to these alone - great empires and original cultures flourished. Influential personalities appeared, men such as Sundjata, Mansa Moussa and Matope, and also splendid cities, like Timbuktu, Gao, Benin and the Great Zimbabwe.

Sundjata, the Lion of Mali

The empire that was incontestably the most brilliant of this period is that of Mali, and Mali is synonymous with Sundjata; the poet-musicians of this country still today sing of him as the "lion of Mali". He makes his entry in history at the beginning of the 13th century, when the Kingdom of Mali was at war with Soumaoro, the terrible king of the Sosso. According to tradition, the royal prince Sundjata was born lame. He hobbled around on all fours during his childhood and adolescence. But one day, infuriated by Soumaoro's harassments, he decided to stand up and go to the help of his people. He called for an iron rod so that he could stand erect, but this bent under his weight. A second and then a third rod met the same fate. Finally someone exclaimed, "Give him his father's sceptre to hold on to!" And by supporting himself on the royal insignia the young prince at last stood upright.

The decisive battle between Sundjata and Soumaoro took place about 1234 at Kirina, on the left bank of the Niger. What was at stake was nothing less than hegemony over the Sudan, that is to say the part of Africa between the Sahara and the tropical forests of Guinea. The account of this battle from oral tradition is just as miraculous as that of Sundjata's accession. At the approach of the enemy army Sundjata asked, "What is that cloud to the East?" He was told, "That is Soumaoro's army". For his part, the latter asked his followers, "What is that mountain towards the West?" He was told, "That is Sundjata's army." What can a cloud avail against a mountain? The answer is easy to guess - the lion of Mali carried the day, and he thereafter established Mali's suzerainty over all the neighbouring kingdoms.[1] In the interior of the country he launched a new social organisation and gave much attention to farming. He is credited with the introduction of cotton growing and peanuts, also stock-breeding. He died in 1255 from an accidental shot, it is said, during a festival.

A vast empire of peace

His successors extended the bounds of empire still further, so that by the 14th century it embraced practically the whole of the western Sudan, from the Atlantic coast in the West to the Aïr in the East, and from the Guinean forests in the South to the salt marshes of Teghazza in the North. In this immense territory, with its very diverse inhabitants, it was possible for people and ideas to circulate freely; as Ibn Battuta, the great Arab geographer who lived there for a long time, noted, complete safety reigned throughout the country. It was not even necessary to travel in caravan because "the traveller has no more to fear from bandits, thieves or abductors than the man sitting at home".

This prosperity and peace encouraged exploration, and one of Sundjata's successors, his nephew Abubakr II, achieved fame by his attempt to explore the Atlantic. He dispatched 200 ships to the West to find the end of the sea because he refused to believe that it had no end. Only one came back. On hearing the sailors' account, the emperor had 2,000 ships fitted out and himself took command of this armada to sail to America. He was never seen again.

Mansa Moussa - the great negro Sultan of Mali

But the most illustrious of Sundjata's successors was Mansa Moussa. During his reign (1312-1332), the Mali empire became famous throughout the Islamic world, from Spain to Iran. In the Arab chronicles of the time it is stated that "there are four sultans in the world, without counting the supreme Sultan of Constantinople, namely the Sultan of Baghdad, the

---

[1] These two stories from oral tradition are found in J.Ki-Zerbo, *Histoire de l'Afrique noire,* D'hier à demain, Paris, Editions Hatier, 1978, pp. 132-133.

Sultan of Cairo, the Sultan of Bournou and the Sultan of Mali".[2] And there is a European map of 1339 which shows a route crossing the Atlas and the desert and ending at the "rex Melli", the King of Mali, lord of fabulous golden treasure. At that time there were some 400 towns in Mali, of which the most important like Niani, Djenné, Timbuktu and Gao each numbered some 100,000 inhabitants. Commerce flourished and the magnificent monarch, revered like a god, kept a brilliant court. His mighty power however did not by any means exclude criticism, and the emperor accepted warnings about the abuse of his power. The ballad-makers who recounted the good deeds of his ancestors could tell him with impunity: "You must do good too and be remembered for it."

The flowering of Afro-Islamic culture
One of the celebrated events of Mansa Moussa's reign was the great pilgrimage to Mecca that he undertook in 1324, accompanied, it was said, by a retinue of 60,000. After crossing the desert he arrived at Cairo as if from the fabled city of El Dorado. His servants were carrying almost two tons of gold, and this was shared out in alms with an unprecedented generosity. Arab authors describe Mansa Moussa as a man of great dignity with refined manners. Among other gifts, he presented the Sultan of Cairo with an essay on etiquette, which he had written himself in Arabic. He was a fervent Moslem, and after returning from Mecca he stepped up the Islamisation of his empire: he built many mosques, including the great mosque of Timbuktu, and also Koranic schools. He laid the foundations of Afro-Islamic art, literature and science, and these were to attain the height of their florescence in the 15th and 16th centuries in the great cities of the Niger valley, especially Timbuktu and Djenné. During this period, the Mali empire was governed by a different dynasty, that of the Askias who originally came from Senegal and established their capital at Gao; the empire now attained its greatest expansion and incorporated parts of central Sudan.

---

[2] Kati Mahmoud *Tarikh el-Fettach (1520)*, trans. into French Houdas et Delafosse, Paris, P. Leroux, 1913. 2nd edition, Maisonneuve, 1964, quoted in Ki-Zerbo, *op.cit.*, p. 136.

Timbuktu - city without equal

At that time Timbuktu numbered some 180 Koranic schools, numerous libraries and several institutions of higher education. "In those days," according to *Tarikh el-Fettach*, Timbuktu had no equal among African towns for the quality of its institutions, political liberty, purity of morals, safety of persons and possessions, mildness and compassion towards the poor and strangers, and respect shown to students and men of science."[3] Leo Africanus, the Moslem geoprapher from Spain, wrote in 1550: "There are in Timbuktu many judges, doctors and priests and they are all well paid by the king, who highly honours men of letters."[4]

The Saharan kingdom of Kanem-Bornou

To the East, the Mali empire adjoined another great African empire, that of Kanem-Bornou, whose influence extended from Tripolitania (in the North of modern Libya) to Cameroon, and on its eastern wing from Mali to the Nile valley, with its centre in the region of Lake Chad. It was a decentralised feudal monarchy. Its sultan, called the Maï, was worshipped as a god and never spoke to his subjects except through a curtain. His cult showed striking parallels to that of the sacred monarchy of the ancient Kush civilisation in Nubia, and some archaeological remains point to relations with Christian Nubia during the first centuries of our era. Kanem-Bornou went over to Islam at the end of the 11th century and became a mighty warrior kingdom with an army of 180,000 men, of whom 100,000 were horsemen, some of them wearing armour.

Benin - the artistic kingdom

In the lower course of the Niger valley, in the region of modern Nigeria's tropical forests, these centuries of greatness witnessed the florescence of several black kingdoms with a high cultural standard. The most famous of these, on account of its artistic marvels, was Benin. It reached its height in the 15th century, under Ewaree the Great, who was both a respected physician and a great conqueror. After ascending the throne around 1440, he conquered vast territories and, according to what tradition tells us,

---

[3] Kati Mahmoud , *op.cit.*, p. 313.

[4] Léon l'African, *Description de l'Afrique*, ed. Epaulard, 2 vol., Paris, Maisonneuve, 1956, pp. 468-69.

travelled to the distant Congo. He constructed fine wide roads through his country and embellished the town of Benin. In its urban attractions the City of Benin surpassed most of the great European cities of the time. It was laid out on a rectangular plan and surrounded by a huge wall with nine gates and a deep moat. Four wide, tree-lined avenues led to the principal gates. The houses had interior courtyards so constructed that the rain water could run away. The houses were also provided with verandahs and with altars in their doorways devoted to their ancestors and gods.

A royal palace as big as the city of Grenoble
One of the first French travellers along the coast of Africa, the Sieur de la Croix, wrote this description in the 16th century of the royal palace of Benin: "It consists of buildings stretching over an area as large as the city of Grenoble and is enclosed by city walls. There are dwellings for ministers and beautiful galleries, most of which are as large as the Amsterdam merchants' exchange. These galleries are supported by wooden columns in copper casing on which the kings' victories are engraved..." And the same author says of the people of Benin: "These people yield nothing to the Dutch so far as cleanliness is concerned. They wash and scour their houses so thoroughly that they shine like the glass of a mirror. Their laws are good and their police well organised; they live on good terms with one another and show a thousand kindnesses to foreigners who come to work there."[5]
Benin remained unaffected by the large-scale religious conversions that took place, first to Christianity and then to Islam. Like all the other kingdoms of the forested zone along the Gulf of Guinea, Benin stayed profoundly loyal to its traditional religion and the culture flowing from it. Its art was derived from that of the sacred kingdoms of Ife (11th century) and Igbo Ikwu (9th century), and further back from the ancient Nok civilisation. Among its justly celebrated masterpieces the terracottas and bronzes have pride of place and they are recognised today as a precious part of mankind's cultural heritage.

---

[5] Sieur de la Croix, *Relation universelle de l'Afrique ancienne et moderne,* Lyon, 1688, quoted in Ki-Zerbo, *op.cit.,* p. 163.

The Ouaklimi of Monomotapa - a spiritual people

Between the Zambesi and the Limpopo, in the south of the African continent, the Bantu kingdom of Monomotapa also attained its zenith in the 15th and 16th centuries. The name Monomotapa, by which it was known to the first European visitors in the 16th century, comes from that of its king Muntoba Shuru Chamutapa, who reigned at the beginning of the 15th century. But the Arab historian Al-Masoudi, who visited the country in the 10th century, calls it "the kingdom of the Ouaklimi" and says of its inhabitants that they enjoyed spiritual discussion and worshipped numerous gods, all of which were however subject to the supreme god, called Mwari.[6] A great elliptical temple in the royal capital, Great-Zimbabwe, was dedicated to this deity. As demonstrated by recent archaeological research, the huge fortified acropolis of the Great-Zimbabwe, south of Harare, dates back to the 7th century. This raised city was built entirely of granite and successively enlarged over a period of a thousand years. It was said to have required no less labour than the pyramids of Egypt, and certainly constitutes one of the most fascinating sites of ancient Africa. About 150 similar structures, but smaller in size, have been found in other parts of this ancient kingdom.

A powerful king, master of fire

Monomotapa produced large quantities of gold and other metals such as copper, iron and tin. These metals and ivory were the basis of its trade with India and China, whence it imported silk, pearls, porcelain and glassware. The mineral extraction was done underground and travellers' accounts speak of extensive mines and tunnels where hordes of labourers toiled. Duarte Barbosa, a Portuguese traveller who visited Monomotapa in the 16th century says of its ruler: "He is a very great prince who has suzerainty over many other kings... Every year he sends to all parts of his kingdom, and to his vassals, a large number of notable persons whose task is to extinguish every single fire and to concede new fire only to those who request it and give evidence of obedience and submission. Those who

---

[6] Al-Masoudi, *Le Livre des Prairies d'Or et des Mines de Pierres Précieuses,* French trans. C. Barbier de Meynard et Pavet de Courteille, Paris, Impr. Impériale, 1861-1877, quoted by Ki-Zerbo. *op. cit.,* p. 188.

The motive for my painting is "Thy Kingdom come".
When I was a kid, my grandmother used to pronounce "Thy Kingdom come" every day, and she tells me
that she always wished God would give a better life to the family, a life devoid of hunger, poverty, sickness
and premature death.
The carving, as you see it in the painting form, represents a young girl raising her arms towards the skies,
praying God that His Kingdom may come.

Joe Ekow Newton   1980 Ghana / Afrika

PATER NOSTER

Akan

Awurade Mpaebo
Yen agya a wowo soro,
Wo din ho ntew,
W'ahenne mmra,
Dee wope nye asase so,
Sedee eye osoro.
Ma yen daa aduane nne,
Na fa yen aka firi yen,
Sedee yede firi won a wode yen aka.
Na mfa yɛn nko sohwe mu.
Na wo na ahennie ne ahooden ne
Animuonyam ye wo dea daa.
Amen.

From E. F. Smidak's book "Pater Noster"

refuse are considered rebels, and the king immediately dispatches as many troops as may be necessary for their destruction."[7]

This fire that was borne to the four corners of the empire originated from the royal fire which was kept permanently burning in the king's palace at Great-Zimbabwe. It symbolised the life and power of the sovereign. When he died it was put out and not relit until his successor was enthroned. As in the first African kingdoms, the King of Monomotapa was thus the master of fire and its secrets.

[7] Duarte Barbosa, pub. 1550 in *Navigationi e Viaggi* by Ramusio in Italy. Quoted in Robert Cornevin, *Histoire de l'Afrique,* vol. II, l'Afrique précoloniale, 2nd edition, Paris, Payot, 1976, p. 73.

IV. THE TURNING-POINT

The major turning-point in the history of Africa, the arrest of her development and the gradual decline into under-development, coincides with the start of Europe's enormous expansion. Europe had, for the last seven centuries, been isolated by Islam in the western peninsula of the land mass joining her to Asia. At that time Islam was the dominant power, not only in the political and economic domain but also in respect of knowledge - philosophical, scientific and technical - and from the 15th century Europe cherished an intense desire to break out of her isolation and rejoin the mainstream of history. She therefore undertook an exploration of the wider world. Marco Polo's accounts (13th-14th centuries), although they were long held in doubt, brought new revelations. And since land routes through Moslem territory were still closed to Europe, it was at sea that she attempted the breakthrough.

Europe launches forth

The first nation to fit out its caravels to sail towards new horizons was Portugal. The stated objective of the undertaking was to find "Christians and spices", as Vasco da Gama put it. Henry the Navigator, the Portguese infante, conceived the plan of taking Islam from the rear by joining the Christian forces of Europe with those of the legendary Prester John, or the Emperor of Ethiopia, so as to break the Moslem monopoly on oriental trade and discover a direct route to India that bypassed Africa. In 1450 the Portuguese reached the mouth of the River Senegal, in 1482 that of the Congo, in 1487 they were at the Cape, and in 1498 they landed in India. During this time, Christopher Columbus set sail for the West, in the name of the King of Spain, trying to find India by that route. In 1492 he arrived in America, or more precisely on the islands of the Caribbean, which he baptised the West Indies. He struck the South American continent six years later, in 1498.

Amazing acquisitions

These voyages of exploration were far from just being scientific discoveries, for they took on the character of conquests, with proprietary claims to the territories they embraced. From 1481 John II of Portugal, with the Pope's consent, assumed the title "Ruler of Guinea" and Vasco da Gama was called "Viceroy of India" in 1504. To avoid any conflict of interest, Pope Alexander VI in 1493 drew a longitudinal line on the map of the world 100 leagues from the Azores and declared all the territory to the West of this line the property of Spain and everything to the East the property of Portugal. He thus handed over the Americas to the kings of Spain and Africa to the kings of Portugal. This high-handed act may well seem risible in view of the means available - a handful of men in a few ships set against vast areas of the globe and all the peoples who were being appropriated. But to all appearances the course of history was destined to evolve along these lines, with greed and gunpowder propelling Europe towards mastery of the world.

Africans to replace the Indians

Like the American "Indians", most of whom were to be rapidly exterminated, the Africans went through severe suffering as a result of this world conquest. The Europeans needed a labour force adapted to tropical conditions in order to work the gold mines and plantations in the Americas, so they began to import black slaves from Africa, and they were to develop this trade to the extent that it drained Africa of her vitality. The forced labour of the Africans helped Europe to appropriate the riches of the Americas, but in addition she was able to employ unscrupulous mercantilism, the policy of divide and rule, and superior weaponry to grasp the riches of Africa itself, thus relegating the peoples of Africa to a sub-human level and to the status of under-development.

The tragedy of the Congo

One of the most moving and at the same time most revolting chapters in the history of relations bewteen Europe and Africa is to be seen in the Congo.

It was in the 1480s that Portuguese seafarers first made contact with the kingdom of the Congo. Following their accounts, the German African specialist, Leo Frobenius (1873-1938) wrote in his *History of African Civilisation*: "In the kingdom of the Congo the first Portuguese explorers discovered crowds of people dressed in silk and velvet, great principalities well-organised down to the last detail, powerful rulers and rich industries -

all civilised to the very backbone!"[1] This kingdom was indeed rich. Its wealth derived mainly from iron-working, the salt trade and highly developed handicrafts. The Congolese weavers were pastmasters in their art and could work vegetable fibres into fabrics that looked like silk and satin velvet. Apart from their clothing, what also impressed European visitors was Congolese music, which they considered refined and delightful. "They play the lute with mastery", wrote the Italian humanist Pigafetta in his book on the Congo.[2]

The king, whose title was Mani-Kongo, resided at Mbanza-Kongo, some 300 kilometres south of the present Kinshasa. He was a divine king according to the ancient African tradition, and was the kingdom's supreme judge. He ruled without recourse to writing, sending his orders by relay-runners. He commanded a powerful army, and his archers had the reputation of being able to shoot 28 arrows before the first of them hit the target. In 1491 the king Nzinga Nkouyou was converted to Christianity. He was baptised on 4 May of that year by a missionary, who was a member of a Portuguese delegation that was received at Mbanza Kongo with full honours. The king invited his people to follow his example, and the multitudes came demanding to be baptised too. One of the neophytes was the king's son, baptised Alfonso. It was he who made the Congo a Christian kingdom after succeeding to the throne in 1506.

It is said that if Alfonso had been white he would undoubtedly have been canonised. Indeed, all accounts agree in attributing to him characteristics worthy of a saint; his faith and his theological knowledge are described as extraordinary. For instance, it says in a letter which the Apostolic Vicar Ruy de Aguiar wrote to the King of Portugal in 1516: "I feel that he is not a man but an angel whom the Lord has sent here to this kingdom to convert it ... He knows the prophets and the gospel of our Lord Jesus Christ, together with the lives of the saints and the affairs of our Holy Mother Church, better than we do ourselves ... He does nothing but study. Often he falls asleep over his books, and often he forgets to eat and drink for talking of our Lord. He is so absorbed by the scriptures that he forgets his

---

[1] L. Frobenius, *Histoire de la Civilisation Africaine*, Paris, Gallimard, 1952.

[2] Filippo Pigafetta, *Description du Royaume du Congo et des contrées environnantes,* pub. in Rome 1591, French trans. W. Bal, Léopoldville, Univ. Lovanium, Paris, 1963.

Beniho Whyte 1981 Nigeria / Afrika

PATER NOSTER
Kalabari Dialect

Wamịna Ḍaḅo, soḅio simearị Ḅo,
Fiafia sime I erẹ prị.
I ama ḅo.
I minini-ye tomikiri ḅu miẹ soḅio anị sime bara.
Ene mangba ḅe fị-ye mingba ḅe ye kẹ wa prị;
Wamịnẹ a-si weriso wa prị,
si ke wa miẹ apụ wa weriso in priari ḅra;
wa kẹ mu tolumafama ḅio su ma,
kuma si ḅu wa ḍua ḅrọma,
Ama mẹ I nye erẹsị,
krọ mẹ sọ,
ebube mẹ sọ,
ḅesakị ḅesakị.
Amẹn.

From E. F. Smidak's book "Pater Noster"

own needs."[3] Alfonso taught the people himself. He had churches and schools built in every province, even girls' schools and one of his own sisters taught in them.

His son Enrique was also a remarkable person. In 1513, at the age of 18, after studying at Lisbon, he made a speech in Latin before Pope Leo X and the assembled cardinals at Rome. In 1518 he was appointed Apostolic Vicar for the Congo, and this required a special dispensation from the Pope because of his youth. He returned to the Congo in 1521, but he was prevented from exercising his office properly by delicate health and by the obstacles thrown up by the European clergy, who were jealous and suspicious. He died around 1530, at the age of only 35.

Although the Portuguese had at first shown the Congolese much respect, treating them on a equal footing and granting Alfonso all the honours due to a sovereign, they soon changed their attitude and became increasingly insistent on total alignment with the court at Lisbon. Alfonso had at first, out of sympathy for his co-religionists, willingly yielded to certain demands, but there came a point when he could no longer accept them. The 22 letters in the Portuguese archives from the Mani-Kongo to the King of Portugal are revealing in this respect. Alfonso takes particular exception to the moral lapses of the clergy sent by Lisbon and to the conduct of certain Portuguese residing in the Congo, which was hardly consistent with the Christian faith. These complaints multiplied as the Portuguese took more and more liberties in the country and disregarded the Congolese king's authority in their hunt for slaves. Some Congolese students on their way to pursue their studies at Lisbon were arrested at Sao Tomé, the centre of the Portuguese traffic in negroes that was then expanding in the Gulf of Guinea, and treated as no more than slaves. Emissaries from the Mani-Kongo were abused as "heathen dogs" by the Governor of Sao Tomé, and the precious gifts they were bearing to the King of Spain were confiscated. When Alfonso requested that the island of Sao Tomé be subjected to his authority so as to safeguard freedom of communications, Portugal responded by elevating Sao Tomé to the status of diocesan centre controlling the whole coast and therefore the Congo too. Thereafter the slave traders made free of the Congo, stirring the

---

[3] Cornevin,R., *Histoire de l'Afrique*, vol. 2, L'Afrique précoloniale, 2nd edition, Paris, Payot, 1976, p. 47.

Mani-Kongo's vassals to revolt and even shipping off princes and the king's relatives. In his exasperation Alfonso wrote to Lisbon: "We wish to receive nothing from your kingdom but priests and teachers for our schools, and in merchandise nothing but wine and flour for the holy sacrament."[4]

In 1540 Alfonso formally prohibited all export of slaves from his kingdom. The response of the Portuguese slavers was to try to assassinate him during mass on Easter day. Miraculously he was spared, and he died in 1543 at the age of more than 80. During his 37 year-long reign the slave trade advanced as rapidly as conversion to Christianity. And this was only the beginning, for in the succeeding centuries, like tens of millions of other Africans, more than three million Congolese were to be snatched from their homeland, sold like cattle and shipped off to the Americas to suffer martyrdom.

The effect of firearms - the fall of the Mali empire

In other parts of Africa too there were undeniable signs that the turning-point had come. At the end of the 16th century, the Mali empire collapsed before the first cannon shots sounding under a Sudanese sky. The Mali army was defeated by an expeditionary force made up of assorted allies - Moroccans and Europeans, among whom were many Spaniards but also English, who provided the artillery contingent.

The Malians were easily superior in numbers to this enemy that had appeared from beyond the desert but they did not possess firearms. Realising the hopelessness of the struggle, the elite warriors of the Mali army refused to flee but threw their shields on the ground and squatted on them. They were shot down in this position, and the foreign soldiers, in search of booty, removed the golden bracelets they were wearing. This memorable battle took place not far from Gao in 1591, and it was followed by many others that were equally overwhelming. By 1595 the destruction of Mali was completed. The Moroccan sultan Al Mansour had all the empire's gold confiscated and forced the Malians to make regular deliveries of slaves.

From this time on, the Afro-Islamic civilisation of the Sudan went on declining, and the final calamity came through a series of natural disasters, with droughts alternating with floods to devastate the Upper Niger during

---

[4] Quoted by Ki-Zerbo, *op. cit.*, pp. 204-205.

The prayer "Our Father" I can define with one word: HUNGER. The man who suffers from hunger and is to ask himself continually if his wife and children will have something to eat the following day, has not much time to think about religion, because a man who suffers from hunger is not a free man. For this reason, religion seems to be far off the simple mortal's mind. When you speak about hunger, you speak of that you know from hearsay, hunger you have been told of. If, in your life, you had suffered only once from hunger - from great hunger - without any hope for even a very simple meal, then you would understand me and the reason why I chose from the prayer "Our Father" that part saying "Give us this day our daily bread".

Ismaila Diabagate   1980 Mali / Afrika

PATER NOSTER

Bambara

I togo ka sènouya
i ka fanga ka sé
I sago bikè ardyana na tyoko min
a ka kè dyen na tén
I k'an tlé-o-tlé balo di an ma bi
Iko minou bagara an ma
an bè hakèto ou yé tyoko min
I ka hakèto an yé tén
I kana to an ka do konosouli la
Nka I k'an kissi kodyougou ma. Amina.

From E. F. Smidak's book "Pater Noster"

(en bambara) * an ka bɛ dahirimɛ nɔgɔ y'an yɛ *

D. ISMAEL . 26.9.80. GAMAKO

the 17th and 18th centuries. The famine from 1738 to 1756 was the most terrible of all afflictions and wiped out 30 to 50 per cent of the entire population of the Sudan.

The end of a chapter for Africa

The chronicle *Tarikh-es-Soudan* (1655) gives this description of the consequences of the fall of the Mali empire: "Everything was changed thereafter. Safety gave way to danger, wealth to poverty; insecurity, calamities and violence took over from peace and calm. On all sides, people destroyed one another. In every quarter, robbery was rife and the fighting spared neither the goods nor the way of life of the inhabitants. Disorder became the norm and spread everywhere with great intensity."[5]
After this nothing could ever be the same again. A chapter had closed for Africa. Her sons, her riches and hopes were to be swallowed up in the holds of slave ships, while Europeans established themselves as absolute masters to exploit what was left of Africa.

---

[5] Abderhamane Es-Saadi, *Tarikh-es-Soudan*, pub. in 1655, trans. O. Houdas, 2nd edition, Paris, Maisonneuve, 1913, quoted by Ki-Zerbo, *op. cit.*, p. 201.

V. THE SLAVE TRADE

The crimes perpetrated under Nazism against Jews, gypsies and others are generally known and abundantly documented, but those against the black man under the system of European mercantilism are far less familiar. Perhaps the explanation for this is that the holocaust on the slave ships and the oversea plantations is less obvious because it extended over several centuries and over a vast geographical area - even though it far exceeded the number of victims in the concentration camps. Perhaps another explanation comes from the fact that the victims' cries were not so much calls for vengeance as outbursts of song, which were so moving that they overcame the oppressor. The Blues, and the musical styles that derived from them, won over the white tyrant's world and overcame the memory of the conditions of which they were the resounding echo.

Traditional systems of slavery
The practice of slavery had existed since early antiquity among numerous peoples, for instance in Egypt, Babylon, China, Greece and the Roman empire, but in very different forms. In Africa it had been relatively mild. Slaves had certain fundamental rights such as marriage, property and inheritance. Their children were often brought up with those of the master in his house. In the Congo, for example, the father of a family called a slave by the name "nvana" (child); the ambiguity was such that a slave-owner wishing to refer to one of his own offspring used the expression "child of the womb". Slaves were rather like adopted children and duly benefited from their master's responsibility towards them. No doubt the position was not always as favourable as this, but under the traditional African system slaves were not regarded simply as goods and chattels. In spite of their status they remained human beings.

The slave system created by European mercantilism
The slavery practised by Europeans in Africa and in America from the 16th century was a totally different phenomenon. It robbed the slave of his humanity and made him a piece of merchandise in the most literal sense of the term - a "movable object". It is horrifying that the 18th century, the very century of enlightenment and the triumph of reason, witnessed the

I wish to indicate by this picture my profound sentiment of pity for all peoples who suffered or are suffering from hunger, wars, the destruction of the environment, bad government, and all the evils that reign in this world today. (Prayer written in Wollof)

Ebou M Sallah 1980 Gambia / Afrika

PATER NOSTER
Wollof

Suñu bai bi chi asaman,
na sa tur sela,
na sa ngur dika,
lo buga na am chi suf
neke chi asaman.
Mei ñu tey suñu dundu gir gu neka
te bal ñu suñu ton,
naka le ñu bale nha ñu ton,
te bul ñu bayi ñu tabi chi bolis,
wande musal ñu chi lu bon.
Amen.

From E. F. Smidak's book "Pater Noster"

zenith of slavery and its trade, and that this period that passes for one of the most brilliant in European history was in fact, in this respect, one of the most barbarous. In Europe of the later Middle Ages trading in slaves was widespread, and most of the victims were Slavs. In the 10th century the Latin term "servus" was replaced by "slavus" or "sclavus" because the word Slav had already become synonymous with the condition of servitude. One of the leading slave markets of the time was in Verdun, where captives from Dalmatia and Central Europe, brought back from the conquests of Otto the Great, were on sale.

The origins of the negro slave trade

The traffic in black slaves for the European market began around the middle of the 15th century. The first Africans deported by Portuguese mariners were rather like "souvenirs", that is curiosities such as might be brought home from distant voyages. The demand for this kind of "curiosity" grew rapidly, and thus a very lucrative business evolved, for the European nobility made it a matter of good taste to have some of these exotic creatures in their retinues, their stables and even their drawing-rooms. In Lisbon for example black slaves constituted a tenth of the urban population by the end of the 15th century.

Up to this point, this system of slavery was hardly different from what had existed in Europe and Africa itself since antiquity. But at the beginning of the 16th century a radical change set in. The position of black slaves changed from being relatively well-treated servants to being a living commodity, sold by weight and exploited without the slightest scruple.

Dying in America for Europe's prosperity

Less than ten years after Christopher Columbus's arrival in America, the Spanish conquerors had played such havoc with the Indian population that they had insufficient labour to work the gold mines they had taken from the Indians. Therefore in 1501 the Kings of Spain and Portugal authorised the first import of Africans to the West Indies. Officially, the slave trade to the Americas was initiated in 1520, with the support of a tax system that brought considerable revenues to the Spanish and Portuguese treasuries. It will be recalled that the monopoly of Spain and Portugal over America and Africa had been consecrated by Pope Alexander VI in 1493.

With the expansion of the mining industry and of the sugar, cotton and coffee plantations, the need for slaves mounted drastically. Because it offered huge profits, the slave trade soon attracted adventurers from all the nations of Europe. In the middle of the 16th century, the Portuguese were overtaken in their predominance by the Dutch, closely followed by Danes, Swedes and Germans. At the time of Colbert, the prime architect of European mercantilism, it was the turn of the French. The slave trade became the exclusive privilege of certain high-ranking figures of the court, and Louis XIV himself was among them. The English were the last to join the race but, after the French, they eventually occupied the leading position among the slave traders.

The slave traders

The best-known English slave trader was John Hawkins. He started his raids on the Guinea coast in 1562, in a ship named - with sublime irony - "Jesus", burned a village of 8,000 inhabitants and seized the survivors to deport them for sale to the West Indies. He rapidly became one of the richest merchants in England, had a knighthood conferred on him and was eventually appointed treasurer of the English navy. He stopped at nothing in his trickery. After having duped a black king and extorted captives from him, he had him seized too, together with his wives and all his court, and sent them off to America.

The traders - kings, dukes, bishops and scholars

But other traders were by no means more scrupulous, and it should be emphasised that all these men were at bottom simply "front men" for kings and other dignitaries who derived enormous profits from the business. The principal instruments in the negro traffic were in fact the Companies (the West Indian Company for France, and the Royal African Company of Merchant Adventurers for England), and their share-holders were dukes, peers and also members of the clergy. Men such as Voltaire did not disdain supporting these Companies in the 18th century. Of the Encyclopaedists only one, the Abbé Raynal, raised his voice against slavery and colonisation. For most Europeans the slave trade was quite a normal activity and no attempt was made at concealment. It was argued that colonies were necessary for the prosperity of Europe and that colonies could not be maintained without slaves. This logic was supported by a racist ideology enshrined in law.

The mechanisms of commerce in human beings

The companies engaging in the slave trade enjoyed official privileges, especially regional monopolies and high import quotas. Thus in 1696 the Portuguese Company of Guinea obtained the right to supply the Spanish colonies with "10,000 tons of negroes".[1]

How was the "merchandise" obtained? There were various methods. The least strenuous was to "buy" well-placed African agents, who were familiar with local conditions, and to furnish them with the requisite "means of acquisition", particularly firearms. Partly by force and partly by gifts, bribery and intrigue, the European traders turned the Africans against one another, taking care that no local chief should secure a predominance that might prove threatening. By exploiting internal rivalries, they managed to ensnare African princes in shameful treaties and make them sell their own brothers. Pitre de Mesurade is a case in point, and he became one of the traders' most faithful allies. At first such sales were conducted in kind, but later the conventional trading units of the time were adopted. And what was offered in exchange for those taken captive? Firearms, iron bars and alcohol were most in demand, but also glass beads and textiles. Alcohol served not only the purposes of barter but also as a "means of direct acquisition", for individuals with a powerful physique were offered a drink and, when they were sufficiently inebriated, trussed up for export. Also it often happened that the European slave traders themselves mounted raids into promising territories. Reliefs found in Benin preserve the memory of such daily scenes, showing a man-hunter armed with a gun overpowering a negro with his bow.

Whole populations were wiped out in this way, while others were scattered by flight. During the four centuries the slave trade lasted, Africa was helplessly caught up in a chain reaction which dragged it further and further into decline.

---

[1] J. Merrien, *Histoire Mondiale des Pirates, des Flibustiers et Négriers,* Paris, Grasset, 1959, p. 393.

The slavers' catalogues

Which African peoples were most affected by the slave trade? The slavers' own catalogues are the best source of information. They list the advantages and disadvantages of the different varieties available: "Cayor negroes - war slaves who encourage revolt; Bambara - stupid, gentle and strong; Gold Coast and Ouidah - good farm workers but inclined to suicide; Congolese - jolly and good workers". There were also the Mandings - "refined, docile, well-built but somewhat light-fingered", and the Peuls - "fighters and good workers, fine women" etc. These varieties were quoted in all the slave trade ports of Europe and America.[2]

A terminology for the slave trade evolved and remains a monstrous monument to the mercantile mentality. It shows a detailed care for precise definition and classification. So we find that the best captives were classed as "India units". These were individuals between 15 and 25 years old "without any blemish, with all their fingers, all their teeth, without any membrane over the eye and in excellent health". Three children between 8 and 15 were worth two India units. Two children between 3 and 7, 1 unit. One mother and child, also 1 unit.

The valuation was based exclusively on physique. It would be vain to look in the instructions to receivers for any qualities but those relating to the physical condition, in other words to the capacity for work. This did not mean that all the captives were illiterate. Wilberforce, the English champion of the abolition of slavery, quotes the case of a slave cargo of which one fifth could write Arabic.[3]

Methods of Export

Slave shipments were carried out from the trading posts which Europeans had established all along the African Atlantic coast. The principal ones were Gorée (Senegal), El Nina (Ghana), Ouidah (Dahomey), Fernando Po, Sao Thomé, Loango (Congo) and Louanda (Angola). These trading posts had none of the opulence of the European ports which were the home base of the slave traders and which derived their wealth from the

---

[2] Quoted in Ki-Zerbo, *op. cit.*, p. 214.

[3] Quoted in Ki-Zerbo, *op. cit.*, p. 220.

Franco Gordon 1980 Sudan / Afrika

PATER NOSTER
Bari

Baba likaŋ lo ki.
Ti karin kunök bulani bula.
Ti tumatyan inot ti po.
Ti kulya kunök konani i kak gwoso ki.
Ti yi kinyo likaŋ lo lo lor.
Pitöki yi i toronjin kaŋ,
Gwoso nagon yi a pitökindye
lepeŋat lo kondya yi arabat kilo.
Ko nyömörö yi i möriesi;
Nagon lwöki yi i kulya narok.
Amin.

From E. F. Smidak's book "Pater Noster"

traffic, like Nantes, Bordeaux, St. Malo or Liverpool. They were desolate places, veritable concentration camps where captives were gathered from the hinterland and amassed in disease-ridden barracks - or, to use the terminology of commerce, where the merchandise was warehoused pending shipment.

Few accounts exist of the dramas that were enacted in or around these camps. One of the few that have come down to us is that of Pruneau de Pommegorge of the French West India Company. In his book, *Description de la Nigritie*, he tells us among other things: "One day I went to one of the traders. I was shown several captives, among them a woman of between 20 and 24, extremely depressed and weighed down by grief. Her breasts were hanging but full, and this made me suspect that she had lost her baby. I asked the trader and he replied that she had no baby. Since it was forbidden on pain of death for the unfortunate to speak up, I ventured to press the tip of her breast. Sure enough, milk came out and I ascertained that the woman was breast-feeding. I therefore insisted that she must have a baby. He was annoyed by my insistence and said that anyway this need not stop me buying the woman because her child would be thrown to the wolves that evening. I was dumbfounded. I was on the point of leaving to collect my thoughts on this terrible prospect when the idea came to me that I could save this child's life. I therefore told the merchant that I would buy the mother on condition that he included the child. He had it brought at once and I handed it to the mother. Lost for means of expressing her gratitude, she picked up some earth and tossed it at her forehead. Although I had done no more than any other decent person would have done, I went away with a delightful feeling - mixed with horror. As this kind of crime was almost a daily occurrence, I had to refrain from visiting the merchants because my means did not suffice for further good deeds."[4]

When they had been gathered in these concentration camps the captives were sold in the "day markets" run by the agents of the various slavers. After a careful anatomical examination in great detail, the purchasers bargained hard with the sellers before clinching the deal. Next, the slaves were branded with the purchaser's initials on the chest, the buttocks or the breast, and this mark was indelible.

---

[4] Pruneau de Pommegorge, *Description de la Nigritie*, Amsterdam, Etud. Dahoméennes, 1789, pp. 210-212.

When the cargo was complete, new separations succeeded those that had already been suffered during capture and during the long march to the trading post. Those leaving had to turn their backs on relatives and spouses who had not yet been bought. Leaving the soil of Africa and walking up the gangway was one of the most heart-rending moments. Some of the slaves managed to hurl themselves in the water and drown, while others choked themselves with their own hands. The remainder set off on the long two-month voyage.

The hellish crossing

The slave ships had descriptive names like Concord, Justice, The African, The King of Dahomey, The Senegalese etc. They were specially fitted out with irons, chains and between-decks so as to control and pack in their human cargo as economically as possible.

Shaven and naked, the slaves were crammed like sardines in the ill-ventilated between-decks, sometimes in the spoon position to save space. It did not take long before they were afflicted with sea-sickness and epidemics, so that they literally wallowed in a bog of vomit, blood and excreta. The mortality rate was frightful - on an average, three or four died for every one who arrived alive. To keep them alive, they were driven out on deck to get some air and get used to doing a little work. Dancing was even organised, with the aid of the whip where necessary, to lift the spirits of the most wretched.

Rebellion was nevertheless quite frequent, and it even happened that members of the crew were lynched. The leaders were executed, drowned or openly flogged until they bled. Sometimes a gash was made in their skin and filled with a mixture of capsicum, vinegar and gunpowder. One leader of a hunger strike was killed, cut up in pieces and forcefully fed to those who had followed him. For these wretches death had lost its sting, it was a liberation. The French abolitionist B.S. Frossard wrote about the sentencing of some rebels: "They heard the sentence of death with demonstrations of the greatest joy. They delayed its execution only to embrace their relatives and friends, and then with gaiety on their faces they threw themselves in the sea to find a prompt remedy for their ills."[5]

---

[5] B.S. Frossard, *La cause des esclaves nègres et des habitants de la Guinée*, Lyon, A. Delaroche, 1789.

Arrival in America
Before arrival in the American ports, all those were thrown overboard who
were not fit for sale but would otherwise attract taxation - the sick and
injured, for instance, and among these there were many children.
Before resale on the American markets, the "cargo" had to be smartened
up. At the end of the voyage, the slaves were crammed with food and
sometimes drugged so that they appeared to be in good shape. The slave
traders came to develop various techniques of restoration, and vigilant
buyers responded with appropriate precautions, for instance tasting the
slaves' sweat to ensure that a shiny skin was not produced by the application
of polish.
After all these humiliating procedures, and when the male or female slave
had been bought by a master in Brazil, Cuba, the West Indies or North
America, a new round of suffering began. On average a slave did not
survive longer than 5 to 7 years from the moment of disembarkation in the
New World. It was considered more economic to replace a sick slave with
a new one than to give him or her proper treatment - "Africa is a good
mother" was the ironical way the colonists summed up the fact that their
source of supply was inexhaustible. For this reason, and because the
plantations never stopped expanding, the slave trade went on increasing
until in the 18th century it reached an annual import rate of some 100,000.

The incredible bleeding of Africa
How many human beings were removed from Africa during the four
centuries of the slave trade? The total number is reckoned at 80 to 100
million.[6] This figure comprises at least 10 million actually sold in
America, 40 to 50 million dead at the hands of raiding parties or during
the middle passage and 30 to 40 million sold within the framework of the
oriental slave trade. The last of these developed particularly in the 19th
century, when the Atlantic trade started to decline following the anti-slavery
movement in Europe, and it was mainly in the hands of Arab slave traders
even though European shipowners continued to play a very important
part. It should be noted that the conditions of slavery in the countries of
the Middle East were very different from those in America. Slaves enjoyed

---

[6]Ki-Zerbo, *op. cit.*, p. 218, where various sources are quoted.

certain fundamental rights, and emancipation, which was considered meritorious under Islam, was quite common.

It is hardly necessary to say that the slave trade had profound consequences for Africa, not only because of the enormous population drain it brought about but also because of the chronic state of war and turmoil that resulted, together with the general and increasing impoverishment of human, cultural and material resources throughout the continent.

Austin Hleza   1980 Swasiland / Afrika

PATER NOSTER

Si-Swati

Babe wetfu lose Zulwini,
Ligama lakho malibongwe,
Umbuso wakho awute,
Intsandvo yakho ayentiwe emhlabeni njengase Zulwini,
Siphe namuhla sinkhwa semalanga okhe,
Usitsetselele tono tetfu,
njengoba natsi sibatsetselela labosonako;
Ungasingenisi ekulingweni,
kodva usivikele kulokubi;
Njengoba umbuso ungowakho,
nemandla nebukhosi,
Kuze kube phakade.
Ameni.

From E. F. Smidak's book "Pater Noster"

VI. IN THE AMERICAS - The cricifixion of the black man

"God of Angola, God of Angola!
You will teach us a three-fold prayer,
Three Our Fathers, three Ave Marias,
So that the African is allowed
To go back home to Guinea."

This chant of the black slave in the Americas is the most poignant expression of his pain and suffering. For many slaves death was the only hope, for the dead were thought to go back again across the terrible ocean, back to their ancestral home, which symbolised a lost paradise.

"Moving things"
What was the real status of a slave in the colonies beyond the Atlantic? The "Code Noir", the royal edict of 1685 that defined the situation of slaves in the French colonies, termed them "movable possessions". But this definition was sometimes felt to be inadequate. In his comment on Article 44 of the "Code Noir", the lawyer Loysel wrote: "Strictly speaking, slaves are not movables but moving things, in the same way that horses, sheep and other animals are included in this word movable".[1]
However, it was also true that slaves were often immovable, in the sense that they were attached to an estate and could not be sold except with the estate. This advertisement is therefore typical: "House for sale situated at Trou du Chat, 16 square metres, kitchen, storeroom, rabbit-hutch, furnished rooms, a horse, four negroes etc." (Gazette de la Martinique of 18 May 1780).
"They were put in a category outside the human species, and literally considered on a par with domestic animals," according to Victor Schoelcher, the famous French abolitionist. "A white woman would no more blush at washing in front of a slave than in front of dog".[2] And Captain Malenfant, a planter and himself a slave-owner, tells how young

---

[1] D. Bellegarde, *Histoire du Peuple Haïtien,* Port-au-Prince, 1953, p. 42.

[2] Victor Schoelcher, *Vie de Toussaint Louverture,* (original edition by Paul Ollendorf, Paris, 1889), Editions Karthala, Paris, 1982, p. 7.

ladies freshly arrived from France, who complained about the slaves' being naked, were told, "You might as well ask us to put clothes on our cows, our oxen and our dogs?"[3]

In the same vein, a notice board at the entrance to the public gardens in Martinique said: "Negroes, mulattoes and dogs not allowed". This notice was not to be taken down until 1848.

A human lottery

Sometimes these wretched people were bid for in a lottery: "We prepared tickets corresponding to the labels on the negroes' arms... These tickets were initialled by us and then put in four different hats. The first of them contained the adult males -prime specimens as well as the elderly, who were specially marked; the second contained the tickets for adult females; the third for young negroes, and the fourth for the babies. Then lots were drawn for ownership after someone had called out the price of each negro unit together with the quality and value attached to the ticket."[4]

The black slave was treated like currency, a bill of exchange that could be cashed in, or an I.O.U. covering a debt. In himself, he had no rights. He was allowed no possessions and could make no savings except to the extent his master permitted. He could acquire nothing, either by gift or legacy, and if his master allowed him any possessions, he could not dispose of them, whether by transfer to someone else or by bequest.

If he was lucky enough to gain emancipation, which was a possibility provided for in principle by law but seldom realised and then circumscribed by official edicts, it was never definitive and could be rescinded at any moment. "The threat of being sent back to slavery is the bosom companion of the emancipated, especially when they are poor."[5] From 1740, emancipation was subject, among other things, to the payment of a tax of 1000 livres for a man and 600 for a woman. The effect of this was to increase robbery among male slaves and prostitution among the female, for they had no other way of amassing such a large sum. It is clear

---

[3] Malenfant, *Des Colonies, et particulièrement de celle de Saint-Domingue,* Paris, 1814, p. 232.

[4] Quoted in J. Ki-Zerbo, *Histoire de l'Afrique noire,* D'hier à demain, Paris, Editions Hatier, 1978, p. 216.

[5] P. Pluchon, *Histoire des Antilles,* p. 177.

"Thy will be done" (on earth as it is in heaven); this line wishes us human beings to use "godly justice". But what do we have instead? The threat of the human race doing "justice" to itself through a nuclear holocaust. "The Kingdom come".
The "skull" at the front of the long carrying soldiers suggests that humanity will only wipe itself out trying to bring peace by using war.
"Give us this day our daily bread." Failure to feed our poor, is present in the sad faces of the chidren.
"Forgive us our trespasses" or "Forgive us our debts". As you said in the letter you sent, a better world can only be built by correcting our mistakes. Mistakes like greed and corruption.

Petro Miano 1981 Kenya / Afrika

PATER NOSTER
Gikũyũ / Ghikuiu

Jthe witũ wĩ Jgũrũ,
Rĩĩtwa rĩaku nĩrĩamũrũo.
ũthamaki waku ũũke.
O ũrĩa wendete wee,
nĩwikagwo gũkũ thi,
o ta ũrĩa wĩkagwo Kũu Igũrũ.
Tũhe ũmũthĩ irio cia gũtũigana.
Na ũtũrekere mathiri maitũ,
o ta ũrĩa ithuĩ tũrekagĩra arĩa marĩ
mathirĩ maitũ.
Na ndũgatũtware magerio-inĩ,
no Kũhonokia ũtũhonokagie ũũru-inĩ.
Ni ũndũ ũthamaki nĩ waku, o na hinya,
o na Kũgoocwo, tene na tene. Amen.

From E. F. Smidak's book "Pater Noster"

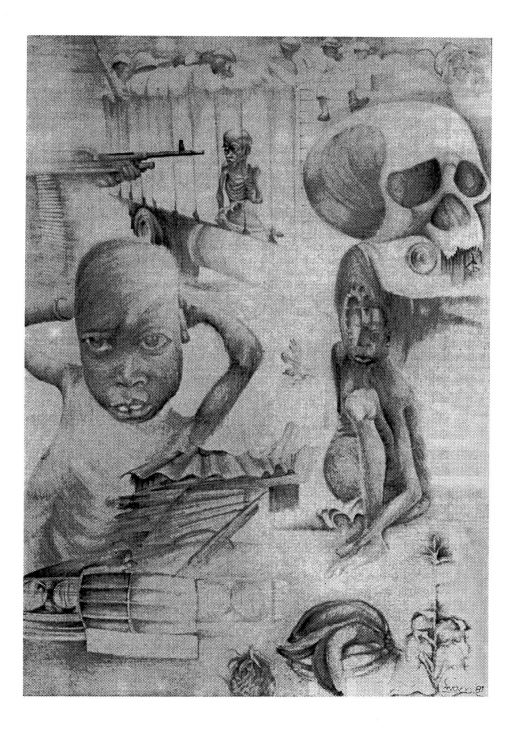

that the threat of losing their "liberty", when it had been bought at such a high price, was one of the most effective means of keeping the emancipated in a submissive mood.

By a surprising inconsistency with the legal status of "movable possession", the Code Noir obliged owners to have their slaves baptised. But far from raising slaves from their miserable condition and giving them a place in the religious community, in the overwhelming majority of cases baptism was no more than an empty formality, without any social benefits.

Punishment, torture and death

The Code Noir was said to be relatively liberal legislation, but it gave masters absolute power over their slaves. True, it forbade masters to "maltreat" them, but it also bestowed the right to mete out punishment. For instance, the Code authorised cutting off ears if a slave ran away for a period of a month. Additionally, the slave was to be branded with the sign of a fleur-de-lys on the shoulder. If the offence was repeated, his hamstring was severed and a fleur-de-lys burned into the other shoulder. A second repitition was punishable with death.

Flogging was the universal punishment, and could be made to fit just about every misdemeanour. Some masters flogged their slaves to the point of incapacity and even death. Excesses multiplied, and Schoelcher wrote about the West Indian planters: "They were corrupted through and through by the terrible atmosphere which they imbibed from childhood, and by the fact that the barbarous excesses they witnessed always went unpunished. If they had a wicked disposition they became monsters, and some of them carried ferocity to mind-boggling lengths. Women received no more mercy than the men when it came to staking them out. If one of these unfortunate women was pregnant then a hole was dug in the ground to hold her belly and she still received the 29 prescribed lashes that tore into the flesh!" (The punishment of staking-out consisted of whipping a slave stretched out and prostrated, with the four limbs tied to pegs in the ground.)[6]

To deal with the harshness of masters such as these, an order was promulgated in December 1784 imposing a maximum number of lashes, and 50 was decided upon. "But this order was executed with the same laxity as the others... It was reckoned that a hundred lashes could cause

---

[6] Schoelcher, *op. cit.*, p. 8.

death, but there were still cases in Martinique, in 1838 and 1840, when slaves were punished with 100 lashes."[7]

Under this wanton flogging, slaves came to imitate the attitudes of their masters, and this had consequences that would be comical if they were not so tragic. Colonel Malenfant tells the story of a slave working as a carter who was chastised for beating his mule too hard. He thought that very unfair and protested in Creole French: "You beat me if I no work, I beat mule if he no walk. He my nigger."[8]

The lash was followed by chains and irons if the slave was a long-term runaway, had committed a major theft or had a fight with another slave. Chains could have a heavy iron ball attached, and the slave had to drag this around on one foot day and night, at work and in his cabin. Constant runaways were moreover fitted with an iron collar with long spikes that made hiding in the undergrowth very difficult. Women who aborted - and this often happened when slaves wanted to save their offspring from the miseries of slavery, or to obliterate the consequences of rape by a white master - had to wear a large piece of wood on their back until their next pregnancy. The point of this punishment was not based on morality but on the fact that the master had lost the free gift of another slave to be.

In a memorandum which the abolitionists submitted to the National Assembly in 1789, we find moreover: "A certain white master was so well known for his ferocity that disobedient slaves could be made to quake at the threat of being sold to this monster. One owner did not stop at exhausting his negresses with hard labour but actually robbed them of their immoral and shameful earnings. Another was threatened by Monsieur d'Ennery, the Governor, with being sent back to France if he continued to shoot his negroes. Yet another filled his estates with the incessant wailing of his slaves until the plantations ran with their blood; and it gave him pleasure to be served at table afterwards by these wretches with their skin hanging in shreds. Another even broke one of the legs of any negro guilty of running away and then abandoned him so that gangrene set in and the leg had to be amputated."[9]

---

[7] P. Pluchon, *Histoire des Antilles*, p. 151.

[8] Malenfant, *op. cit.*, p. 205.

[9] Quoted in D. Bellegarde, *Histoire du Peuple Haïtien*, Port- au-Prince, 1953, p. 44.

Not all planters were as cruel as this but good masters were in the minority. Thus the Chevalier de Cotignon said, in writing about his travels to the West Indies: "I cannot pass over in silence the cruelty of the colonists towards their blacks. I shall never forget what happened one day when I was shooting around Pointe-à-Pitre in Guadeloupe. I was working the undergrowth when I suddenly heard heart-rending groans. As I drew near the place they were coming from, I saw a flock of hungry birds making off. I fired and killed one of them. But imagine my surprise when I spotted an iron cage with a blood-stained negro. I realised with horror that the birds had been devouring him. I think that if the person who had condemned him to this brutal death had appeared at this moment, I would have killed him. The pitiful wretch begged my help and he did not need to ask twice. I tore at the bars and beat them with stones until I managed to rescue him from his tomb and set him free. He kissed my hand and ran off. He had been there two days, without food or drink, with his arms behind his back and his feet in an iron band."[10]

There are also accounts of owners who had their slaves thrown into furnaces or boiling cauldrons, or had them buried alive and in an upright position, with only their heads sticking out, and left them to die in this way. One inspector on a West Indian estate never went on his rounds without hammer and nails, so that he could punish the slightest shortcoming by nailing slaves to a post by their ear. Many of the planters maintained that to make their slaves work they had to kill some of them.

A human working machine

Basically, slaves were working machines intended for a maximum yield at minimum cost. They were fed in the most rudimentary manner. In many plantations slaves had to provide their own food by cultivating small plots of land during their rest periods. To live in, they had cabins that were usually badly maintained, being made of mud and leaves and unable to withstand bad weather. As for clothing - if, as was not always the case, they were given any - they had to make do until it was no more than rags. Disease was naturally rampant - bronchitis, chronic fever, tuberculosis, dysentery, parasitosis, skin infection, and also earth-eating, which could

---

[10] Quoted in Pluchon, *op. cit.*, p. 152.

never be eliminated. Melancholia was also very frequent, and often proved fatal.

The day's work on a plantation usually began at five in the morning with a reveille call. When the bell or overseer's horn sounded, the field-workers among the slaves mustered to march off in columns. The overseer brought up the rear and kept them together so that there were no stragglers. In the fields the slaves worked in rows and the overseer with his whip saw to it that there was no slacking. Apart from breaks for breakfast and the midday meal, the slaves worked until sunset. Before returning to their cabins, all the slaves had to gather some grass for the animals or some wood for the evening cooking, and no one was allowed to come back empty-handed. Their burdens were examined on arrival to make sure they were satisfactory. After a quick supper the overseer gave his daily report and the manager, or the master himself, meted out punishments. For those who were not in chains the night was in theory their own.

Flight and insurrection - Mackendal's crusade.

Many slaves tried to escape. Some fled the day after disembarking, others after many years of servitude. The fugitives were known as maroons, the same term as was used for domestic animals that had returned to the wild. There were some inveterate maroons who fled again as soon as they were caught and there were some who escaped for good.

There are no statistics on marooning but its extent is evident from the unremitting concern shown by planters, managers and colonial administrators. Petty marooning lasted anything from a few days to a few weeks, but large-scale marooning produced permanent organised bands hiding in the mountains. Hunting parties and even military expeditions went after them, but without much success.

Uprisings were frequent, and one of the most important was the one led by Mackendal in Haiti from 1755 to 1757. He is one of the few slaves about whom some biographical details are known. He was an African prince from the Guinea coast who possessed a lively mind and stout heart. After becoming a maroon, he gathered a numerous band together and launched a veritable crusade against the colonists, with the stated objective of making Haiti an independent African kingdom. His exploits and elusiveness made him a legendary hero. After fighting for three years he was eventually caught and burned alive.

Other reactions

Marooning and insurrection - even open warfare - were one set of responses from Africans in the grip of the hell of American slavery. But there were many others too. Perhaps the finest was that, in spite of all the horrors to which they were exposed and the hatred with which they might have reacted, slaves usually showed a common humanity and a generosity of heart. There are abundant examples from life in the colonies: the slave sacrificing his life for the white master who oppresses him, the black mother tenderly suckling the children of the master in his great house. Such examples illustrate the trait that was so characteristic of ancient Africa and which the African historian Joseph Ki-Zerbo calls, "a gut feeling of sympathy for all those who belong to the tribe of Adam."[11]

At the end of this chapter on the martyrdom of Mother Africa, we wish to say that, although this book is dedicated to the survivors of the incredible holocaust resulting from slavery and the slave trade, we very much hope it will also be read by those who are not of African origin. For this tragedy concerns us all. Of all the various aspects of this tragedy there is one to which we should pay very special attention - the negation of so much human potential. We can never know how many other victims of slavery possessed similar gifts to those of Saint-Georges or Toussaint Louverture without ever being able to develop and express them. Of course it is true in general that a lot of people have not had the chance to realise their potential because they died prematurely through war, epidemics or whatever. But in the case of the Africans there was, in addition to wars and epidemics, the misfortune of being born black.

The scale of this human tragedy brings the miracle of Saint-Georges's life into focus. In spite of the misfortune attaching to his colour, he attained heights beyond the reach of others more favoured by their birth. Born into and moulded by a world that knew nothing but suffering, torture and humiliation he dispelled the shadows in his own being by the beauty of his music.

It was to highlight this miracle that we went into the details of the horrors of slavery and the slave trade, and not to make any accusations. Any human accusation would be idle before the monstrosity of what happened.

---

[11] Ki-Zerbo, *op. cit.*

Only life itself can tell the story behind the events. As a rule, there was hardly any hope of survival for the victims of the slave trade. For how can one talk of hope when out of 50 million slaves embarked only 10 million arrived alive, and of these the majority lived no more than seven years after their disembarkation?

It meant in fact the death of Africa - Africa the cradle of humanity. Henceforth her children were no longer regarded as human beings. They were hunted like animals, captured like animals, shut up like animals, sold like animals and finally exploited like animals.

Death became their best friend, and yet there were some survivors. Among the millions hunted down on the African continent there was a certain girl, a girl like many others. Captured and maltreated like her companions, she survived by a sheer miracle. She was embarked on a ship bound for the West Indies - a meaningless destination for her because she had never heard of the West Indies. This girl was the mother of Joseph Bologne, Chevalier de Saint-Georges. Some historians of the time say she was called Nanon, so we shall call her by this name.

My wish is that this prayer "Our Father" will become a reality to your hearts and that God's light will shine into your hearts, minds and reveal Jesus Christ as the Lord to you. God bless you!
I have tried to combine all the ideas given to me by you to a point of an illustration. The soldier is symbolic of all the wealthier lands, waring against the weaker, poorer lands being presented by the boy liberated by death.

Robert Hooper | 1980 Südafrika / Afrika

PATER NOSTER

Zulu

Baba wethu osezulwini, malingcweliswe igama lakho;
mawufike umbuso wakho;
mayenziwe intando yakho emhlabeni njengasezulwini;
usiphe namuhla isinkwa sethu semihla ngemihla;
usithethelele amacala ethu,
njengalokhu nathi sibathethelela abanecala kithi;
ungasingenisi ekulingweni;
kodwa usikhulule kokubi;
ngokuba umbuso ungowakho, namandla,
nenkazimula, kuze kubephakade.
Amen.

PATER NOSTER

Sepedi (Lebowa)

Tataweso wa maxodimong!
Leina la xaxo a le kxêthwê;
Mmusô wa xaxo a tlê thats ya xaxo a
e dirwê mono lefaseng byalo ka xe
e dirwa lexodimong;
Re fê lehono boxôbê bya rena bya ka mehla;
Re lebalêlê melato ya rena byalo ka xe
re labalêla ba ba naxo le melato xo rena;
O se re isê molekong;
xomme O re pholosê bebeng;
xobane mmusô ké wa xaxo, le matla,
le tumisô, ka xo sa felexo. Amene.

PATER NOSTER

Tsonga (Gazunkulu)

Tata wa hina l'a nge matilweni,
vito ra wena a ri hlawuriwe,
a ku te fuma ka wena;
ku randa ka wena a ku endliwe
misaveni sa nga hi le tilweni;
U hi ha namuntlha vusa bya hina bya
siku rinwana ni rinwana;
Hi rivalele milandu ya hina,
tani hi loko na hina hi rivalela vanwana
la va nga ni milandu ka hina;
U nga hi yisi miringweni,
kambe u hi lwela ka lo' wo biha. Amen.

PATER NOSTER

Xhosa (Transkei et Ciskei)

Bawo wethu osemazulwini,
malingcwaliswe igama lakho;
Mabufike ubukumkani bakho.
Makwenziwe ukuthanda kwakho nasemhlabeni,
njengokuba kusenziwa emazulwini;
Siphe namhla isonka sethu semihla ngemihla;
Usixolele amatyala ethul,
njengokuba nathi sibaxolela abo banamatyala kuthi;
Ungasingenisi ekulingweni, sihlangule enkohlakalweni.
Ngokuba bubobakho ubukumkani, namandla,
nozuko kuse kuwo amaphakade. Amen.

From E. F. Smidak's book "Pater Noster"

OUR FATHER who art
in heaven hallowed be thy name t-
hy kingdom come thy will be done
on earth as it is in heaven give us
this day our daily bread and forgive us our debts as we forgive
our debtors lead us not into te-
mptation but deliver us from
evil for thine is the kingdom the power and the
glory for ever Amen

VII. THE MUSIC OF AFRICA

Since this book is devoted to a child of Africa who is remembered by posterity above all for his musical gifts, we must add some information and reflections on African music to this first section about the Great Black Mother. As in every human society, music has played an important part in the life of African peoples from the very dawn of time. In the earliest civilisations on our planet music, beginning with song, was mankind's most important means of entering into communion with the divine. Through song, man merged his vital breath with the afflatus of cosmic being and joined in the music of all creation.

In a sense, we can say that African music has never entirely abandoned this initial purpose, and that is no doubt why traditional African music sometimes sounds alien or even off-putting to the European ear, accustomed as it is to the European art music. Clearly, the musicality of human beings who have remained in intimate communion with elemental pulsations and the mysteries of life as a whole cannot be judged on the basis of an aesthetic code deriving from theoretical speculation, from which the intensity of living experience is absent. That would be like reproaching birds for singing false notes.

A very telling example in this respect is the music of the pygmies, which for a European must seem the most "primitive" African music. But it is probably the most ancient music in existence and in its essence one of the most moving expressions. The life of the pygmies of Zaire, like that of pygmies in other regions of Africa, is governed by their relationship with the forest and by their knowledge that singing gives pleasure to the forest. They avoid sounds that might injure the forest, such as a sudden noise or a strident cry. All pygmy songs are sacred because they are all dedicated to the forest. They have the power to "awaken" the forest and to attract its attention to its children's needs. And the forest itself is a universe full of sounds that the pygmies can interpret and use. When the forest stops "talking" they take this as a sign that something is seriously wrong and danger threatens.[1]

---

[1] See Zaire in Grove's *Dictionary of Music and Musicians*

Judging this music according to European standards would not only show a lack of piety but also a lack of intelligence. We must acknowledge that every human community expresses its innate musical sense in the manner most appropriate for it, and that the value of this expression depends less on aesthetic criteria than on the feeling that inspires it and the message it conveys.

After political prejudice, musical prejudice

This is what we should bear in mind when, as Europeans, we speak of African music or of any other non-European music. For some decades now, musical prejudice has tended to decline. It no longer attempts to rate the music of Africans, Asians or American Indians far, far below European so-called art music, and to attribute to it at best some merit for its ethnological curiosity; but the prejudice is still present in many minds. We must learn to accept without sniggering the fact that there are hundreds of millions of people on our planet whom the gravelly singing of an old negro, the ragas of an Indian singer, or the rhythmic patterns of a Javan gamelan orchestra make happier than the most immortal works of Mozart and Beethoven.

Musical prejudice also has an impact on what is called "popular" music in Europe itself. Musicologists tend to draw a very sharp division between the different kinds of popular music and "art" music, and to treat the former with condescension or even contempt, whether it is a matter of traditional folklore or modern folk, pop or rock, or the love song in all its innumerable forms. This attitude amounts to putting theories and established codes above the feelings of all those who find moments of happiness, peace or liberation in their particular kind of musical expression. Music teaching in our schools, governed as it is by these codes and theories, must have discouraged more children from the spontaneous expression of their innate musical sense than the complete absence of instruction could ever have done. Teachers are in the habit of blaming young people's musical passivity nowadays on the listening facilities afforded by modern technology. They do not realise that it is their own methods and the general attitude prevailing in the world of "serious music" that are responsible for this situation.

When music is turned into a mere ceremony, a codified ritual for public performance according to its own rules, without any involvement of the deeper levels of human feeling, it is obviously moribund. Is it surprising then that popular forms of music, be they western, African or Asian, have remained so vigorous, and either kept their ancient characteristics or incorporated new elements with the spontaneity that distinguishes all mankind's authentic creations?

The arbiters of musical theory are not just a modern phenomenon. Plato (426-348 B.C.) in his "Laws" postulated a strict censorship of musical expression in order to preclude anything "deviating from the harmony of the spheres" that might provoke "dangerous emotions". Eight centuries later, Saint Augustine insisted on the necessity of observing a strictly mathematical basis for music so as to prevent its taking precedence over the word and thereby prejudicing religion. He says in his "Confessions": "It is not good if the spirit is carried away by this pleasure of the senses... Each time I find myself being more moved by the music than by the words that are sung, I must confess that I have committed a great sin." One can feel nothing but pity for the man who was so intimidated by theologians that he denied the lifting of his heart when God spoke to him in the first voice to touch the human soul, music.

The dread of emotion was a constant preoccupation of men of the church who were concerned with music, and it was the main cause of imposing on music an artificial mathematical structure that came from reason rather than from musical intuition. The philosophers played their part too. In the 18th century Kant put music at the bottom of his hierarchy of the arts, allowing it value only when it was combined with carefully reasoned words. Hegel (18th-19th centuries) granted that music expresses the divine but demanded that it should be subordinated to philosophy. This dichotomy, typical for European intellectuals, between thought and feeling, or mind and body - nebulous concepts further confused by their philosophical definitions - naturally led them to call African music sensual or earthy, because in Africa music has never become a matter of the intellect, but has remained true to itself as an expression of the whole man - body, mind and soul.

What does music mean for Africans?

In so far as a non-African may pronounce on the subject, we quote here the observations of a European who has approached African music from an angle quite different from the one mentioned above: "Black people have a remarkable innate musical talent. We should bear in mind that they all participate. There are indeed professional musicians but it is very unusual for them to be the only performers in a community... Whatever the occasion might be - birth or death, initiation or marriage, magical ceremonies or the events of war - invariably all the people take part by dancing, singing or playing instruments. Thus, for black people all of life's pulsations are turned into music, and what touches their soul is translated into rhythmic vibrations. Their emotion becomes a powerful cosmic unison carrying them beyond their individual limits, uniting them with their fellows and merging them in the great rhythm of the universe... African music knows both the heights and the depths of human emotion, but even in its greatest ecstasy it never employs artifices or forced and unnatural devices. Contrary to widespread opinion, African music is far less "erotic" or "lascivious" than European music at certain periods of our history. There is a total absence of those decadent characteristics that we often find "artistic" without realising the extent to which music of this kind is artificial, pretentious and forced...African music has an intensity to which even the European listener cannot remain indifferent. This intensity can attain a fevered ecstasy of singers and dancers but never loses the character and expressiveness of an truly elemental art form." And the author concludes by quoting another European scholar who has brought a sincere interest to his study of African music, A. Schaeffner. In comparing it to European music, he sums it up as "less elevated but also less secular and perhaps for this reason more genuinely religious."[2]

A multitude of musical idioms

It is the task of historiography to record, classify, date, compare and interpret the data left on this earth of ours by human activity over the ages. Music is perhaps the most ephemeral of all these activities but it too is the subject of research and has therefore given rise to the history of music. So far as African music is concerned, research is very recent since the Africans themselves have never felt the need to address something so non-essential when they were preoccupied with making music and living it. Thus it was Europeans who engaged in this research at the beginning of

---

[2] *Afrikanische Musik*, by H. Hickmann in *Musik in Geschichte und Gegenwart*, Leipzig, 1949.

the twentieth century, when recording machines were invented and it became possible to collect "musical specimens" throughout the continent. The first thing that struck these researchers was the multidude of musical idioms present in Africa, and indeed this is natural enough in view of the vastness of the continent, the diversity of cultures that have developed there and above all the extraordinary musical creativity of the Africans. Each of the countries of present-day Africa has its own musical traditions, and within each country every cultural community offers an infinite number of variations in the music of the human soul.

We cannot take it upon ourselves here to present a complete survey of Africa's musical landscape, especially since ethno-musicological analyses afford little interesting information for the non-specialist. We shall therefore confine ourselves to certain matters of general interest.

The instruments

One of Africa's most ancient instruments is the bow. Invented some 15,000 to 30,000 years ago, this appears not to have been intended primarily or exclusively as a weapon. There are in fact plenty of indications that it has always been used to produce sounds as well. In the course of thousands of years the bow has taken on more sophisticated forms, for instance that of the arched harp, and then with the addition of a resonator it gave rise to a whole range of well-known string instruments such as the lute and the zither. But it is noteworthy that the musical bow still exists in its original form in several parts of Africa, and that in Zimbabwe it is played with the mouth.

The xylophone is another very ancient and typically African instrument. It has a calabash for resonator and exists in infinite variety. Some xylophones are so big that they are played by several musicians. Then there is the *mbira* or *zanza*, also called the lamellophone or thumb piano (because it is played with the thumbs), which is also found in innumerable forms. This consists of a keyboard (often double) of small metal lamellas stretched over cross-bars, with many different kinds of resonator. One interesting detail is that each *mbira* is normally tuned individually, although this by no means prevents the performance of music for two or three musicians. Furthermore there is the vast range of wind instruments including transverse flutes, whistle flutes, long flutes without mouthpiece, nose flutes, double flutes, clarinets, oboes, oliphants (horns carved from elephant tusks), trumpets, whistles etc. Finally come the percussion instruments, whose variety is practically unlimited.

African music, both instrumental and vocal, is notable for its variety of timbre and sound intensity, which is incomparably greater than that of European music. "Nowhere else in the world but in African music does one find a combination of sounds with such intensity, fulness and simplicity, or tonal nuances of such almost unreal delicacy."[3]

Musical creativity

Modern ethno-musicologists also voice their amazement at the spontaneity, vitality and richness of African musical creativity. Some ascribe this to the intimate relationship between music and daily life in Africa, where each event and activity finds musical expression. Others see it as the fruit of the special way in which African children are brought up. And indeed until the age of two, until weaning, African babies spend practically their whole day on the back or the haunches of their mothers. They are thus constantly in close contact with their mother, sensing each of her movements like an unbroken dance and registering as omnipresent music each inflection of her voice when she speaks or sings. And the African mother sings a great deal - at her household tasks, in the fields and of course at festivities.

This ancestral custom was doubtless kept up by Africans shipped to America, and one can well imagine that this was how little Joseph, our Chevalier de Saint-Georges, spent the first years of his life - on the back of his young, beautiful and wretched mother, Nanon.

Another reason for this musical creativity is no doubt the fact that African musical life is devoid of the rigid division between musician and listener, or artist and layman; or, to put it more crudely, between performer and consumer, such as we find in the musical life of the West. Admittedly, among some African tribes certain kinds of music are reserved for a caste or for special musicians, for instance initiation music or that performed at magical rites or sacred dances; but in general making music belongs to everyone, with a certain allocation by genre according to sex and generation. In certain communities of southern Africa, for instance, every young man and girl has to compose their own repertoire of songs, and at festivities each is expected to make their original contribution in accordance with

---

[3] *Afrikanische Musik*, loc. cit.

certain traditional precedents. The art of improvisation is also encouraged in many communities.

Rhythm

"The rhythm of African music has too often been misunderstood," according to H. Hickmann. "It is by no means as free, wild and arbitrary as the uninformed often tend to believe, but is structured like the rhythms of other kinds of music and follows similar laws of sequence and periodicity." The subtlety of this structure is however such that the uninformed are incapable of even perceiving it and cannot understand it without resorting to learned calculations.[4] It is hardly necessary to add that African musicians master this rhythmical structure without engaging in mathematical exercises. The ethno-musicologist A. Schaeffner, quoted above, maintains that "the rhythmical virtuosity of black Africans has no equal except in Arab, Hindu and Malaysian music".[5]

One of the distinctive features of African rhythms is their ability to assume an independent melodic character and to develop a theme with variations through a subtle interplay of light and dark nuances. Another interesting characteristic, related to this, is the link between melodic rhythm and the spoken language. In fact a large part of instrumental music - as in the playing of a xylophone ensemble among the Lobi of the Upper Volta - is really a discursive dialogue which the performers can easily translate into words if they are asked to.[6] This reminds us of one of the primary functions of African drums in conveying messages over a distance. This connection between music and language has multifarious expressions and is considered one of the fundamental features of African music. It also explains the dominant role of pitch, to which Africans seem to be much more sensitive than Europeans.

Musical genres

The musical genres found in Africa today encompass all conceivable levels, from sacred songs of the most ancient origin to modern Afro-jazz. They embrace ritual and funeral music, magical incantations, music linked

---

[4] *Afrikanische Musik*, loc. cit.

[5] See *Africa* in Grove's "Dictionary of Music and Musicians".

[6] Ibid., p.148.

with work, the seasons and festivities, court music with its songs to the
glory of past kings, recreational and dramatic music, and love songs. The
only genre one would seek in vain is academic music because this is
essentially alien to the vitality of the Africans' musical sense.

Ancient Egyptian music

We cannot conclude this brief sketch of African music without a few
words on one of its expressions that is now extinct but nevertheless
preserved for human memory by pictorial representations and instruments
found by archaeologists - the music of ancient Egypt dating back to the
fourth millenium B.C. As is shown in the Nile valley's tomb and temple
paintings, music played a leading role in pharaonic civilisation. The cults
of divers divinities such as Amun, representing the divine breath, the
goddess Hathor, Osiris and Isis, Thot and many others, including the pharaohs
themselves, were inalienably linked to their expression in music. A Roman
author, who admittedly witnessed only the final period of Egyptian
civilisation, states that the music of the Egyptians was closely linked to
knowledge of the stars. And Plato, who took up a similar position, praised
the excellence of the teachings of Egypt's musicians. Pythagoras is
thought to have learned from them.[7]

Although numerous texts of Egyptian songs have been preserved, no one
has the slightest idea of their melody, and experiments carried out on the
instruments discovered have not so far allowed scholars to reconstruct the
actual sound of Egyptian music. Very little can therefore be said about it,
and researchers' findings are limited to the description and dating of
ancient instruments. These are essentially the same instruments as in the
rest of Africa, that is the arched harp (recorded in the Nile valley from
2,600 B.C.) and its various derivatives, bamboo flutes of all kinds
including the long flute without mouthpiece which was played obliquely
and survives in the contemporary *nay*, single and double clarinets, and also
trumpets which were used first and foremost in funerary cults for the
voyage of the dead on special boats to the beyond, and finally percussion
instruments, among which one must single out the *sistrum*, a kind of rattle
associated from early on with religious ceremony.

---

[7] See the article on Egypt by R. Anderson and J. Pacholczyk in Grove's *Dictionary of
Music and Musicians.*

One interesting detail is that in numerous paintings the musicians depicted are mentioned by their names, which is an indication of the high esteem in which professional musicians were held in the court of the pharaohs. While string instruments were played by both men and women, wind instruments seem to have been the prerogative of male musicians. Curiously, from the time of the New Kingdom (1567-1085 B.C.) harpists were represented as being blind.

The music of ancient Egypt went through many transformations as a result of repeated invasions of the Nile Valley, but it disappeared for good after the introduction of Islam in the seventh century, and Arab music took its place. Nevertheless it is to be presumed that elements of that ancient music have survived until today in the musical traditions of Nubia, among the Bedouin of the Egyptian desert and the boatmen and fellahin of the Nile valley, as well as in the liturgy of the Coptic church.

SECOND PART - THE FATHER

Let us now leave the world of the mother of the Chevalier de Saint-Georges and turn to that of his father. Here too we have made every effort to draw as authentic a picture as possible. We have used such information as is available to us on this world of 250 years ago and avoided customary rationalisations and euphemisms that conceal the facts. For it is not enough to say, "I was born in Europe and so I know all about Europeans." What do we actually know about the life of Europeans two and a half centuries ago and above all about those who lived in the colonies?

We have learned some things at school and others from historical novels. Young people have picked up certain ideas watching films in the cinema and on television, but these too are often based on a romantic, idealised vision rather than on historical fact. The literature and painting of the colonial period, and those who were inspired by them, naturally endeavoured to convey the image of a white world at the height of progress and civilisation conducting a praiseworthy battle against "primitive barbarism" in its colonial territories. And the image served up by the cameras of Hollywood and other centres of the film industry encourages the notion of the "good old days" that knew no sickness, fear or other ills.

We might note that the world of the Chevalier de Saint-Georges was also that of the grandfather of another famous man of colour, Alexandre Dumas, the author of "The Three Musketeers", who through his numerous novels helped create the ideal, heroic world that still shapes our imagination. Alexandre Dumas was the son of a mulatto, born at Jérémie in Haiti, named Alexandre Dumas Davy de la Pailleterie, who like Saint-Georges was the son of an African slave and a white landowner. Moreover the connection between Saint-Georges and Dumas does not end there, for as we shall see Dumas Davy de la Pailleterie was to serve under Saint-Georges at the time of the French Revolution. In view of this link, one might have expected Dumas to choose Saint-Georges as the model for D'Artagnan, Athos or Porthos in the novel since he so well embodied the musketeer ideal. There is however a reason why he did not. Dumas was indeed a man of colour but he was second generation and, since he identified himself with his European antecedents, preferred to make his musketeers white.

I. THE COLONIAL SCENE - The world of the white masters

Having sketched a picture of Mother Africa and followed her unfortunate children to the Americas, we now turn our gaze on the world of the white masters and Saint-Georges's father. The scene is the French West Indian colonies.

A paradise with two faces

The West Indies - enchanted isles of a thousand fragrances and an emerald sea, white beaches and coconut palms, glorious dawns and flaming sunsets - by their name alone evoke dreams in the soul of the European, and seductively invite him to satisfy his untiring quest for happiness. Of course it is an illusion. Historical truth is forgotten in the desire for happiness. "This handsome mulatto has about him the scent of cinnamon and distant islands", someone said dreamily when talking about Saint-Georges, forgetting the horror behind appearances and the abominations these islands had witnessed. We find the same misrepresentation in painters of the past who have passed down to us idyllic scenes of well-dressed, well-fed and smiling slaves.

The majority of the tourists who descend on the shores of this archipelago today - and it is one of the most important tourist areas in the world - see the external beauty and nothing more. They come to have a good time and want to forget rather than remember the past. The dark shadows are dispelled by the good humour of the black population, the rhythms of its music and the bright colours of the crowded scene. Tourist publicity is aimed at an image of serenity. Its purpose is far from raising a monument to the unknown slave or pointing up the contrast between the luxury hotels that line the beaches and the poverty of West Indians driven to emigration to western capitals, where they form an underclass exposed to racial discrimination. Has slavery really been abolished, or has it just changed its face?

The Spanish conquest

The first "tourist" to set foot on West Indian soil was Christopher Columbus. In October 1492 he discovered Cuba, and then having heard from his Arawak guides of a great island to the East, famous for its riches, he changed course and on 6 December of the same year dropped anchor in a magnificent bay. It was a sunlit morning, and at the sight of the high terraces encircling the bay, and beyond them the blue mass of mountains in the interior, he was overwhelmed by the splendour of sun, sea and sky. "Es una maravilla!", he cried.

This marvel was Haiti. Columbus, as the King of Spain's emissary, disembarked on this happy island and planted the cross there to signify its incorporation into the European world. The name Haiti comes from the language of the Tainos, Indians of Arawak origin who inhabited the island at that time, and it means mountainous country. There are indeed mountain peaks higher than 3000 metres. Columbus substituted the name "Isla Española" or "Hispaniola", which were later replaced by Santo Domingo. The Tainos did not survive long after the arrival of the Spanish. By 1533 there were only 600 left of the estimated million inhabitants.

The French West Indies

France established its sovereignty over the western part of the island in the seventeenth century, which was then known as Saint-Domingue, and also over several other West Indian islands such as Guadeloupe and Martinique. Thanks to the forced labour of the African slaves who had replaced the extinct Tainos, the French West Indies experienced a boom and soon became the main focus of French external trade. There was a rapid development of sugar, and then coffee and cotton, plantations. The boom was most spectacular on Saint-Domingue. It was called the pearl of the West Indies and became France's pride and glory in the Americas, for on the backs of slaves it created the most glittering society yet seen in the New World.

The island received a military, administrative and judicial organisation. Towns and villages were built, irrigation works set up and roads constructed over the plains and mountains for the traffic in merchandise. Vast settlements spread throughout the territory as well as thousands of plantations for tropical crops and factories for processing them and meeting the needs of development. Fine roads, lined with orange and lemon trees and palms, linked the principal towns. Stagecoaches and mail-coach services facilitated communication. Practically every parish boasted a post office and mail left for Europe twice a week.

Paris in miniature

The towns were full of bustle. Le Cap, which was the colony's first capital, was the richest of all. Because of its opulence and amenities the colonists called it "the Paris of the West Indies". Elegant ladies and fine gentlemen of the colonial aristocracy promenaded along the Cours Brasseur and the Cours Villevard, dressed in the latest Parisian fashions. There was a theatre where the current Parisian hits were performed. Port-au-Prince, founded in 1749, ran Le Cap close in its splendour. Other important towns were Saint-Marc in the Artibonite, Les Cayes in the South and Jacmel in the West.

While there were many opportunities for pleasure in the towns, they were surpassed in sumptuousness by life on the estates of some of the major planters. Their life-style was princely. They had fine horses and luxurious carriages. They held magnificent hunting parties, where the colony's belles chased the wild pig mounted on magnificent hunters imported from North America. And on a smaller scale this colonial scene was duplicated on the smaller islands such as Guadeloupe and Martinique.

A heterogeneous society

Although the whites were uncontested masters in relation to the blacks and those of mixed blood, in their own society there was a very strict hierarchy which reflected that of the metropolis. At the bottom of the ladder came the "little whites", artisans or small-time planters who earned their living by the sweat of their brow and were often quite poor. But that did not stop them feeling superior to coloured people on the strength of their white skin, even when these were well-off and educated. Indeed, they were the bitterest enemies of the blacks and mulattos.

There were also people who had come from metropolitan France to seek their fortune on the islands. Some of them were agents and representatives of commercial firms in Dieppe, le Havre, Bordeaux and Marseilles; but some of the less respectable included fugitives, bankrupts, discharged or demoted officers, defrocked priests and the like.

The "Big Whites"

In their turn, the little whites were at the beck and call of the big whites, a small exclusive caste that owned vast plantations, mostly sugar, and hordes of slaves. They formed a kind of colonial aristocracy who were consulted by the administration and officered the local militias. They were entrenched in the French colonies for generations and developed their own distinguishing features. Writers on the period mention their elegance and beauty, their lively and impetuous temperament as well as their extreme indolence. These rich sugar planters were attached to the amenities of France and sometimes spent long periods there, making the most of their fortunes and business connections. They also educated their children in France. The colonies afforded no higher education, in accordance with the French government's measures to preclude too strong a sense of independence in its overseas possessions by imbuing its young citizens with a sense of loyalty towards the mother country as well as with its culture.

The allure of black women

Liaisons between white men and black or mulatto women were very common right through the colonial period. Few colonists did not have a coloured mistress. This was true even of the big landowners, and they gave these liaisons a semi-official character that wives could do nothing but tolerate. On the other hand, mixed marriages were frowned upon and therefore few and far between. White men who nevertheless married coloured women were subjected to general contempt from colonial society, and were sometimes affected by sanctions such as refusal to recognise their aristocratic titles and banning from positions in the army and administration. This state of affairs helped multiply illicit relations, and these were looked upon more kindly than marriage because they kept black women in a subordinate position where they enjoyed no rights.

The status of mulattos

These liaisons produced a special caste in its own right, the mulattos. And since the Chevalier de Saint-Georges belonged to this we must give it some scrutiny. The mulattos formed a class that was acceptable to no one. Most of the whites rejected them because they brought together two elements that should be kept apart forever. The blacks feared them because of their ambiguous position between the master and his human mule. As the term mulatto indicates, the half-caste was regarded as a kind of elevated mule, somewhat privileged in comparison with the ordinary beast of burden but a far cry from man created in the image of God.

The desire of white power to keep coloured people in perpetual servitude is expressed with unparalleled clarity in a letter written by the French Minister of the Navy on 13 October 1766 to the Governor of Guyana, Maillart: "We must remember that all the negroes were transported to the colonies as slaves, and that slavery has indelibly marked them for all time, including those of mixed race; it therefore follows that their descendants can never be treated as white."[1] And on 10 April 1770 a communication from Versailles assured the Haitian authorities "how determined His Majesty is to uphold the principle keeping people of colour and their posterity for ever apart from all the advantages enjoyed by the whites". The reason for this was "the distinction set by nature between white and black people, which has been carefully maintained on political grounds as a barrier never to be crossed by coloured people and their descendants; a distinction all the more useful as it exists in the very hearts of the slaves themselves and makes a major contribution to the peacefulness of life in the colonies." His Very Christian Majesty also emphasised that "it is important for law and order not to undermine the humble status intrinsic to negroes whatever their station might be."[2]

And a West Indian historian, Hilliard d'Auberteuil, writes: "Interest and security demand that we overwhelm the black race with such contempt that whoever is descended from it is marked with an ineffaceable stigma to the sixth generation."[3]

Unmixed black people were considered subhuman, but mulattos symbolised vice and sin. There was a willingness to acknowledge certain qualities inherited from the father, but only to emphasise the opposing disabilities, and this in words of sanctimonious hostility. Much was made of the mulattos' love of finery, smart clothing and polite manners, but only to throw up the caricature of monkeys in human dress. The purpose remained to deny the black man any legitimate status beyond servitude.

It was then hardly surprising if some mulattos tried to "whiten" their posterity and to make them "jump the barrier", as used to be said. Through successive white marriages a line could achieve whiteness after two or

---

[1] Bellegarde, *op. cit.* p. 41.

[2] ibid.

[3] ibid.

three generations. These "parvenus of the skin" were among the fiercest enemies of the stigmatised colour and they took great care to hide their black ancestry. The worst insult that could be made to "new whites" was to call them "descendants of coast people", and this was an insult that could be wiped out only by killing the offender in a duel.

Colonial apartheid

Although mulattos constituted a majority among the enfranchised, this did not mean that all mulattos were free simply by virtue of their whiter colour. About half of them stayed slaves. And even when emancipated, mulattos always had to show respect to white people, their natural superiors. For instance, it was not permissible for a half-caste to keep his hat on in the presence of a white, whoever he might be. And he had to let him go first through doorways. At church, in the theatre and in public conveyances, on boats and at table, the half-caste had his separate place.

The liberated mulattos' life was governed by all sorts of taboos imposed by the king or the colonial administration. In the second half of the eighteenth century these taboos multiplied. In 1758 they were forbidden to carry a sword except when on duty. Certain professions, such as physician or goldsmith, were barred to them. In 1767 the king expressly confirmed that "all those descended from a negro race are banned from every kind of public function and office, and even more from membership of the nobility". In 1774 the emancipated were forbidden to assume the names of whites. In 1777 entry to France was formally prohibited for all coloured people - with the exception of the military. In 1778 mixed marriages were forbidden in France. Even though the enforcement of these regulations was sometimes arbitrary - this was a time when "the king's pleasure" could override any law - the result was that coloured people were constantly subjected to vexations and humiliations.

The mulattos in France

We must emphasise that the situation of mulattos in France was more favourable than in the colonies. They constituted a small minority which in no way threatened the establishment, whereas in Haiti they were almost as many as the whites. In 1789 the colony numbered 40 000 whites, more or less the same population of mulattos, and an overwhelming majority of

700 000 blacks.[4] And then in France the mulattos were often the sons of rich or noble whites and as such enjoyed powerful protection. Some of them had access to the best schools. Some of them even served in the royal household; others were actually officers in different regiments, and we shall see that this happened to Saint-George. But when these young coloured people returned to their colonies they suffered the cruellest humiliation. Laujon, a young metropolitan jurist who disembarked in Haiti, described this return to the fold in 1787: "Many of them held rank in the army. Their mere appearance was enough to command respect, and yet as soon as they set foot on the soil of Haiti they were subjected to public scorn and to any insult that might occur to the first white face they encountered."[5]

These educated young mulattos were to become such a dangerous ferment threatening colonial order that on the eve of the French Revolution every attempt was made to stop them returning to their native colonies.

---

[4] Victor Schoelcher, *op. cit.*, p. 1.

[5] Bellegarde, *op. cit.*, p. 176.

II. GEORGE DE BOLOGNE SAINT-GEORGE

Fictitious fathers

There has been a great deal of confusion as to the father of the Chevalier de Saint-George. Its source seems to have been a novel by Roger de Beauvoir[1] which attributes the Chevalier's paternity to Jean de Boullongne, Count of Nogent, who was Treasurer of the Order of the Holy Spirit and Controller-General of Finance under Louis XV during the years 1757-1759; he was descended from the family of the celebrated painters, Louis and Bon de Boullongne, of Flemish origin. Now, Jean de Boullongne never lived in the West Indies, as is indisputably proved by the dates of his career as high magistrate. Other authors, notably the Count of Caix de St-Aymour[2], identify as the Chevalier's father a cousin of the former, Guillaume-Pierre de Boullongne-Tavernier, Marquess of Busancy, Vice-Treasurer of the French Colonies in the Americas from 1750 to 1758, and then Extraordinary Treasurer-General for War and Treasurer-Commander of the Order of St-Louis until 1779. And then others have opted for his brother, Philippe-Guillaume de Boullongne-Préninville, the lord of Magnanville and farmer general.

All these retrospective paternities completely contradict the testimony of one of the first biographers of the Chevalier de Saint-George. This was his friend and contemporary, the Anglo-Italian fencer Henry Angelo, who said that the father was "a rich planter" from Guadeloupe.[3] In fact, none of the three persons mentioned above matches this designation, and there is no reference to possessions in the West Indies in the various accounts of their careers or in such testaments as survive. Moreover, neither the genealogy nor the nobility titles of the Boullongnes bear the name Saint-George, and the only connection with it is a place called Landres et St-Georges in the marquessate of Busancy (in the Ardennes, Vouziers district), which was bought around 1766 by Boullongne-Tavernier, and

---

[1] R. de Beauvoir, *Le Chevalier de St-Georges*, Paris, edit. Dumont, 1840.

[2] Caix de St-Aymour, *Une famille d'artistes et de financiers aux XVIIe et XVIIIe siècles - Les Boullongne*, Paris, Henri Laurens, editor, 1919, pp. 92-93.

[3] H. Angelo, *Angelo's Pic Nic*, memoirs publ. in London, 1905, pp. 9-10.

LE CHEVALIER

DE

SAINT-GEORGES

PAR

ROGER DE BEAUVOIR

NOUVELLE ÉDITION

PARIS

MICHEL LÉVY FRÈRES, LIBRAIRES-ÉDITEURS

RUE VIVIENNE, 2 BIS

—

1839

Reproduction et traduction réservées.

Title page of biography by Roger de Beauvoir:
Le Chevalier de Saint-Georges, Paris, 1840

another place called Fontaine St-Georges in the Nogent-sur-Seine district where Count Jean de Boullongne had his seat.

In search of the true father

We next carried our researches to the Archives Nationales et des Territoires d'Outremer (TOM) in Paris, starting with the data we possessed on the Chevalier de Saint-George that was verified by official documents. We knew his name, Joseph Bologne Saint-George; his place of birth, Guadeloupe; and the approximate date of birth, in the 1740s. We consulted the records of the Guadeloupe civil registry, and although we unfortunately found neither an entry for the birth of Saint-George nor cast-iron evidence of the father's identity, we did make a series of significant discoveries which, we believe, allow us to claim that we have succeeded in identifying the real father.

George de Bologne Saint-George - a typical West Indian landlord

The father's name is George de Bologne Saint-George - he always signed his name without the final "s", just as the Chevalier did. He was a gentleman of the King's bedchamber, and an important planter at Basse-Terre/Guadeloupe. He was the first citizen with the name Bologne Saint-George to appear in the records of the civil registry of Basse-Terre, the principal island and capital of Guadeloupe. The details of his biography emerging from our researches tally with the accounts of the Chevalier's first biographers - La Boëssière junior and Henry Angelo - and also elucidate some of the most obscure aspects of the Chevalier's life, such as his financial circumstances. In pursuing our research we also established that long before ourselves, Odet Denys, the author of a fictionalised biography published in Paris in 1972 under the title "Qui était le chevalier St-George?", had already scoured the archives and had reached the same conclusion as ourselves. However, he did not relate the vicissitudes of the life of George de Bologne St-George, either because he had not had access to the source documents or because he chose to preserve silence on the subject.

George de Bologne Saint-George was a typical rich landlord of the French West Indies. He was the youngest son of Pierre de Bologne, a wealthy colonist and major in the Lonvilliers Regiment in Guadeloupe.

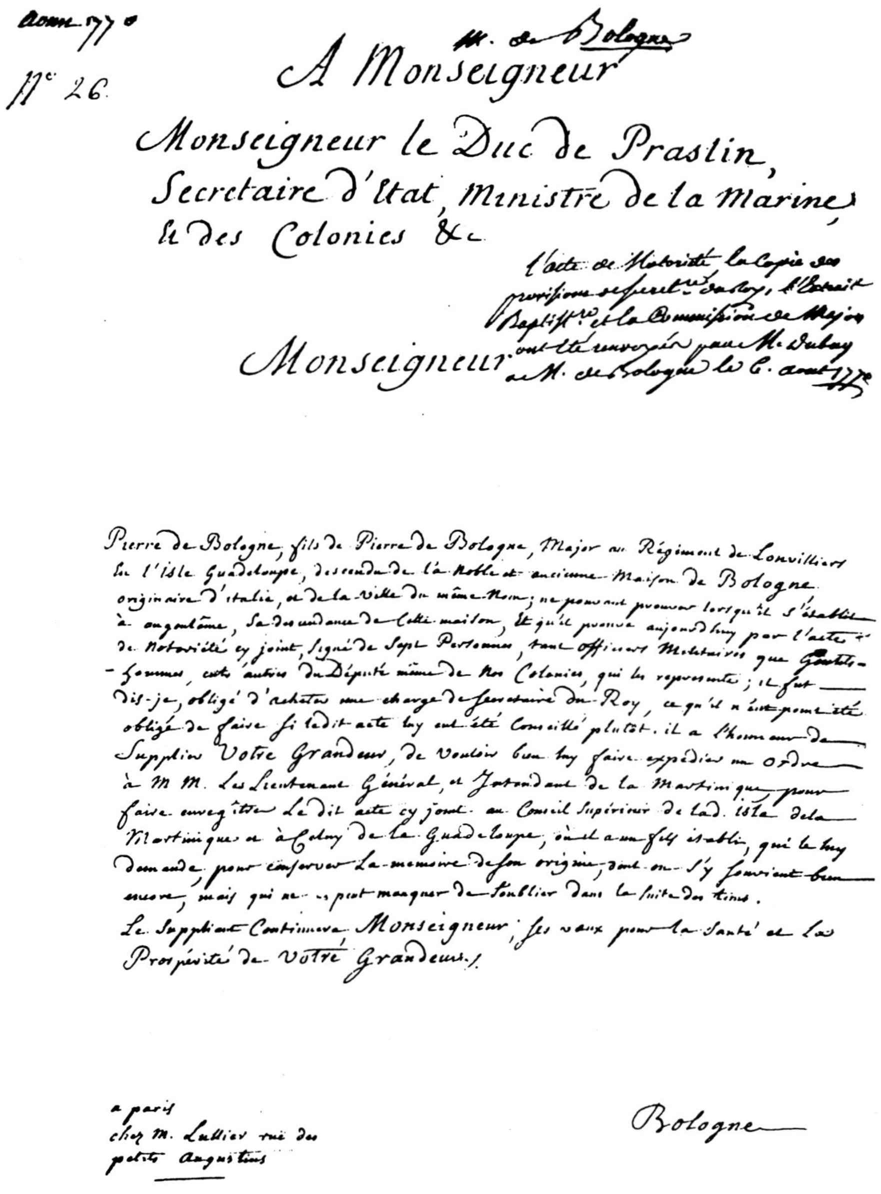

Anné 1770

N° 26

M. de Bologne

A Monseigneur

Monseigneur le Duc de Praslin, Secretaire d'Etat, Ministre de la Marine et des Colonies &c

l'acte de Notorieté la Copie des provisions de Secret.re du Roy, l'Extrait Baptist.re et la Commission de Major ont été envoyées par M. Dubuc a M. de Bologne le 6. aout 1770

Monseigneur

Pierre de Bologne, fils de Pierre de Bologne, Major au Régiment de Lonvilliers en l'isle Guadeloupe, descendu de la Noble et ancienne Maison de Bologne originaire d'italie, et de la ville du même Nom; ne pouvant prouver lorsqu'il s'établit à angoulême, sa descendance de cette maison, et qu'il prouve aujourd'huy par l'acte de Notorieté cy joint, signé de Sept Personnes, tant officiers Militaires que Gentilshommes, entr'autres du Député même de nos Colonies, qui les represente; il fut dis-je, obligé d'acheter une charge de Secretaire du Roy, ce qu'il n'eût point été obligé de faire si ledit acte luy eut été conseillé plutôt. il a l'honneur de Supplier Votre Grandeur, de vouloir bien luy faire expédier un Ordre à M M. les Lieutenant Général, et Intendant de la Martinique pour faire enregistrer Le dit acte cy joint au Conseil Supérieur de lad. isle de la Martinique et à Celuy de la Guadeloupe, où il a un fils établi, qui le luy demande, pour conserver La memoire de son origine, dont on s'y souvient bien encore, mais qui ne peut manquer de s'oublier dans la suite des tems.

Le Suppliant Continuera Monseigneur, ses vœux pour la Santé et la Prospérité de Votre Grandeur./

a paris
chez M. Lullier rue des petits Augustins

Bologne

Letter of Pierre de Bologne to the Duke of Praslin, Minister of the Navy, which must have been written at the end of 1769 or the beginning of 1770. In this he requests the registration of an official declaration establishing the line of descent. Dossier Bologne, Serie E 37, Archives Nationales, Paris

Italian origins

His family probably derived from "the noble and ancient house of Bologne, of Italian origin". That at least is the claim made by his older brother, Pierre de Bologne, in a letter to the Duke of Praslin, Minister of the Navy, which must have been written at the end of 1769 or the beginning of 1770. In this he requests the registration of an official declaration establishing the line of descent. This is the complete text of the letter:

"To His Grace the Duke of Praslin, Secretary of State, Minister of the Navy and the Colonies
Sir,
Pierre de Bologne, son of Pierre de Bologne, major in the Lonvilliers Regiment on the Isle of Guadeloupe, a descendant of the noble and ancient house of Bologne, originating in Italy, and from the city of the same name, presents this petition. Being unable, when he settled in Angoulême, to prove his descent from this house, establishes the same today by virtue of the enclosed declaration, signed by seven persons who are army officers and gentlemen, among them the Deputy of our colonies who is their representative. He found himself obliged to purchase an order from the King's Secretary, which would not have been necessary if the said declaration had been suggested to him earlier. He has the honour of entreating Your Grace to have an order transmitted to Their Honours the Lieutenant-General and Intendant of Martinique so as to secure the registration of the enclosed declaration by the Higher Council of the said Island of Martinique and also Guadeloupe, for there he has a son living who asks this of him in order to preserve the record of his origin. This origin is still well remembered there but may otherwise fall into oblivion in the course of time.
The supplicant will, Sir, maintain his wishes for the health and prosperity of Your Grace.
From the residence of M. Lullier,
Rue des Petits Augustins, Paris.   signed: Bologne"[4]

---

[4] Dossier Bologne, Series E 37 in the Archives Nationales. The document in question is no longer attached to the letter but there is a note in the hand of the recipient indicating that it was returned to Pierre de Bologne on 6 April 1770.

This Pierre de Bologne, who must have been the uncle of the Chevalier de Bologne, acquired something of a reputation as a poet. He was born on Martinique in 1706, enlisted in the Musketeers and, after being discharged at the time of the Peace of Aix-la-Chapelle, settled in Angoulême. Here in 1749 he married Bénédictine Husson, the daughter of a rich bourgeois who had a senior position in the financial department of La Rochelle. In the same year, he bought the office of King's Counsellor-Secretary, with the right to attend the Metz parliament. This office raised him to the first order of nobility, with the title of Squire, and he exercised it until 1781. He secured the registration of his titles with the Superior Council of Guadeloupe in 1764. Also he secured his admission to the Academy of the Inestricati of Bologna in Italy. His poetic works mainly comprise sacred odes, and a collection of these was published in 1758. According to Sabatier de Castres, he was among the best poets of his time for this genre. In 1786 he also published a book entitled "Amusements d'un septuagénaire". He must have died about 1789. He had two sons, Clément-Pierre and Pierre-Clément, both of whom married in Guadeloupe where their father had left them a coffee estate.

A family of sugar planters and officers

The Bologne family (sometimes Boulogne - both spellings are found, sometimes in the same document) seems to have settled on Guadeloupe as early as the mid-seventeenth century. From 1664 one finds them established as sugar planters at Montagne St-Louis in Basse-Terre. In that year's census (Archives Nationales, Séries G 1) they are listed as associated with the Vander Stratin family, and a certain Louis Bologne is registered as a "heretic" (protestant). At least one branch of the family seems to have come from Rotterdam, for in the 1687 census we find a certain Sieur Pittre (Pierre) de Bologne "native of Rotterdam", with his wife whose maiden name was Vaney Bergen (or Vanden Bergen), as the owner of some thirty slaves. Alongside him there is a Sieur Guillaume de Bologne, sugar planter and cavalry officer, owner of 45 slaves, who is also a native of Rotterdam. These Bolognes were perhaps brothers, and they are both mentioned among the leading citizens of Basse-Terre and St-Louis who in 1686 made voluntary contributions for the island's fortification.

In succeeding generations the Bolognes are seen to increase in number and in wealth, with sugar and coffee plantations. Many of them held high

rank in the colony's armed forces. We can see then that the father of the
Chevalier de Saint-George was born of a typical rich colonialist family.

A legitimate daughter - Elizabeth Bénédictine de Bologne

According to the records of the Basse-Terre civil registry office, George
de Bologne Saint-George was born in 1710 as the youngest son of Sieur
Pierre de Bologne and Catherine d'Hérigoyen. On 8 September 1739 he
married Elizabeth Françoise Jeanne Mérican, and the wedding took place
in the parish of St-François in Basse-Terre where her parents lived. On
21 January 1740 a daughter was born of this marriage, Elizabeth
Bénédictine de Bologne. The certificate of baptism was not signed by the
father. In 1745, when the girl was five, she was sent to France, presumably
for the sake of her education.[5]

A revealing document - Father Archange's statement

In all the documents relating to the family affairs of George de Bologne
St-George there is reference to this child only - but there is one notable
exception. In a statement written around 1782, in connection with a
dispute between the parish and the Bologne family over its burial rights in
the chapel of the Holy Virgin of the church of St-François in Basse-Terre,
the parish priest wrote quite definitely that Bologne St-George had <u>two</u>
children, a girl and a boy, "both living in France" (that is, in 1782).[6] Father
Archange's statement, and the total silence otherwise on the subject of this
son, notably in the documents concerning Bologne St-George's inheritance,
lead one to think that the second child must have been an illegitimate son,
a bastard. In the absence of formal proof, we have here an indirect proof
that the Chevalier de Saint-George really was the son of Sieur Bologne St-
George. To this must be added the name itself, which is an indication that
at some time and place the father must have acknowledged his illegitimate

---

[5] According to a document relating to Bologne St-George's inheritance, the "Extrait des
Registres du Conseil d'Etat" incorporated in the Bologne Dossier, Série Colonies E37 of
the Archives Nationales.

[6] This document is in the same Bologne Dossier. The certificates of marriage, the
daughter's baptism and Bologne St-Geoorge's death are however all to be found in the
civil registries of the parishes of St-François, Basse-Terre, or St-Dominique, Le Baillif,
kept in the DOM-TOM Archives.

mr Pierre Bologne a mis la premiere pierre
à cette eglyse à peuprès vers l'année 1742
Ce Pierre Bologne n'a eut que deux fils dont l'un
etoit St george Bologne et l'autre marié en france
Ce St: george Bologne n'a eut qu'une fille et un garçon
qui est le beau pere de mr: galard tous deux etablij en france

Pierre de Bologne a eul pour frere samuel et louij
de Bologne tous deux changers a la pojition de
jas premiere pierre de mr: de ... pierre de Bologne
maj personne ne dira qu'en posant la premiere pierre
a un edifice on en acquiert le domaine il s'en juiveroient
les plus grandes absurditez

Facsimile of the Memoire of Père Archange, Paroisse St-François,
where is mentioned, that Bologne St-George had two children, a daughter
and a son (important document as indication of paternity) -
Dossier Bologne, Serie E 37 Archives Nationales, Paris

son, even though there is no official record of this recognition in the records we have studied. And then there is Henry Angelo's description of St-George's father as a "rich planter of the colony" (of Guadeloupe).[7]

Sieur Bologne St-George's misadventure

George de Bologne St-George initially followed the habitual life style of one of the "big whites", as the owner of an important sugar estate at La Montagne St-Robert, Baillif/Basse-Terre, with a large number of slaves. But in December 1747 something happened that was to bring turmoil to this grandeur. The incredible story that we have unearthed from the archives may provide the reason why the first biographers of the Chevalier de St-George were so reticent about his father's identity and thus occasioned all the speculations we have mentioned above as to his presumptive paternity.

One Sunday, as was the custom, Bologne St-George was among several guests at his uncle's, Samuel de Bologne, a sugar planter whose estate was situated not far from his own. After dinner he got into a quarrel with one of his cousins. It was not a serious affair, just some teasing banter between family members who had drunk a little too much. But a third guest, Le Vanier St-Robert, intervened and this led to some sword play. Honour had been offended, and this occurred all the more readily because the colonists were known for their hot blood. In the ensuing scuffle Bologne St-George wounded Le Vanier on the nose. This did not seem particularly serious because Le Vanier got up and went home unaided. But three days later he died.

Accusation of homicide and flight

Although death was probably caused by tetanus rather than the wound itself, Bologne St-George found himself accused of homicide, and took to flight.

In the trial that followed, one deposition in particular deserves our attention, because if true it indicates a harsh or negligent aspect of Bologne St-George's character. When Le Vanier's brother-in-law, Captain Brunbeaupain, came to announce his relative's death to Bologne St-George and ask what action he intended to take, he offered the sum of

---

[7] H. Angelo, *op. cit.*, p. 9.

10,000 francs in compensation. Since the widow was left penniless with seven children, Brunbeaupain replied that this could not even be contemplated. Bologne St-George is said to have retorted, "In that case, I'll settle for the sum of a thousand *écus* (3,000 livres) and a trip to France."

Condemned to death and executed in effigy

However, on 31 March 1748 Bologne St-George was sentenced in his absence to "be hanged and strangled until death ensues on the gallows erected in the corner of the public square in this town of Basseterre" and to the confiscation of all his goods. The widow who had claimed 100,000 livres was awarded 30,000 in damages. A full transcription of the record of the trial, with all the testimony presented, is included in the Bologne Dossier mentioned above (Série E in the National Archives).

The hanging was carried out in effigy on 25 October 1748. As for Bologne St-George we know nothing of his whereabouts at the time.

The King's pardon

A note appended to the dossier subsequently tells us that the condemned man obtained the King's pardon, but the date of this decree is not stated. We find Bologne St-George back in Basse-Terre in 1755, when on 23 April of that year he signed the death certificate of his uncle Samuel. (It is noteworthy that in the various documents signed by him and included in the Baillif registry office he sometimes signed himself Bologne St-George and sometimes St-George Bologne.)

A mysterious exile

It is possible, but by no means proven, that during the seven year period between his disappearance and the signature at Basse-Terre, Bologne St-George withdrew temporarily to Haiti. Two writers, Roger de Beauvoir in his book already quoted, and Odet Denys[8], maintain that the Chevalier's father bought an estate on that island. Odet Denys even specifies that he obtained a free concession from the King for a vast sugar plantation. We have not however been able to find any reference in the Boulogne Dossier

---

[8] Odet Denys, *Qui était le chevalier de St-Georges?* Paris, Le Pavillon, Roger Maria, e-ditor, 1972.

to any activity of this kind or to a property in Haiti, and the documents of his inheritance make no mention.

Nanon and the birth of her son

It was probably from among his household slaves that Bologne St-George selected a mistress in the person of the beautiful Nanon[9], a girl who according to Odet Denys was of Senegalese origin. Nanon's son seems to have been born on Christmas day, and he was given the name of Joseph. So far as the year of birth is concerned, there are various suggestions in the biographies of Saint-George, as we shall see in the following chapter. The most reliable undoubtedly is the one given by himself in two official documents[10], and this dates his birth at the end of 1748. This means that he was born during his father's exile.

Journey to France

After being pardoned and having his possessions restored to him, definitely before 1755, Bologne St-George decided to leave for France a few years later. He seems to have established himself there in 1759, taking with him Joseph, aged ten, Nanon and also his legal wife. A document in the archives relating to Bologne St-George's legacy[11] tells us that Elizabeth Mérican-Bolgone came to France in 1759 and lived there until her husband's death on a "modest allowance" he had granted her. The date of 1759 also tallies with the information provided by La Boëssière, that Saint-George was taken to Paris by his father. As for Nanon, it is Angelo who says she accompanied him.

A Parisian Maecenas

As we shall see later, Bologne St-George's life in Paris seems to have been very distinguished and full of generous hospitality towards practitioners of the arts. According to the contemporary testimony of the autobiography of

---

[9] The name Nanon was first mentioned by Angelo, op. cit. It was a very common name among female slaves.

[10] Census and "Registre des Volontaires nationaux", both of Lille, 1791. See subsequent mentions in this book.

[11] "Extrait des Registres du Conseil d'Etat", Boulogne Dossier, Série Colonies E 37, Archives Nationales.

John Adams, the second President of the United States, who was his country's envoy to France at the end of the 1770s, St-George even passed himself off in the capital's high society as a former governor of Guadeloupe. But it may be a question of one of those deformations that come about when remarks are passed from mouth to mouth. One can read in John Adams's journal:

> "17 May 1779 - Landais gave us an account of St-George at Paris, - a mulatto man, son of a former governor of Guadeloupe, by a negro woman. He has a sister married to a farmer-general. He is the most accomplished man in Europe, in riding, running, shooting, fencing, dancing, music. He will hit the button, - any button on the coat or waistcoat of the greatest masters. He will hit a crown-piece in the air with a pistol-ball."[12]

Return to Guadeloupe and death

Bologne St-George may have spent too liberally, or his West Indian possessions may have been in straits, but for whatever reason in 1764 Bologne St-George took out a large loan before a notary in Paris - about half a million French livres, "in order to buy negroes and improve his property on the island of Guadeloupe".[13] He then had to return to Basse-Terre, and left behind in Paris not just his son and Nanon, to whom according to Angelo he paid an annuity of 7,000 or 8,000 francs each, but also his legal wife and daughter. With the borrowed money he set about restoring his possessions, and lived there completely rehabilitated and in lonely splendour until his death in 1774. He was buried on 26 December of this year in the church of St-Dominique at Le Baillif.

---

[12] *The Works of John Adams, Second President of the United States,* ed. by his grandson Ch. F. Adams, Vol. III, Boston, 1851, p. 205. We owe our knowledge of this source to Ellwood Derr, who has written on St-George and to whom we express our gratitude. In the Guadeloupe archives we have not found any Boulogne or St-George as governor of the island.

[13] Papers relating to the Bologne St-George inheritance, Boulogne Dossier, Série E37, Archives Nationales.

THE

WORKS

OF

JOHN ADAMS,

SECOND PRESIDENT OF THE UNITED STATES:

WITH

A LIFE OF THE AUTHOR,

NOTES AND ILLUSTRATIONS,

BY

HIS GRANDSON
CHARLES FRANCIS ADAMS.

VOL. III.

BOSTON:
CHARLES C. LITTLE AND JAMES BROWN.
1851.

Title page of "The Works of John Adams", Second President of the United States:
With a life of the author, notes and illustrations, by
his grandson Charles Francis Adams, Vol, III., Boston: Charles C.
Little and James Brown, 1851.

The Bologne St-George inheritance

His inheritance gave rise to an epic dispute between his heirs and creditors, and we owe some invaluable documents to this, particularly the extract mentioned above from the records of the Conseil d'Etat. For the heirs had requested and obtained the help of the King in their defence against their adversaries. As this document - included in the Boulogne Dossier - says, Bologne St-George left two estates, both of them situated in Le Baillif, parish of St-Dominique. One for sugar was called Saint-Robert, with 212 slaves, and one for coffee was called Mont d'Or, with 61 slaves. The total was put at a value of 1.5 million silver livres of the islands. No mention is made of any possessions on the island of Haiti.

The principal creditor was the Count of Kearney, a former colonial officer, who had lent Bologne St-George the sum of about 200,000 livres. The other creditors were merchants of Nantes and Bordeaux and the brother-in-law of the deceased, Varège de Servanches. In a letter of 25 June 1775 to de Sartines, the Minister for the Navy of the time, the Count of Kearney calls Bologne St-George "the worst-disposed debtor on earth", and he adds in brackets "as M. de Sartines has every reason to know." The main objects of his claims were the slaves on the two estates, and he demands payment "in negroes". In a letter of 10 July 1776 to the same minister he argues that since the sum lent had been used to buy negroes these "represent the amount of the loan", and that they should therefore be exempted from the general rule attaching them to their estates, and treated as movables belonging to him, the Count of Kearney. This was a classic argument of the slavery system.

The sole heirs

In all these documents the sole heirs mentioned are the widow of the deceased, Elizabeth Mérican, and her daughter Elizabeth Bénédictine, the wife of Sieur Le Velu de Clairfontaine, cavalry captain in the King's Regiment. Both ladies were resident in France, the first in the Saint Joseph community in Paris, and the second at Agen in the Garonne. Their representative in Guadeloupe was Clément de Bologne (son of Pierre de Bologne, the poet), respectively their nephew and cousin, who had taken over the management of the two estates.

We can see that Nanon's son counted for nothing in this business. So far as his father's family was concerned he did not exist. We do not know whether his father wanted it this way or not; it might of course have been the son's own wish not to benefit from plantations nourished with the blood and sweat of slaves. However that may be, he was at the time very much in the limelight in Paris.

It may well be that future researchers will find more data on the father of the Chevalier de Saint-George and on the Chevalier's relationship with his paternal family. But in our estimation the most important question is why George de Bologne St-George took his little son Joseph to France.

Given the hardships of the voyage and the mentality of the time, it certainly seems surprising that a white gentleman should so much have wanted to take with him a child who was not even his legitimate son, but a bastard, a mulatto born of his illicit liaison with a slave. Some people may say the reason was that at that time a coloured page boy cut a figure in the household of a rich colonialist back in Paris. But we should give George de Bologne St-George his due. Not only did he take little Joseph to Paris and thus spare him the degrading conditions to which half-castes were exposed in the colonies. He also sent him to the best schools in the French capital and thus allowed his extraordinary gifts to develop.

Some biographers believe that he took Nanon to Paris too. That would indeed have been a way of taking part of the colonies with him and facilitating Joseph's adaptation to Parisian conditions. We do not know how old the mother might have been at that time - perhaps 25 or 26. Nor do we know whether she was still as beautiful as when George de Bologne first noticed her. But such questions are of little importance when love takes over, and we like to think that Bologne St-George's motive in taking Nanon and her son with him was indeed love. Love is, after all, the only force capable of transcending all divisions between groups of human beings, even those divisions decreed by a decadent society to be eternal and insurmountable.

THIRD PART - THE LIFE OF THE CHEVALIER

DE SAINT-GEORGE

THE YEARS 1748-1789

I. CHILDHOOD IN THE WEST INDIES

Realms of light and wisps of anguish

Childhood in the West Indies can mean many different things depending on the colour of your skin. Recalling his own childhood as a white born in Guadeloupe in 1887, the poet St-John Perse wrote a eulogy: "What cause I have for praise! O, what a splendid fable, what a table of abundance!" His childhood world in the West Indies was like the land of Baudelaire's dreams where all is order and beauty, luxury, peace and voluptuousness. Or in St-John Perse's own words, "Realms and horizons of light". It was a pampered childhood, cradled in gentleness: "Palms... One was bathed under green leaves, and the water was like green sunshine. One's mother's servant girls, tall and glistening, moved their warm legs close to one and made one tremble..."[1]

It is hardly necessary to say that the life of those servants' children at the end of the nineteenth century was a long way from anything so idyllic; and this was even truer of the children of their forebears, the eighteenth century slaves, who were born in servitude or shipped to Africa and sold in the colonial markets. Their everyday experience of humiliation and brutal treatment left memories of a different kind. Compare the example of a black Caribbean poet, Aimé Césaire, who was born in Martinique in 1913 and one of the founders of the "negritude" movement. His evocation of his childhood is full of bitterness and despair:

"That town, lifeless after the early morning bustle, with its undercurrent of leprosy, consumption, famine, with fear crouching in ravines, fear perched in the trees, fear dug into the soil, fear drifting in the sky, fear piled on fear - and with that wisp of anguish...

So much blood in my memory! There are lagoons in my memory, but they are full of corpses' heads, not of waterlilies. There are lagoons in my memory, but their shores are not lined with women's loincloths. My memory is enclosed with blood and has a girdle of corpses round it!"[2]

---

[1] St-John Perse, *Pour fêter une enfance,* in "Eloges", 1911, Editions Gallimard, 1960, p. 14.

[2] Aimé Césaire, *Cahier d'un retour au pays natal,* Paris, Présence Africaine 1983, p. 10 and p. 35.

Which of these two childhoods applied to the Chevalier de Saint-George? Listening to his music, with its characteristic interplay of light and dark, we might conclude that there was something of each in his recollections. With the heart and soul of a child, he no doubt drank in the beauties of nature and knew moments of intense joy. But we can equally assume that he came to know fear early in life, and the anguish described by Aimé Césaire. For a child in his situation fear was as much a daily experience as was the beauty of his surroundings, and he had to come to terms with it.

The childhood scenes in Roger de Beauvoir and Odet Denys

In the absence of details about the Caribbean childhood of the Chevalier de Saint-George, authors like Roger de Beauvoir and Odet Denys have tried to supply them from their own imagination, and the results vary with their individual taste. The version of the novelist Roger de Beauvoir[3] is dramatic and embellished with deeds of gallantry and amorous adventures. He devoted half of his two-volume novel, published in 1840, to the childhood, but his story reflects the spirit of his age rather than historical fact, and bears the stigma of European racialism. According to him, St-George spent his childhood as a slave in Haiti, attached to the estate of de Boullongne but without knowing his master was also his father - indeed, he did not meet him until later, when he was living in Paris. (We have already pointed out, at the beginning of the chapter on the father, that de Beauvoir's book was the source of the error, repeated to this day in almost all the biographies, attributing Saint-George's paternity to Jean de Boullongne, Controller-General under Louis XV.) In his novel, de Beauvoir has Saint-George grow up in a wretched bamboo hut, exposed to all the sufferings and humiliations of slave status, where he lives with his mother, whom the author chooses to call Noémi.

The childhood described by Odet Denys in 1972[4] is completely different. The author, a Parisian lawyer born in Guadeloupe, has drawn extensively on historical sources, and like us has discovered the true identity of the father in the National Archives, but without referring to the vicissitudes of his life which we have detailed in the previous chapter. His book is like de

[3] Roger de Beauvoir, *Le Chevalier de Saint-Georges,* Paris, edit. Dumont, 1840.

[4] Odet Denys, *Qui était le Chevalier de St-Georges?*, Paris, Le Pavillion, Roger Maria, editor, 1972.

Beauvoir's a mixture of fact and fiction, but more sober in tone and more humain in outlook. According to Odet Denys, Nanon enjoyed an honourable position in the de Boulogne household and was treated like a second wife and not a slave. Saint-George is shown growing up in his father's mansion, where he spent a relatively protected childhood imbued with a deep feeling of compassion towards the unfortunate slaves.

Which of these pictures is the true one - the infant slave in rags, beaten and rejected by his father, or the cherished son brought up in his father's house? We simply do not know. Let us content ourselves with a summary of what little we do know.

The birth of Joseph de Bologne Saint-George

The Chevalier de Saint-George was probably born at the end of 1748 in Guadeloupe. He was the son of George de Bologne St-George, gentleman in ordinary of the King's Bedchamber, a large-scale planter in Basse-Terre. His mother was a black slave whose name is said to have been Nanon, of Senegalese origin and very beautiful. He was the second child of Bologne St-George and was given the name Joseph.

In the absence of certificates of birth, baptism and of acknowledgement by his father, the place and date of his birth cannot be established with certainty. In different biographies the dates vary considerably, from 1739 to 1749. This is not of course so very surprising in the context of the time. It quite often happens that the exact date of birth of famous people from the past is unknown. But ten years is a long time. This has a major effect on the chronology of the Chevalier's life, especially since historical sources normally identify the principal stages of his life in terms of his age. We have therefore given careful scrutiny to the different dates of birth, their sources and their credibility.

The date of 1739 comes from the death certificate of 1799[5] , witnessed by Nicolas Duhamel, formerly a captain who served under Saint-George, who on signing it indicated that the age of the deceased was 60. This is clearly incorrect, for if Saint-George was born in 1739 he could not have become a pupil of La Boëssière before reaching the age of 20, since the

---

[5] Archives de la Seine, Fonds des Insinuations du 3e et 6e arr., table no. 39, quoted by La Laurencie, *L'école française de violon*, 3 vol., Paris, 1922-24, p. 487.

latter did not open his fencing school until 1759.[6] But La Boëssière's son always said categorically that Saint-George entered his father's school at the age of 13.[7] This is indeed the normal age to begin formal training in the use of arms, especially for someone who was to have a career as brilliant as Saint-George's.

The La Boëssière son himself gives 25 December 1745 as the date of birth[8]. There may be no reason to question the day and the month, but the year is contradicted by two official documents signed by Saint-George himself. These are the Register of National Volunteers of Lille, in which on 25 July 1791 he declares his age as 42[9], and the census of the same town later in the year 1791, in which he declares his age as 43[10]. This indicates that he was born at the end of 1748. We shall therefore adopt this date since the evidence of the subject himself should take precedence. And it might well be that the date of 1745 given in La Boëssière's text derives from a reading error on the part of the printer, since confusion between 5 and 8 could easily happen with eighteenth century manuscripts, as we can confirm from our own researches in them.

The question of the father's exile

As for the exact place of Saint-George's birth, a fairly recent declaration of the Town Council of Basse-Terre states that he was born there.[11] Now, if St-George was really born on 25 December 1748 we must take into account the fact that at that time the father's situation was at its most critical. As we saw in the previous chapter, he had been found guilty of homicide and was condemned to death on 31 March 1748. All his goods had been confiscated and he had been in flight since his indictment at the beginning of 1748. And on 25 October 1748 he was executed, in effigy, on the main square of the town of Basse-Terre.

---

[6] La Boëssière, *Traité de l'Art des Armes,* "Notice Historique sur feu La Boëssière", Paris, l'imprimerie de Didot, l'Ainé, 1818.

[7] ibid., "Notice Historique sur Saint-Georges".

[8] La Boëssière, *op.cit.*,"Notice Historique sur St-Georges".

[9] La Laurencie, *op. cit.*, p. 449.

[10] ibid., p. 475.

[11] La Laurencie, *op. cit.*, p. 489. The declaration was made on 28 November 1912, when the council decided to rename one of its roads "rue du Chevalier de St-Georges".

The bonds of affection suggest that Nanon accompanied Bologne St-George in his mysterious exile and, if this is so, it is extremely unlikely that Joseph was born in Basse-Terre. So there is a question mark over this too. The only thing that seems certain is that the mulatto boy's early childhood must have been marked by the precariousness of his father's - not to mention his mother's - situation. Be that as it may, after 1755 Bologne St-George had been pardoned by the King and resumed possession of his property in Basse-Terre. The lives of Nanon and her son must then have taken a more normal course.

Departure for France

In general terms, the life of the great European composers in past centuries has been contained within the familiar geographical area of Europe. With the Chevalier de Saint-George it was different. His life may be said to embrace three continents: Africa, where his mother's roots were; America, where he was born and spent his early childhood; and Europe, whence his father originated. It was to the last of these, beyond the vast Atlantic Ocean, that fate was to direct the child's future.

It was probably at the beginning of 1759, when Joseph had reached the age of ten, that his father decided to leave the islands and go and live in France, taking with him not only his son but also, it seems, his legal wife and Nanon. The date of 1759 derives first and foremost from La Boëssière's statement that Saint-George was brought to live in France by his father "at the age of ten".[12] Again, it is known that Elisabeth de Bologne St-George settled in France in 1759. As for Nanon, it is Henry Angelo, Saint-George's friend, who affirms that she came to France with them.[13]

What was Nanon's role in this "foursome", which may strike us as odd but was probably not so unusual for people from the colonies? Was she just an accessory, a servant to the married couple? Or was she rather a kind of second wife, as Odet Denys suggests, whom the legal wife would have been forced to accept? Did Madame de Bologne actually live with her husband or did she withdraw to the Convent of St.Joseph as soon as she arrived in France? We have no definite answer to these questions, but it

---

[12] La Boëssière, *op. cit.*, "Notice Historique sur St-Georges".

[13] Angelo, *op. cit.*, p. 11.

seems that one of the motives inducing George de Bologne St-George to bring Nanon to France must have been his desire to save his son the pain of separation from his mother.

A new life for young Joseph

A new and extraordinary life was about to begin for Joseph, unique in the history of European music and moving in many other ways. But for him at the time the voyage simply meant plunging into the unknown. And unknown is the right word, for we must bear in mind not only the great distance separating the Caribbean from France but also the hazards of transatlantic sea travel at a time when ships were at the mercy of storms and pirates, and often did not reach their destination. We must remember too the illnesses that could afflict people on the high seas, and the limited medical facilities. These were the hazards and hardships of voyaging across the ocean 250 years ago.

The age of the steam-ship had yet to come. The first crossing of the Atlantic by steam was not until 1819. But in the year 1759 great sailing-ships were still the order of the day, and the one that carried the mulatto boy to Europe cannot have been much different, so far as external appearance is concerned, from the ship that bore his mother from Africa to the West Indies.

Let us summon up in our imagination what young Joseph's voyage from the West Indies to Paris must have been like, beginning with the embarkation. Most of us have somewhere deep in our memory a recollection of the fateful moment of embarking for new horizons - the bustle of the port, the scenes of farewell, the shipping of the gangways, the raising of the anchor and finally the vessel's gradual departure from the roads for infinite horizons. One fine day, young Joseph was among it all, on the quay of some Caribbean port - we do not know which - waiting to board a ship whose name we also do not know. We can picture him, fascinated but uneasy in the face of the adventure that awaits him. He must have been reassured by his mother's presence, and no doubt by that of his father. He must have been used to excitement. In his life in the colony he must have known many upheavals, and perhaps this taught him the virtue of silence.

The crossing took about two months at that time. The days spent between the water and the sky seemed interminable; the only rhythm came from the wind and the only shapes on the horizon were the sudden appearance of an enemy, or more rarely a friendly, ship. Eventually land was sighted. On a cool spring morning in 1759 the ship entered the roads of a French port. Was it Brest, Le Havre, Bordeaux? We do not know. But it is quite possible that on disembarking the child's gaze fell on a familiar sight - his black brothers chained to the deck of a slave ship or engaged in slave labour in the docks.

A stagecoach soon removed him from this all too familiar scene, and after long hours on rough roads it passed through one of the city gates of the French capital. This was to be the setting for his multifarious exploits. Here he would show an incredulous Europe what "a movable object" was capable of...

II. A PRODIGY IN PARIS - A YOUNG MARS

For the second part of Joseph's youth we have more detailed information, thanks above all to the already mentioned "Notice Historique" from the pen of his faithful friend, La Boëssière, the son of the famous fencing master who presided over Saint-George's career in the martial arts.

A dazzling world

According to this Notice, Saint-George disembarked with his father in France at the age of ten. As one can imagine, arrival in Europe must have been a staggering experience for this mulatto child from the islands. It was his first entry into a completely white world. The only familiar black faces were his own and his mother's, according to what Angelo tells us.[1] And for the first time he got to know cold and the absence of light. He had come a long way from the glorious dawns and flaming sunsets - and, heaven be praised, from the ubiquitous contempt and the heavy atmosphere of violence and oppression. Now it was to be Paris, capital of joy and of "the land of song", as certain authors like to describe France in the middle of the eighteenth century: Paris with its magnificent buildings, its splendid squares and well-planned gardens, its elegant and refined society of the age of Louis XV.

He must of course have felt intimidated, but also fascinated by all this novelty. What boy of ten could fail to be attracted, especially one as alert as he was? His first reaction was to go out exploring. With the help of a rich father's patronage, he must have explored to his heart's content. The capital was unlike the colonies in that good taste prevented those in society from openly expressing racial sentiments; a coloured child aroused more benevolent curiosity than anything else.

The pupil who astonished his masters

In spite of his years, Saint-George won people's hearts with his extraordinary gifts, and charmed away any hostile feelings. As the Notice tells us, his learning facility astonished those who were appointed his instructors. No doubt these were private teachers employed by his father

---

[1] Henry Angelo, *Angelo's Pic Nic,* London, 1905, p.11.

to prepare the boy for entry to a regular educational institution, and to make him fit in with the ways of Parisian aristocracy.

The life of children of the nobility was strictly regimented and controlled. Good manners and proper speech were instilled in them from their earliest years and occupied a much more important place in their education than scholastic teaching. "The rules of propriety and Christian civility", as defined for instance in the famous manual by St-Jean-Baptiste de La Salle, laid down what was required of a "civilised" person from the manner of sitting down and standing up to the various formulas of polite behaviour in different circumstances. Such rules constituted a code of behaviour which simply had to be observed by anyone wishing to enter high society. Any deviation from this code was possible only for lords and ladies of the highest rank, and they could get away with setting new fashions which in their turn soon became the norms of etiquette.

And so from his arrival in France young Joseph was submitted to this social moulding, and learned how to move with ease in the glittering Parisian society of the eighteenth century.

Angelo lauds Nanon's beauty and describes her, with a euphemism typical of the time, as "one of the most beautiful women that Africa has ever sent to the plantations". And he tells us that "St-George combined in his person his mother's grace and good looks with his father's vigour and assurance". The boy's agility greatly entertained M. de Bologne who, watching his son's frisky and high-spirited games, "often laughed and said he thought he had sired a man but in fact he had sired a sparrow."[2] However, this sparrow was to turn into an eagle.

At La Boëssière's school

When St-George had reached the age of thirteen his father, intending him for the career of a swordsman, boarded him with La Boëssière. This famous fencer, whose real name was N.B.T. Texier de la Boëssière,[3] had been admitted to the Royal Academy in 1759 as a Master of Arms, and in the same year he opened a fencing school in the Rue St-Honoré.[4] He was

---

[2] Angelo, *op. cit.*, pp. 9-10.

[3] From Maran in Bas-Poitou, 1723-1807.

[4] For this academy term, see A. Robaglia, *L'escrime et le duel*, Paris, 1884, p.25: "Before the Revolution, the Paris masters of arms formed a corporation called an academy,

an excellent teacher and soon became one of the best exponents of his art in France, and also one of the first to evolve a complete theory of fencing. It was he who introduced the use of the mask in France. His academy produced leading swordsmen like Pomart, Cauvin and La Madelaine, and moreover a man of whom we shall have more to say, Alexandre Dumas Davy de la Pailleterie, the father of the novelist who was also a mulatto born in the West Indies. But it was St-George who was far and away La Boëssière's most celebrated pupil and who became his hallmark.

St-George's development is recounted by La Boëssière the son, who knew what he was talking about. "From the age of eight when my father put the foil in my hand", he writes in the introduction to the second edition of the *Traité de l'Art des Armes*, his father's masterwork, "I had the inestimable advanatage of being trained under his instruction and brought up with M. de Saint-Georges, who was my friend and companion in arms right up to his death."[5]

"The inimitable"

He knew Saint-George as "the inimitable" and as "perhaps the most extraordinary man ever seen in the art of arms and in all physical exercises", to whom one might have applied "what Ariosto said of Zerbino: nature made him and smashed the mould".[6] On the other hand, he stresses: "It is not enough to have a generous share of natural gifts alone, for they do not fully emerge unless they are guided by absolute principles; M. La Boëssière knew the triumph of developing those that M. de Saint-Georges brought to the task. The illustrious pupil was so fully aware of this truth that he always paid homage to the master's talent, and even though envy tried to undermine his gratitude M. de Saint-Georges never yielded to the base insinuations of jealous mediocrity. All his life he was

---

whose members, numbering 20, were the only ones allowed to take pupils. To become a member a six-year novitiate as assistant or overseer was required, and then a public examination before a competent jury." In his examination, La Boëssière fenced with the brilliant Donadieu, the leading master of the time. The date 1759 is provided by the La Boëssière son in his "Notice Historique sur feu La Boëssière" (his father), prefacing the second edition of *Traité de l'Art des Armes*, Paris, 1818.

[5] La Boëssière, *op. cit.*, Introduction, p. vi.

[6] ibid., "Notice Historique sur St-Georges", p. xv.

my father's friend; the two men were made for mutual esteem. M. de Saint-Georges always liked to repeat that he owed his great success to the excellent principles he had been taught."[7]

Saint-George shared his master's passion for hunting, in which he also acquired a high reputation for his ability. Moreover La Boëssière was not only a skilful swordsman and hunter, but also a poet. In 1786 he published an elegaic poem on "The generous death of Prince Leopold of Brunswick". He also wrote a comedy and an opera.

A dazzling career

This is what La Boëssière the son has to tell us about Saint-George's years of apprenticeship:

"The morning was devoted to his education and the rest of the day was spent in the exercise hall.[8] At the age of fifteen he had made such rapid progress that he could beat the strongest fencers. By seventeen he had developed superlative speed. The acquisition of experience set him beyond compare.

The other arts have monuments to show for the skill of their distinguished practitioners: pictures survive the painter and statues the sculptor; compositions and verse survive the musician and the poet. But with the performing arts it is otherwise. Dancing, fencing and swimming leave behind no trace of the perfect execution of those who have practised them with distinction. Only contemporaries who have witnessed these prodigies retain the memory. Many people who have seen Saint-Georges in action are still alive. They can attest that all praises that might be spoken of that marvellous man fall short of how he took their breath away.

I saw him at close quarters, indeed never left his side, and I confess that I am still full of admiration at the bouts he fought, each of them more amazing than the others.

---

[7]ibid., "Notice Historique sur feu La Boëssière", p. xiii. The author seems to be referring here to disputes within the Academy, perhaps the one around 1766-67 which set La Boëssière senior against the fencing master Danet.

[8] Education in the academies of the time included, besides the usual school subjects (maths, geography, history and modern languages), the dancing and music (instrumental and singing) that were considered indispensable for a young gentleman.

Saint-Georges had reached the height of five feet six inches[9], was well-built and endowed with great physical strength. He was quick, supple and slim and had an astonishing agility. No on else under instruction showed as much gracefulness and discipline. His stance was superb and with his hand held high he could always exploit the faults of his opponent. His left foot was firm and never wandered, and his right leg stayed absolutely straight. This combination gave him the poise he needed to recover his position and go back on to the attack with the speed of lightning...

There is nothing a fencer cannot do who possesses this speed... He had an incredible thrust, but kept out of his opponent's reach and had the most impressive guard... But he managed his weapon with such skill that he was always on target... His precision was such that it was impossible to strike back however hard one tried. He made good use of the gracefulness and talent that nature had bestowed on him, and those watching were amazed. When he was fencing with friends he was full of consideration, but woe betide anyone who tried to take advantage! If he noticed this he took his revenge with interest. The full extent of his gifts could not be estimated just by watching him. One had to be well-advanced in the art of fencing to have a bout with him, and only then did one really get the measure of his superiority."[10]

It may be that La Boëssière junior in presenting this testimony displayed an admiration that was heightened by the fact that St-George was his father's pupil and his own friend. Let us also take into account another authority on the art of fencing at the time, Henry Angelo, who ran an academy in London which was frequented by the most illustrious fencers. He was a friend of St-George too, though he was not above envy and backbiting. In his biographical sketch, "The Life of the Chevalier de St-George", included in his *Picnic*, Angelo describes St-George as "a man who was universally admired for his numerous accomplishments" and who in the art of fencing "surpassed all his contemporaries and predecessors". "No professor or amateur," Angelo says, "ever showed such a high degree of precision and strength, such a long thrust and so great a speed. His attacks were an uninterrupted sequence of blows, and his parrying was so

---

[9] 1.78 metres

[10] La Boëssière, *op. cit.*, pp. xv-xix.

impenetrable that one could not touch him. He was indeed the personification of energy."[11]

At the Tuileries riding school

Saint-George excelled not only in fencing but also in riding. It was at the Tuileries riding school, one of the royal academies controlled by the "Grand Ecuyer de France", that he mastered the art that was considered at the time the foremost and most important of all the martial arts. The Chevalier Dugast, the school's principal, thought him one of his best pupils.[12]

So we can see that Saint-George received an excellent education of the kind prescribed for young nobles engaging on a military career. His father had no hesitation in devoting the large sums required for attending an academy, somewhere between 1,500 and 3,000 livres a year. "The academies of Paris", says Babeau, who gives these figures, "were accessible only for a small number of the gentry."[13]

St-George in the King's Guards

As we learn from a document signed in St-George's own hand, the list of officers drawn up at the formation of the American Hussars Regiment in 1792,[14] the young mulatto became a member of the "Gendarmes de la Garde du Roi" in 1761. Thus at the age of thirteen, in the same year as he became a pupil of La Boëssière's academy for the martial arts, he made his first steps in military life.

This need not surprise us. In times past, young people were initiated in practical exercises at a much earlier age, in contrast to our modern education with its insistence on theoretical instruction which compels them to spend years on the school bench. As we have seen, La Boëssière's son began his training in fencing at the age of eight. Moreover, we should not lose sight of the fact that the fencing schools, though geared to the academic or artistic aspects of the discipline, remained

---

[11] Angelo, *op. cit.*, p. 10.

[12] La Boëssière, *op. cit.*, p. xx.

[13] J.F. Babeau, *La vie militaire sous l'Ancien Régime,* 1889-90, Paris, Firmin-Didot, p. 35.

[14] Archives administratives du Ministère de la Guerre, Dossier St-George, cote 91/47

essentially para-military institutions. Like the riding schools, they offered a high-level education to young nobles, many of whom had hereditary obligations to fulfil in the army. Entering military service at thirteen was not at all unusual. To take only one other example, Alexandre Dumas Davy de la Pailleterie joined the Queen's Dragoons at the age of fourteen. The Company of the Gendarmes was then part of the King's Ordinary Guards, and was attached to the royal household. For young members of the nobility destined for a military career, entry as a volunteer into the Companies of the King's household was usually the first rung of the ladder. A noble title was the indispensable qualification, and the fact that St-George was allowed into the Guards proves that in spite of his colour -which in principle was a barrier to recognition as a member of the nobility - he was accorded his rights as the son of a Gentleman of the King's Chamber. We shall see in the next chapter that before being called "chevalier" St-George was called "écuyer", the title of nobility preceding that of chevalier; it was also the title of an officer who looked after the stables of a prince or other grandee.

Nineteenth century biographers like Fétis[15] and the author of the article on St-George in the "Biographie Universelle de Michaud" affirm that St-George joined the Musketeers, that is to say the Horse Guards. Although this company also formed part of the Royal Guards, it was quite separate from the Gendarmes, and the information is therefore incorrect.

Apart from various mentions of his belonging to the Royal Guards, we have found no other information on St-George's military career until the Revolution. It is however probable that his career went on, alongside his other activities, right through the 1770s and 1780s, for in 1790 we discover St-George again, this time with the rank of captain. And he could scarcely have attained this rank overnight.

Champion in all sports

"Never," Angelo says, "did any man combine so much suppleness with so much strength. He excelled in every physical exercise he took up, and was also an accomplished swimmer and skater."[16] He could often be seen

---

[15] Fétis, *Biographie universelle des Musiciens et Bibliographie générale de la musique*, Paris, 1837-44.

[16] Angelo, *op. cit.*, p. 10.

swimming across the Seine with only one arm, and in skating his skill exceeded everyone else's. As to the pistol, he rarely missed the target. In running he was reputed to be one of the leading exponents in the whole of Europe. Fétis for his part states that "no one could catch him up when he ran; at dancing he was a model of perfection; he was an excellent horseman who could ride the most difficult horses bareback and render them docile".[17] To summarise all these superlatives, we remind the reader of the poem dedicated to St-George by an author of the time: "Dans les armes, jamais on ne vit son égal..."

Contests with Picard and Gianfaldoni

One can imagine that a prodigy such as St-George soon dazzled Parisian society, with its appetite for the extraordinary. Doors opened to him, his company was fought over, and when there was still some sign of jealous hostility, St-George managed to disarm it in no time. One example came from a master of arms from Rouen and former officer, named Picard, who in 1765 publicly challenged him and called him contemptuously "La Boëssière's mulatto".

He boasted that he would beat St-George with ease. Angelo tells us that St-George's father insisted on acceptance, and promised him an English-style cabriolet if he won. So, at the age of seventeen, St-George went to Rouen and "like Caesar came, saw and conquered".[18] Picard was obliged to acknowledge his opponent's superior skill.[19]

A year later, on 8 September 1766, St-George distinguished himself in another sensational public contest, this time against the celebrated Italian fencer Giuseppe Gianfaldoni. This match took place before an exceptionally grand audience which brought together the leading names of the aristocracy and the capital's finest swordsmen. In a letter quoted by Angelo, Gianfaldoni relates the ups and downs of the encounter. It ended with four hits to the credit of the master and two for the young St-George,

---

[17] Fétis, *op. cit.*, article on St-George.

[18] Angelo, *op. cit.*, p. 10.

[19] This Picard or one of his relatives may be the same man as Picard Alessandro Bremond, who in 1775 published in Milan a treatise on fencing translated from French into Italian, *Trattato sulla scherma* , the sole illustration in which is a portrait of St-George.

Brevet d'armes of the Académies de Paris, with portrait of St-George, Cabinet des Estampes, Bibl. Nationale, Paris

then eighteen. Gianfaldoni therefore emerged victorious, but he heaped praise on his opponent, granting him incredible speed and strength and describing his parries as "almost impenetrable". He predicted that the young mulatto would become the best swordsman in the whole of Europe.[20]

The "God of Arms"

Gianfaldoni was not mistaken. After his six years with La Boëssière (approximately 1761-1767), in the course of the succeeding years St-George developed such perfection that he came to be known as the "god of arms", just as Vestris was called the "god of dance". He became one of the leading authorities in the art and science of arms, and taught as a master. He was admitted to the Royal Academy, whose official certificates were issued bearing his effigy together with that of three other celebrated masters, La Faugère, La Boëssière and Daressy. The text beneath the four portraits runs: "We, the professors of the Academies of the Capital..."[21]

We do not possess any details on his activities as a master of arms. They were somewhat overshadowed by the musical activities in which St-George engaged round about the mid-1760s.

The "other" St-George

Indeed, within the brilliant swordsman, the fighting hero, the spirited horseman and the sporting genius, there lay another Saint-George, a man of great sensibility, vulnerable and melancholic - the musician. This is what makes him such an extraordinary figure, both in the history of classical music and in that of arms. Of course we can find a large number of musicians of genius in the eighteenth century, but we would search in vain for another who attained similar distinction in so many other fields. As for those who reached comparable heights in the martial arts, we would search among them in vain for another person with such distinguished achievements in music. His uniqueness is as amazing for us as it was for his contemporaries. He epitomised the classical ideal of harmony between body and soul.

---

[20] Angelo, *The reminiscencesof Henry Angelo,* London, 1828.
[21] Bibliothèque Nationale, Print Room.

In the following chapter we shall turn to this other aspect of his life - the violinist, director of orchestra and composer.

DEUX
SIMPHONIES
CONCERTANTES
Pour deux Violons principaux, deux Violons ripieno,
deux Hautbois obligés, deux Cors ad Libitum, Alto
et Baffe, avec un Violoncello obligé en fuprimant le
fecond Violon principal.

COMPOSÉES

PAR

M.ᴿ DE S.ᵀ GEORGES
ŒUVRE VI.

Mis au Jour par M.ᴿ BAILLEUX.
Prix 9.ᵗ

A PARIS

Chez M.ᵣ Bailleux, M.ᵈ de Musique, des Menus-plaisirs du Roy, Rue S.ᵗ
Honoré, à la Regle d'Or.
à Lyon, chez M.ᵣ Castaud, à Toulouse, chez M.ᵣ Brunet
à Bordeaux, à Bruxelles et à Lille,.
Chez les Marchands de Musique.

Écris par Ribère?

Title page of "Deux Simphonies Concertantes" composées par Mr. de
St. Georges, Oeuvre VI, Bibliothèque Nationale, Paris.

III. THE MUSICIAN

"Enfant du goût et du génie,
Il naquit au sacré vallon,
Et fut de Terpsichore émule et nourrisson.
Rival du dieu de l'harmonie,
S'il eut à la musique uni la poésie,
On l'aurait pris pour Apollon."

(He was born in the sacred valley, A child of taste and genius, Nourished by Terpsichore. He rivalled the god of harmony, And if he had combined poetry with music, He would have been taken for Apollo.)

These lines by the poet Moline were published in the "Mercure" of February 1768, and they were inscribed below a portrait of St-George painted by an American artist, Mather Brown, in the same year. As we can see, they are no longer devoted to the "god of arms" or the "French Hercules" but to the artist, the dancer and especially to the musician who was then beginning to make a name for himself in Parisian concert halls.

Paris, the musical capital

At that time Paris was not only one of the principal centres of musical creation in Europe, but might well be called the continent's musical capital. Apparently, no other European city had so many composers, instrumentalists and music publishers. Foreign musicians flocked to Paris to find an audience or to publish their works. During the 1760s and 1770s, the Parisian publishers, numbering 44 for an urban population of about half a million, published more compositions than the rest of Europe combined. Several of Mannheim's musicians shuttled back and forth between the little court of the Palatine Elector and the French metropolis, where some of them even settled permanently.[1]

---

[1] B.S. Brook, "The Symphonie Concertante" in *Musical Quarterly*, V. 47, 1961, p. 493 ff.

The Parisian patrons

Paris's domination in European musical life of the time can be largely explained by the presence of numerous patrons - high-ranking aristocrats, magistrates and financiers - who maintained private orchestras. They entertained talented people of all kinds in their houses and gave them the chance of developing their creativity.

The most famous of these patrons was, up till 1762, the Farmer-General Le Riche de la Pouplinière, who was the patron and pupil of Rameau. He had appointed Johann Stamitz, the leading representative of the Mannheim school, to take charge of his private orchestra. He did a great deal to promote symphonic composition in France. Other patrons were the Count of Clermont, the Prince of Conti (for whom the infant Mozart gave his first concert in Paris in 1764), the Duke of Aiguillon, the Count of Albaret, the Marshal of Noailles (whose accredited composer was Karl Stamitz, son of Johann), and the Baron Bagge (well-known as the sponsor of the young Rodolphe Kreutzer). Nor should we overlook the Prince of Ardore, the Marquis of Saint-Georges, the Ambassador of Naples to Paris, and a distinguished harpsichordist who gave much sought-after concerts at the Place Vendôme. (In spite of his name there seems to be no connection between him and our Saint-George.) Musicians did of course also receive patronage at court, where Madame Pompadour, the Queen and the King each had their own circle of protégés.[2]

St-George's musical education - his father's patronage

Saint-George's father must also have been active as a Maecenas, or at least that is the impression we get from the homage paid him by several composers. Among them Antonio Lolli should be noted, the famous Italian violinist, who in 1766 dedicated his Opus 4 to him; also Karl Stamitz, who in 1770 wrote at the top of his Six Quartets Opus 1: "To Monsieur de Bologne de St-George, who brings to his good fortune as a lover of the arts the pleasure of also understanding them, and who has given us artists an invaluable gift in the person of his son".[3]

---

[2] Michel Brenet, *Les Concerts en France sous l'Ancien Régime,* Paris, Librairie Fischbacher, 1900, reprinted New York, Da Capo Press, 1970.

[3] B. Brook in his article on St-George, *Musik in Geschichte und Gegenwart* (MGG).

The father was then a lover and connoisseur of music, who subsidised gifted musicians from his income; and it is perhaps here that we shall find the origins of St-George's musical training. Admittedly, he started off with an extraordinary proclivity for music, in addition to all his other talents. La Borde wrote: "Saint-Georges is perhaps of all men the one born with the greatest sum of different talents", to which was added "the rare quality of great modesty and sweetness of nature".[4] And La Boëssière tells us: "He possessed a delicate and sensitive disposition, and all the arts exercised a powerful attraction on him, but music appealed to him most".[5]

According to Fétis, St-George studied the violin under Leclair, and La Laurencie believes that he studied composition under Gossec. It is also possible that he was Lolli's pupil for a time, when Lolli was living in Paris in 1764 and 1766. What is certain is that Lolli dedicated the two concertos of his Opus 2 to him in 1764,[6] and that Karl Stamitz knew him well and appreciated his gifts, as is shown by his dedication of 1770 to the father.

In 1766 Saint-George received another musical tribute, this time from François Joseph Gossec, who was then a member of the Prince of Conti's orchestra, and who dedicated his Six Trios op. 9 to him in these terms:

"To M. de Saint-George, Ecuyer, Gendarme in the King's Guards.
Monsieur,
In view of the reputation you have acquired through your talents and the support you have accorded to artists, I allow myself the liberty of dedicating this work to you, out of homage to an enlightened music-lover. If you lend it your approval its success is assured. I am, Sir, with respect, your very humble servant.
   F.-J. Gossec, d'Anvers."[7]

We should also mention that J. Avoglio, first violin of the Concert Spirituel, in 1768 dedicated to him his six sonatas for the violin (Opus 4).[8]

---

[4] De La Borde, *Essai sur la Musique III*, Paris, 1780.

[5] La Boëssière, *op. cit.*, p. xx.

[6] Brook, *MGG*, article on St-George; *MGG*, article on Lolli.

[7] Quoted by La Laurencie, *op. cit.*, p. 454.

[8] "Mercure" of May 1768, p.179.

THE CHEVALIER DE SAINT-GEORGE
VIOLINIST

By LIONEL DE LA LAURENCIE

THIS strange and romantic personage, one who seems made to tempt the pen of a Lenôtre, was born at Basse-Terre (Guadaloupe), December 25, 1745, the son of a comptroller-general, M. de Boulogne, and a negress. He was given the Christian name of Joseph Boulogne Saint-George. Is this the origin of the surname "Saint-George" under which he became famous? No historical document exists which might authenticate the fact; but M. Roger de Beauvoir, who has written a lengthy novel[1] with Saint-George for its hero, one filled with detail which is not altogether inaccurate, furnishes a quite reasonable explanation of the origin of the name. "This name, Saint-George," he writes, "was not given the young mulatto as a mere matter of choice of name, as is so often the case in the colonies. The handsomest vessel in the harbor of Guadaloupe, at the time the child was born, served him in the stead of a godfather."

Brought to France by his father when he was very young, Saint-George soon gave proof of the extraordinary ease with which he learned. Placed in lodgings with the famous fencing-master La Boëssière, he rapidly became a redoubtable fencer, and showed remarkable endowment for all forms of bodily exercise. The little mulatto's petulance, says Angelo, and his extraordinary vivacity greatly entertained M. de Boulogne, who said that instead of a man he had engendered a sparrow.[2]

Before long La Boëssière's pupil had acquired great superiority, not alone in the handling of the foils, but as a marksman, skater, equestrian and dancer as well. At the same time his rare natural gifts for the arts, and notably for music, were carefully cultivated. Saint-George took lessons from Jean-Marie Leclair, and his talent for the violin soon made itself evident. In 1761 he was numbered among the *gendarmes of the* royal guard; yet his leisure hours made it possible for him to perfect, without interruption, his

[1] Le Chevalier de Saint-Georges. Roger de Beauvoir. Calmann-Lévy, Paris, 1890. The book is well-written, and interesting despite the occasional obtrusion of the melodramatic. It gives vivid pictures of life in the French Antilles and Paris during the closing decades of the *ancien régime.—Transl.*
[2] Henry Angelo: *Angelo's Pic-Nic*, 1905, p. 10.

Lionel de La Laurencie, The Chevalier de Saint-George,

violinist, in The Musical Quarterly 5, 1919 (Extrait)

These are the only surviving testimonies to the young mulatto's musical activities and friendships in the 1760s, but they show that St-George had, even before reaching the age of twenty, become a recognised and respected musician as well as the finest swordsman in France.

St-George, First Violin at the Concert des Amateurs

But it was at the end of the 1760s that his musical career really took off. In 1769 he joined the Concert des Amateurs as first violin. This had just been assembled under the direction of F. J. Gossec, thanks to the support of patrons such as the Farmer-General de la Haye, Baron d'Ogny, general manager of the postal services, and - who knows?- perhaps St-George's father.

The twelve weekly performances of the Amateurs took place from December to March in the sumptuous drawing-room of the town house of Charles de Rohan-Rohan, Prince of Soubise and Epinoy, one of the most beautiful monuments to eighteenth-century domestic architecture, which today houses the National Archives. They were subscription concerts and a lot of new music was played, above all symphonies and concertos. According to Gossec himself, they provided the opportunity to hear "the most skilful performers of Paris in all parts of the orchestra".[9] The most famous instrumentalists of the Opera and the Court took part, as well as celebrated foreign virtuosos. Many soloists made their début at the Hôtel de Soubise before appearing in the Concert Spirituel, which was France's leading musical venue, housed in the Tuileries. Publishers loved mentioning the double glory of performance in both places in the works they published.[10]

The Orchestra of the Amateurs, the largest at the time, had 40 violins, 12 cellos, 8 double basses and the usual number of flutes, oboes, clarinets, bassoons, horns and trumpets, adding up to some 76 players altogether.[11]

---

[9] F. J. Gossec, "Note concernant l'introduction des cors", in Fétis's *Revue musicale*, 1829, t. V., p. 222.

[10] Brenet, *op. cit.*, pp. 360-61.

[11] ibid.

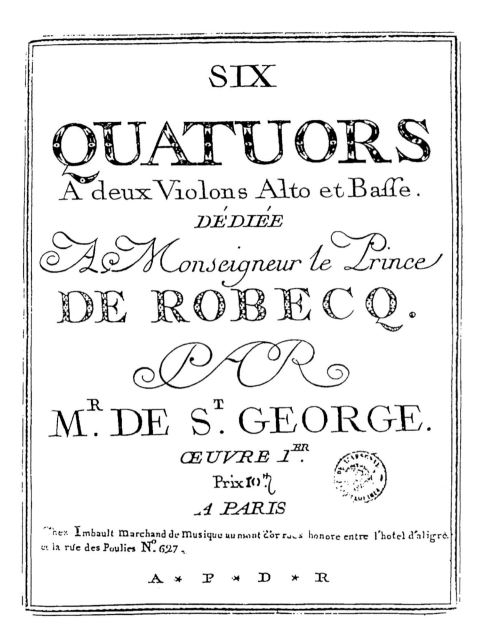

Title page of "Six Quatuors" A deux Violons Alto et Basse, dédiée à
Monseigneur le Prince de Robecq par Mr. de St. George, oeuvre 1er,
Bibliothèque Nationale, Paris.

Conductor of the Concert des Amateurs

In 1773 when Gossec, together with Gaviniés and Le Duc, was summoned to take over the Concert Spirituel, St-George succeeded him at the Hôtel de Soubise. He was twenty-four years old and he was to wield the baton there for eight years. In fact it was St-George, rather than Gossec who conducted for only four years, who won the Orchestra of the Amateurs their marvellous reputation. They were praised for their ensemble playing, precision, sensitive execution and attention to nuances - in short for the superiority of their performances.[12] In the "Almanach Musical" of 1775 they were called "the best orchestra for symphonies in Paris and perhaps in Europe", and it was this orchestra, long before the Concert Spirituel, that introduced Haydn's symphonic works into France.

First published compositions - the string quartets

It was in the spring of 1773, at the age of twenty-four, that St-George published his first compositions. These were the Six String Quartets that the composer dedicated to the Prince of Robecq (Anne-Louis-Alexandre de Montmorency).[13] Since about 1765 this type of instrumental music had enjoyed growing popularity in Paris but it was represented mainly by foreign composers such as Toeschi, Cannabich, Haydn, Boccherini, Karl Stamitz and J. C. Bach. One of the first French musicians to write quartets was Gossec (in 1772), closely followed by St-George, who in 1777 and 1785 published two series of quartets. La Laurencie writes that "St-Georges is, with Maestro Gossec and the violinist Vachon, one of the first French protagonists of the string quartet, and this is another reason why he should receive the attention of historians of music".[14]

People who personally heard St-George play were full of praise not only for his virtuosity but even more for the beauty of his expression. The singer and actress Louise Fusil said of him, "He possessed musical feeling

---

[12] De La Borde, *op. cit.*

[13] One may ask why St-George dedicated his first musical creation to the Prince of Robecq and not, for example, to one of his musical friends. The Prince was a military man, a lieutenant-general, with no musical standing. We have tried in vain to identify his connection with St-George. Perhaps they were acquainted through fencing or the army. But the Prince was born in 1724 and therefore 24 years older than St-George.

[14] La Laurencie, *op. cit.*, p. 458.

SOUVENIRS

D'UNE ACTRICE

————

MÉMOIRES DE LOUISE FUSIL

(1774-1848)

AVEC UNE PRÉFACE ET DES NOTES

PAR

PAUL GINISTY

————

LIBRAIRIE DE "L'ART DU THÉATRE"

CHARLES SCHMID, Éditeur

51, RUE DES ÉCOLES

PARIS

Memoirs of the singer Louise Fusil, a friend of Saint-George

in the highest degree, and the espressiveness of his execution was his outstanding feature".[15]

Fétis puts him among the best violinists of his time, and La Laurencie, analysing the form of his compositions, describes him as a "bold and brilliant violinist" who "performs with bravura and exploits the very extremities of touch, plying his bow with precise fluidity and a great variety of articulation". His concertos, he continues, "earn praise for their graceful themes, their utterly creole langour and melancholy sentiment. The composer likes to repeat his themes twice, the second time in a lower octave".[16]

Concertos and symphonies

The second of St-George's works, the two concertos for violin and orchestra, was published at the end of 1773. It was performed at the Concert des Amateurs by the composer himself and according to the "Mercure" it received "the most rapturous applause, both for its excellent execution and for the composition itself".[17]

In 1775, two years after the publication of these first concertos, the publisher Bailleux acquired a six-year copyright on a whole series of St-George's further concertos.

St-George's creative activity was now at its height. Apart from concertos, quartets and several brilliant sonatas for the violin, and for the harpsichord accompanied by the violin, between 1775 and 1784 he composed three symphonies and some ten concertante symphonies, of which most are unfortunately lost. Barry Brook, the author of several studies on this form of composition, which had just emerged in Paris, puts St-George among its most important exponents, with Cambini, Davaux, Bréval, Pleyel, Gossec, Le Duc and Bertheaume. [18]

---

[15] Louise Fusil, *Souvenirs d'une actrice*, Paris, Librairie de "l'Art du Théâtre", Charles Schmid, editor, 1903, p. 128.

[16] La Laurencie, *op. cit.*, p. 493.

[17] "Mercure", December 1773.

[18] B. Brook, *The Symphonie Concertante*, loc. cit., and *La Symphonie française dans la 2e moitié du 18e siècle*, Paris, 1962.

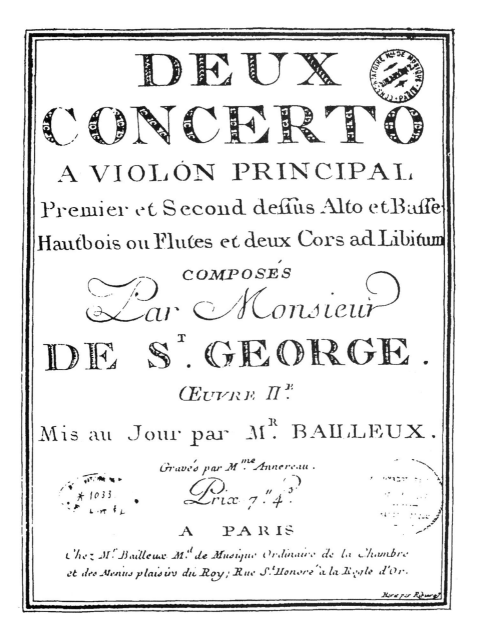

Title page of the second of St-George's works, the "Deux concertos pour violon principal et orchestre, oeuvre IIe", Bibliothèque Nationale, Paris.

A natural musical genius

Another modern musicologist, Joël-Marie Fauquet, has this to say on the subject:

"After a concert performance of a fine concertante symphony for two violins by Saint-Georges, I remember overhearing the remark, 'He is influenced by Mozart'. But the truth is, and today it is too often forgotten, that Saint-Georges remains one of the principal exponents of the French aesthetic of the concertante and the violin concerto; and that it was actually Mozart, with the prodigious faculty of assimilation belonging to his genius, who absorbed into his own violin concertos and his admirable Concertante for violin and viola the quintessence of what he acquired from the works of Parisian violinists, influenced by the Mannheim school, during his second stay in the French capital in 1778. Be that as it may, Saint-Georges's aristocratic vigour of invention, together with his fluidity and variety, make him a musician who is very close to Mozart in spirit, after due allowances have been made."

And M. Fauquet goes on to say:

"There is no better comparison of Saint-Georges's natural genius and distinction, whose spontaneity would certainly have been diminished by excessive theory, than with another French musician, François-Adrien Boieldieu, who also composed as naturally as a song-bird.

It would be hard to say exactly why the Chevalier's unjustly forgotten concertos have the effect today of elating us like an excellent champagne and truly moving us: analysis does not apply to what is pure music."[19]

The operatic adventure

By the end of 1775 St-George's musical reputation was so well established and his fame as a director of orchestra so great that he was considered for the post of artistic director of the Royal Academy of Music, or in other words the Opera. The Paris Opera in the Palais-Royal had been administered by the city for a few years, and was the pride of France. It attracted a select audience consisting of nobles, magistrates and top financiers - not to mention the royal family - who had their own boxes,

---

[19] Sleeve notes on a 33 album of St-George's concertos, Arion, Paris, 1974

sometimes for life. On certain days the auditorium was opened to a more popular audience, in recognition of the fact that the Opera was a kind of national passion, a symbol of nationhood comparable with Versailles. There was talk of "the threat of a major revolution" when St-George's candidature was made known. It became the focus of one of the rare displays of racial prejudice against Saint-George recorded in the chronicles of the time.

As we learn from the "Correspondance littéraire, philosophique et critique" of the Baron von Grimm, a review intended to inform foreign princes about Parisian life, St-George's nomination collapsed in the face of lively opposition from some of the female artistes of the Opera, including the famous singers Sophie Arnould and Rosalie Levasseur and the dancer Guimard. Grimm presented St-George to his readers as "a young American known as the Chevalier de St-George, who combines the most gentle manners with incredible skill in all physical exercises and very great musical talent", but the artistes nevertheless at once addressed a petition to the Queen, "to beg Her Majesty that their honour and the delicacy of their conscience made it impossible for them to be subjected to the orders of a mulatto".[20]

"Such an important consideration," Grimm adds, not without a certain irony, "had the full effect intended". After a great deal of discussion the King found a solution that safeguarded the honour of the petitioning ladies and spared St-George the embarrassment of seeing another candidate given preference. He entrusted the direction of the Opera to the courtiers in charge of the royal amusements, and promised to make up any deficits at the Opera from his own pocket if necessary.

Confrontation with racism

The Opera episode cannot have been the first or the last time that Saint-George was rejected because of his colour. But we have no evidence from his own hand, neither in letter nor diary, as to how he reacted to such annoyances. If he ever confided his most secret thoughts, his suffering and sadness, it must have been to his violin, his most faithful companion. We

---

[20] "Correspondance littéraire", January 1776. (Grimm's text shows the first written mention of the title of Chevalier given to St-George, at least in the biographical data known to us.)

do however know from La Boëssière junior that he could get angry and had a quick temper. It was "dangerous to push him too far", even though, "when he came to himself he did everything possible to remove any offence caused by what he had said".[21]

Beauvoir has a story - and such anecdotes may or may not be authentic - that one day St-George was called "off-white" by someone passing in the street; he grabbed him and dipped him in the gutter, then pulled him up again and said, "Now you're just as off-white as I am!". Or, again, Beauvoir says that in response to an offensive remark about his slave origins, St-George once took his riding-whip and used it as if he were playing a Corelli sonata![22]

The Chevalier's fearsome sword was of course well enough known for others to show respect or at least restraint, for in the eighteenth century questions of honour were settled by the duel. But here too St-George more than once showed his generosity in pardoning weakness and ignorance, and renounced certain victory rather than exact vengeance. For instance, when a musical colleague, the famous violinist Jarnowick (= Giovanni Mane Giornovichi), so far forgot himself as to slap St-George's face, he simply said, "I admire his talent too much to fight him."[23]

St-George was then a man equipped with every means of deflecting white arrogance and contempt - strength, skill, heart and spirit. He had something else too - humour. Again it is Beauvoir who tells us about this, and since he refers to a definite source we may assume authenticity. The source is a sketch attributed to Carmontel and entitled "Duel à l'écumoire" (Duel with a Skimmer). It showed the Chevalier fighting with the ferocious butler of the Prince de Conti, the famous musical patron with whom St-George was, according to Beauvoir, on familiar terms. The sketch was inspired by the following incident. St-George was dining with the Prince at the Isle Adam, and went into the kitchens to complain about a dish that had not found pleasure among the guests. The butler, who must have been new and ignorant as to who this was, called him a nigger and attacked him with a knife. With his customary agility St-George seized a skimmer, and using this as an unconventional sword boldly parried his adversary's attack

---

[21] La Boëssière, *op. cit.*, p. xxi.

[22] Beauvoir, *op. cit.*, pp. 316-17.

[23] Anecdote recounted by A. Pougin in *Viotti et l'école moderne de violon*, p. 19.

and disarmed him, to the enthusiastic applause of the other guests who had come running in to watch the spectacle.

The theatre calls

A lively and active temperament such as St-George's could hardly fail to be drawn to the theatre. In spite of his rejection by the ladies of the Opera, he pursued his interest in the stage and soon began to compose dramas and perform as an actor himself. He found that the doors of other theatres were open to him, like that of Madame de Montesson, the morganatic wife of the Duke of Orleans, first prince of the blood, who appointed him director of her concert at the Palais-Royal. This association was to mean a new phase in the Chevalier's life.

The St-George miracle

Before dealing with this new phase let us pause for a moment to ponder what we have narrated so far. The time is the height of the era of slavery. Africa's "living ebony" is sold by weight, and the black man suffers the worst degradation in his history. The law denies him the expression of his humanity and reduces him to the level of an animal. Coloured people are even forbidden to bear a white man's name (1773) and Louis XVI bans negroes and mulattos from entering France (1777). A royal decree prohibits marriage between coloured and white people in France (1778) and officially there still prevails the principle "which excludes coloured people and their posterity for ever from all the privileges pertaining to whites" (Louis XV's letter of 1770). And yet against this background we find a black man in charge of the greatest orchestra in France. He introduces Haydn's symphonies to French audiences, presents to them some of the best virtuosi in Europe, by his own compositions contributes to creating two new genres in European music - the string quartet and the concertante symphony - and has his works played before an illustrious audience!

More amazing still, this black man was to be admitted to the court at Versailles to make music with Queen Marie-Antoinette herself![24] A "descendant of the coastal people" was received with honour by Her Majesty the Queen of France!

---

[24] Bachaumont, *Mémoires secrets pour servir à l'histoire de la République des Lettres en France, depuis 1762 jusqu'à nos jours*, London, t. XIV, 1779.

Should we just attribute this to the inconsistencies of a régime in perpetual contradiction with itself? That would be a misunderstanding of the flexibility of the French mentality and its capacity to bend dogmatism. And it would be a misapprehension of the extraordinary personality of the Chevalier de Saint-George. Faced with a talent and spirit such as belonged to this chosen one of the gods and the muses, even the law and racial prejudice could only bow their heads. With Saint-George the rehabilitation of the black man began when he had reached the nadir of his fortunes.

We have called this section "The St-George miracle", and after what has been said the reason for the title is clear. If the reader has tried with us to relive the Africans' tragic saga he will understand this miracle, which is the essence of this book.

We have seen the ancient civilisations of Africa, followed by the holocaust that changed its destiny. We, as whites, cannot avoid the question how the white man could do it. There have been holocausts in the Americas against the Incas, the Aztecs, the Mayas in the South and the Redskins in the North, but the most terrible of all was the one that hit Africa because it was aimed at destroying the Africans as human beings.

And yet from this hatred and embittered hostility an infant prodigy was born. Some may say there is nothing miraculous in this because the child's father was white. But the father had another child too, who was white but had none of the gifts of the mulatto son. The miracle therefore was the child of the black slave mother. It was he who possessed that incredible facility for acquiring all the arts, mastering Haydn's works, creating his own compositions and competing with the most brilliant musicians of his time.

Thus, at a time when black humanity from Africa to America was shrouded in darkness and Africa's civilisations burned down to nothingness, a new dawn broke and from the ashes rose the immortal bird of human genius. In the person of the Chevalier a new age began that was to reject the myth of white superiority and move towards the truth of a common humanity.

IV. RELATIONS WITH THE HOUSE OF ORLEANS

According to most biographers, it was around 1777, or perhaps before the Opera affair in 1775, that the Chevalier de St-George formed close ties with the Palais-Royal, that is to say with the House of Orleans, one of the branches of the French royal family. At the time its head was Duke Louis-Philippe, grandson of the Regent, and a generous supporter of literature and the arts who had a particular love of the theatre. After the death of his wife, Louise Henriette de Bourbon-Conti, the Prince of Conti's sister, he remarried in 1773. This time his wife was Charlotte-Jeanne Béraud de la Haie de Riou, the Marquise de Montesson, a woman of spirit but lower down in the ranks of nobility. At the King's insistence the marriage had to be kept secret, but it was known to all, and in fact the point of the secrecy was to stop the Marquise de Montesson from taking the title of Duchess of Orleans.

Louis-Philippe of Orleans enjoyed the good life and had hardly any political ambitions. At the time of the "princes' revolt" against Chancellor Maupéou's reforms in 1771, it was with reluctance that he accepted the leadership of this movement as the oldest of the royal princes. Unlike his young and effervescent son, the Duke of Chartres - the future Philippe-Égalité - he made no bones about seeking reconciliation with the court after Louis XVI's accession. Because he was corpulent and easy-going he was known affectionately in his own circle as "big daddy" but the more malicious called him "bourgeois" and "Monsieur de Montesson".

Madame de Montesson's theatre

Madame de Montesson was described as a friendly person whose "company was like a school for good taste and good manners. Although she loved literature and herself engaged in writing, she was not obsessed with cleverness and her manner was simple and unpretentious".[1] She shared her husband's passion for the theatre and up till 1785 she laid on dramatic performances, concerts and parties in her private theatre at the Palais-Royal and also in the theatre that the Duke of Orleans had built in his residence at Bagnolet. It was a great favour to be invited.

---

[1] The Duke de Lévis, *Souvenirs et Portraits*.

Madame de Montesson's theatre shone with special brilliance among the shows of high society, as Grimm says in his "Correspondance littéraire" - "not only because of the standing of the actors and the distinction of the audience, but also because of the plays selected".[2] Among these were fashionable works such as "The Barber of Seville" by Beaumarchais, Pergolesi's "La Serva Padrona" and Grétry's comic operas, of which some, such as the "Judgement of Midas" were first performed there, and then there were the comedies written by the Marquise herself. The performers numbered not only celebrities from the Italian and French Comedy but also the highly talented lady of the house and the Duke of Orleans himself. Thus we read in Grimm: "The performances mounted this winter in Madame de Montesson's theatre were no less brilliant than the previous year. There were two or three shows a week, and the most distinguished personages of Paris and the court were always to be seen pressing for admission... The leading actors in this illustrious troop are always the Duke of Orleans, the Viscount de Gand, the Messieurs de Ségur, the Count of Ornésan, Madame de Montesson, the Countess of Lamarck and the Marquise Ducrest."[3]

According to the same author, only the royal family shunned Madame de Montesson's performances in the Palais-Royal and kept to those given in the same Palais-Royal as part of the Opera. However, Voltaire, the uncrowned king of the Republic of Letters, went there several times.

"Ernestine" - St-George's first dramatic work

It was at the Marquise of Montesson's brilliant theatre, according to Beauvoir,[4] that the Chevalier de St-George's first dramatic work saw the light of day, probably in the spring of 1777. It was a comedy in three acts interspersed with ariettas and entitled "Ernestine". The score is lost but a few fragments still exist in the library of the Paris Conservatoire.[5] It was

---

[2] Grimm, *Correspondance littéraire*, t. XI, pp. 443-44.

[3] Grimm, ibid., April 1780.

[4] Beauvoir, *op. cit.*, p. 202.

[5] In *Recueil d'Airs et Duos avec orchestre de M. de St-Georges*, Bibl. Cons. no 4077 ms. La Laurencie identified four fragments of "Ernestine" here, using the names of the

taken from a novel by Madame Riccoboni, "Ernestine ou les malheurs d'une jeune orpheline". (Ernestine, or the misfortunes of an orphan girl). The author of the libretto was none other than Choderlos de Laclos, then a young artillery officer, who was later to become celebrated in different ways, first as the author of the novel "Les liaisons dangereuses" (Dangerous Liaisons), an eloquent picture of the immorality of his time, then as secretary to Philippe-Égalité, and finally as a general and specialist in the fortifications of the revolutionary army after 9 Thermidor. A collaborator in the libretto was Desfontaines, the author of "L'Aveugle de Palmyre" and the "Mage".

In spite of the participation of so much talent, "Ernestine" was an utter flop. It had been much applauded at Madame de Montesson's but it lasted only one day at the Comédie Italienne when it was staged on 19 July 1777. According to the "Mercure", this failure was due above all to the libretto, while the music made the best of the text and was distinguished by "very pleasant duets, brilliant arias and its orchestration", showing "a good style, with a great deal of knowledge, facility and talent".[6] On the other hand, "Le Journal de Paris" in reporting the failure of the play nevertheless observed that "several musical passages, including the first two dialogue duets, hold out the promise of a real success".[7] For Bachaumont, Saint-George did not have "as much taste in regard to dramatic works" and "should have realised that excellent music applied to a dull and detestable comic opera loses all its merit".[8]

The worst critique came from Grimm, who wrote: "Messieurs de Laclos and Desfontaines felt that the underlying plot, being interesting rather than comic, needed to be enlivened with some by-play, and so they added the role of a valet, which is the height of platitude and bad taste. Even Pergolesi's talent could not have carried off a plot like this, and M. de Saint-Georges's composition, ingenious and clever though it was, often

---

characters to whom the arias are addressed. They appear on pages 42, 78, 107 and 112 respectively.

[6] Mercure, August 1777, pp. 170-71.

[7] Journal de Paris, 20 July 1777, p. 3.

[8] Bachaumont, *Mémoires secrets pour servir à l'histoire de la République des Lettres en France, depuis 1762 jusqu'à nos jours,* London, t. X, 25 July 1777.

missed its effect. There was grace and finesse, but little in the way of character or variety, and few new ideas."[9]

Since the score is lost we have no means of judging. We should note, however, that Baron de Grimm, who was then Minister Plenipotentiary in Paris of the Duke of Saxe-Gotha, was far from being a dependable judge. As Mozart's correspondence shows, the Duke set such little store by his genius that he refused to support him during his stay in Paris in the spring of 1778 and even obliged him to leave the French capital. Mozart had nothing very flattering to say of Grimm, and when he mentioned the "brutes and idiots" who surrounded him in Paris he no doubt had this literary diplomat very much in mind.[10]

"La Chasse"

St-George was not at all discouraged by the failure of "Ernestine". He went on composing symphonic and chamber music: in January 1778 Le Duc published two new concertante symphonies (Opus IX), and in September of the same year another series of string quartets, not to mention the concertos published by Bailleux from 1775 to 1781. Then St-George wrote a second comedy with ariettas, "La Chasse" (The Hunt), whose première took place at the Comédie Italienne on 12 October 1778. The words were by the same Desfontaines who had collaborated on the libretto of "Ernestine". But this time the outcome was more satisfactory. According to Bachaumont, the première attracted a huge audience and caused quite a tumult. The tumult was certainly favourable, for the "Journal de Paris" reports that the performance was "loudly applauded". "Le Mercure" for its part emphasised that this second dramatic venture of Saint-George's "is infinitely superior to the first. There is every encouragement for him to continue a career that is so promising. The music was much appreciated and deserves to be."[11]

As with "Ernestine", it was Grimm who found the most to criticise in the black composer's music, in which he condemned "above all a large number of imitations and echoes".[12] We shall see later that this was a

---

[9] Grimm, *op. cit.*, July 1777.

[10] Massin, Jean and Brigitte, *Wolfgang Amadeus Mozart,* 1970.

[11] Mercure, 25 October 1778, p. 305.

[12] Grimm, *op. cit.*, October 1778.

constant criticism of Saint-George expressed by the author of the
"Correspondance littéraire", who never took into account the mutual
influences and borrowings among musicians in any period of cultural
history, and who in the end openly admitted the racial prejudice that
inspired his opinions. But it would not appear that St-George took this
pettiness very much to heart. At least we have no evidence that he did. He
could well afford to ignore subtle denigration from a Grimm or a Meister
(the co-author of the "Correspondances") since, as the comments in the
capital's leading journals show, in general he enjoyed a good press.

St-George's romances

The general public might not be familiar with St-George's serious works -
his symphonies, concertos and quartets were played before the select and
restricted audience of subscription concerts and in private preformances -
but they lapped up his ariettas and romances, several of which became
popular songs that were sung in the street. Sometimes the composer wrote
the words for them himself, and the few texts that have been preserved are
examples of languorous love songs. Louise Fusil[13] quotes one (the score
of which is in the British Museum) :

> "L'autre jour sous l'ombrage
> Un jeune et beau pasteur
> Soupirait ainsi sa douleur
> A l'écho plaintif du bocage:
> Bonheur d'être aimé tendrement,
> Que de chagrins vont à ta suite,
> Pourquoi viens-tu si lentement,
> Et t'en retournes-tu si vite?

(The other day under the shade, A young and handsome shepherd, Sighed
his sorrow in these words, To the wood's sad echo: What sadness follows
after The happiness of being tenderly loved. Why does happiness come so
slowly, And leave again so soon?)
Another example:

---

[13] Fusil, *op. cit.,* original edition of 1841, Dumont, pp. 142-43.

Romance Nouvelle, Paroles et Musique de Ch^{er.} de St. George.
Avec Accomp^{t.} de Guittare. A Pariz chez Imbault.
Goethe Museum, Düsseldorf

2

Ma maitresse m'oublie
Amour fais moi mouro
Quand on cesse de nous chero
Quel cruel fardeau que la vie
Bonheur... &c....

"Ma maîtresse m'oublie,
Amour, fais-moi mourir!
Quand on cesse de nous chérir,
Quel cruel tourment que la vie!"[14]

(My mistress forgets me, O love, let me die. When we are no longer loved, Life is a cruel torture!)

On the subject of love, it was primarily Bachaumont, the author of the *Mémoires secrets* - a scandalous chronicle secretly printed abroad for a readership greedy for gossip from the capital - who portrayed Saint-George as a "black Don Juan" by describing him as "a very valorous champion of love". This epithet was slavishly taken up by all the biographers, beginning with Roger de Beauvoir who embroidered the idea and gave it so much prominence in his book that it practically overshadows everything else in Saint-George's life and personality.

Other authors who have written about his life are hardly better, and one is bound to ask whether this is not further evidence of racist feeling, conscious or unconscious, that insists on believing that a black must above all be a creature of almost animal voluptuousness. When we consider the extent to which in France and elsewhere the eighteenth century was a period of general licence, it is hard to understand why these authors, who would never have thought of mentioning the bedroom secrets of a Gossec, Viotti or even of a Mozart, should seize on St-George to repeat the tiresome stereotyping that he "went from boudoir to boudoir" and that he "was the lover of an incalculable number of marquises, countesses, duchesses and other fine ladies", on no more evidence than what was written in a scandal sheet emanating from the feverish imagination of Roger de Beauvoir.

It is very likely that Saint-George was successful with women. They admired his prodigious talents, his intelligence and lively mind, also his gentleness and mysterious beauty. What man with all his qualities would not have gained their favour? In his *Notice Historique* La Boëssière junior even says that "sought after everywhere in society, he often had his music to thank for relations in which love was not far away. Given his lively

---

[14] ibid, 1903 edition, p. 23.

temperament, he loved and was loved".[15] Because of his colour, any notion of a lasting union was forbidden for Saint-George, partly because marriage between white and coloured people was formally prohibited in France from 1778, and partly because none of the noble families with whom he mixed would have wanted to introduce a mulatto descendant into their family tree. St-George's love affairs were condemned from the outset as dreams of an unattainable happiness. He had no prospect of conjugal life and paternity. The fatal moment always intervened when the social barrier came down with its undeniable finality. No doubt he often felt lonely, and for this we have the evidence of the melancholy character of some of his musical compositions and the words of songs he wrote.

The poor bird's loves and death

The most eloquent piece in this respect is a composition for the violin that was very successful at the time but whose score is now lost, so that our only knowledge of it comes from Louise Fusil. Its title was "Les amours et la mort du pauvre oiseau" (The poor bird's loves and death). "The first part of this little pastorale," she writes, "opened with a a sparkling song, full of gaiety and flourish; the bird's chirping expressed its happiness on seeing spring again and welcomed it in accents of joy. But this was soon followed by the second part in which the bird cooed its loves. This was a song full of soulfulness and seduction. One could almost see the bird flit from branch to branch in pursuit of the cruel mate who had already found another and had spread its wings in flight. The third theme was the poor bird's death, with pitiful songs, regrets and memories that sometimes recall the earlier notes of joy. Then the bird's voice gradually faded away and finally ceased. It fell from its lonely branch and breathed forth its life in a few vibrant notes. That was the bird's final song, its final sigh."[16]

This description led La Laurencie to say, "Who knows if this little ornithological drama was not a kind of musical autobiography of Saint-Georges?"[17] The notion is all the more likely in that the composition revives the distant image of the young Joseph whom his father called a sparrow.

---

[15] La Boëssière, *op. cit.*, p. xxi.

[16] Louise Fusil, *op. cit.*, 1903 edition, p. 128.

[17] La Laurencie, *op. cit.*, p. 488.

The intimate world of St-George

Saint-George seems to have peopled his solitude mainly with a few faithful
friends. These included the La Boëssière, father and son, the famous
horn-player and fencer Lamothe - Louise Fusil writes that, "St-Georges
and Lamothe were like Orestes and Pylades; one was never seen without
the other"[18] - and Simon Leduc, the composer and violinist who like
Gossec and Laviniès was one of the directors of orchestra of the Concert
Spirituel, but who had the misfortune to die very young, at the age of
only 32. His death deeply moved St-George, as was shown in the incident
we recounted at the beginning of this book.

Another intimate figure in St-George's world was Nanon, his black
mother. We know less about her, for we have only Beauvoir's account -
Denys simply reproduces what he wrote - but according to the novelist she
spent her remaining days in Paris, living withdrawn and incognito, and
even passing for St-George's servant in the eyes of the world. Anyhow,
this is one of the most captivating chapters in Beauvoir's otherwise insipid
book. Even though we cannot establish its authenticity, his version has at
least the merit of painting a fine and moving image of a mother who
sacrificed everything for her son and, out of love, accepted a hidden life
and concealment from strangers, but was a loving and warm presence for
St-George in his loneliness. He loved his mother, Beauvoir says, as a bird
loves its nest.[19]

It is a pity that we know so little about Nanon, for, even if Beauvoir's
story was born of poetic fantasy, she must have occupied an important
place in St-George's life.

Hunting groom to Duke Louis-Philippe

If it was really Nanon who kept house for Saint-George, she must either
have died or left in 1779, for in that year he moved into the Palais-Royal
and, according to Angelo, joined the staff of the old Duke of Orleans. The
Duke appointed him hunting groom at Le Raincy, a post of honour and
profit that he obtained, as the same author emphasises, "without engaging
in any intrigue or underhand dealings", in the manner practised by many
others seeking a prince's favour. Bachaumont, for his part, reports that

---

[18] Fusil, ibid., p. 127.

[19] Beauvoir, *op. cit.*, p. 264.

"Madame de Montesson wanted to have him available for her performances, so she got the Duke of Orleans to find him a post in the hunt, which involved various pleasant duties, many of which were also useful".[20]

St-George does not figure in the official list of the hunting and falconry officers of Louis-Philippe's household, nor in that of the Duke of Chartres when he succeeded his father six years later, but we find confirmation in the "Tablette de Renommée des Musiciens" of 1785, where St-George is mentioned as "écuyer de Mme la comtesse de Montesson et directeur de son Concert". The title "écuyer" in this context was the designation for a groom - the officer in charge of the stables of a prince or other nobleman. St-George cannot have received it before 1779, and the title of "écuyer" by which Gossec addressed him in his dedication of 1766, that is 13 years earlier, cannot have been the same. Perhaps reasons of etiquette dictated that St-George was called Madame de Montesson's groom rather than that of the Duke of Orleans: the officers of a prince of the blood had by definition to belong to the best of the nobility.

St-George's financial situation

St-George's appointment to the household of the foremost prince of the blood raises a very specific question, that of his financial position. As we learned from the Guadeloupe archives, his father died at Le Baillif in December 1774. And as we learned from the papers relating to his legacy, St-George was not one of the heirs; perhaps, as we suggested in the chapter on the father, he did not want to benefit from the slave plantations. M. de Bologne St-George's estate, with all its income, went to his widow, Elizabeth de Bologne-Mérican, and his daughter, Elizabeth Bénédictine de Bologne, whose married name was Le Velu de Clairfontaine. Both ladies had been established in France for some time and seem never to have had any relations with St-George.

Did that mean that St-George was thereafter deprived of the pension that, according to Angelo, his father had granted him? How much would he have earned as director of the Concert des Amateurs, from the sale of his musical compositions, from occasional benefit concerts and his fencing activities? Although Angelo remarks that "the various talents of St-George

---

[20] Bachaumont, *op. cit.*, t. XIV, 1 May 1779.

Extract from the Symphony Concertante in D major composed by Chevalier de Saint-George with the note "Volti Subito comme le Diable". Work incomplete. Oeffentliche Bibliothek der Universität Basel CH, Musiksammlung.

were like a gold mine", the total revenue was certainly not enough to pay for St-George's life style, bearing in mind the brilliant society of which he became a part and his lack of interest in saving. "He could have collected a considerable fortune if he had added prudence to his other qualities", Angelo says, and stresses that he "was very liberal where money was concerned".[21] In fact, St-George's temperament was not compatible with a judicious hoarding of wealth. He generously shared his income not just with his friends but with anyone who came to request his help.

"With such a good heart," writes La Boëssière, "he could only be generous, and so he was - almost to excess. He cared nothing for money himself, and what he had belonged to his friends. He was generous and charitable, and made sacrifices to relieve the poor. I have myself known old men whom he helped with money and the most touching attentions, within the limits of his means." And the author adds, "He made his gifts more precious by the delicacy with which he got them accepted". He was good to the point of weakness, his friend tells us - "he often got carried away and completely forgot that his own interests called him elsewhere. One could not blame him because it was himself he forgot."[22]

Hence it would appear that the favour of Louis-Philippe must have rescued Saint-George from a good deal of embarrassment; as we have said, he was a generous man who liberally supported artists and his annual charity for the needy amounted to more than 250,000 francs.[23]

Boundless activity and new compositions

Now that he had become an intimate of the Palais-Royal, which was then the centre of artistic and social life in Paris and was occasionally regarded as a kind of alternative Versailles, St-George was able to deploy all his qualities as horseman, huntsman, musician, actor and socialite.

While remaining in charge of the Amateurs at the Hôtel de Soubise, he conducted Madame de Montesson's concerts, performed in her productions and, above all, composed new musical works. These included several concertante symphonies, a bassoon concerto - which was given its first public performance by the famous Ozi at the Concert Spirituel on

---

[21] Angelo, *Angelo's Picnic*, London, 1905, p. 11.

[22] La Boëssière, *op. cit.*, p. xxi.

[23] *Nouvelle Biographie Générale*, 1862.

TROIS SONATES

Pour Le Clavecin ou Forte Piano

avec accompagnement de Violon obligé

Composées Par

Mr DE St GEORGE

1er œuvre de Clavecin

A PARIS

Prix 6 ...

A P. D. R.

V_m
+2372

Title page of St-George's first work for the harpsichord, the "Three Sonatas for Harpsichord or Forte Piano with violin obbligato", Bibliothèque Nationale, Paris,

28 March 1782 -[24], a fresh series of quartets (Opus 14) and a first work for the harpsichord, the Three Sonatas for Harpsichord or Forte Piano with violin obbligato published by Le Duc in 1782.

Two new dramatic works also appeared at this time, "L'Amant anonyme" and "Le droit de seigneur". The former is a two-act comedy with ballet episodes, whose complete score is to be found in the library of the Paris Conservatoire. This indicates that the play was produced in the capital on 8 March 1780, probably in Madame de Montesson's theatre. The libretto was inspired by the comedy of the same name by Mme de Genlis, the celebrated niece of Mme de Montesson, which had enjoyed a certain success and also been performed abroad, notably in Vienna. St-George's music comprises an intricate overture and a whole series of charming solo, ensemble and choral parts. As for the second of these dramatic works, "Le droit de seigneur", hardly anything is known about it. The only surviving fragment is an aria published in the "Journal de la Harpe" in 1784.

Of course, St-George also continued to write romances, and the demand for them soon spread to the provinces.

The theatre of General of Montalbert

St-George complemented all these activities with his work as actor and musician for the Marquis and Marquise of Montalbert, who maintained an extremely elegant theatre in their house in the Rue de la Roquette of the Faubourg St-Antoine. Marc-René de Montalbert was a general and a highly-regarded tactician. Like Choderlos de Laclos he was a leading specialist in the subject of fortifications. His young wife, Marie-Joséphine de Comarieu, was known for her rich and subtle mind; as the author of several novels she left behind her the reputation of a woman of letters.

A mysterious assassination attempt

The Chevalier de St-George was now at the height of his popularity. As La Boëssière tells us, he was sought after in every company and there was hardly any reception or important performance where he was not the focus of attention. "In contrast with the melancholy that seized him when he was alone", wrote Odet Denys, "his gaiety at parties shone forth like his native sunshine. His laughter, although within the limits of good manners, was

---

[24] *Annonces*, no. 728.

magnetic. When he laughed everyone laughed with him."[25] He was a model for all the young people of the time, Louise Fusil comments. "They were like his courtiers, and he was never seen without his followers around him."[26]

Nevertheless, shortly after his entry in the Palais-Royal an incident occurred which shows that he also had serious enemies, even though their identity has never been discovered. The few known details are again due to the tireless pen of Bachaumont. On 1 May 1779 he reports in his *Mémoires secrets*: "Recently, in the night, he was attacked by six men. He was with a friend of his, and they defended themselves as best they could against the clubs with which the unknown assailants tried to overcome them; there was even talk of a pistol shot being heard. The watch came to the rescue and interrupted the murderous attack, so that M. de St-Georges got away with bruises and superficial wounds. He is already to be seen in society again. Several of the assassins have been arrested. The Duke of Orleans wrote to Monsieur le Noir, the head of police, as soon as he was informed of the incident and urged him to make the most thorough enquiries so that the culprits receive exemplary punishment."[27]

But, Bachaumont continues, twenty-four hours later the Duke of Orleans was invited "from on high" not to meddle in the affair. The prisoners, who were all found to belong to police circles and one of whom was the famous detective Desbrugnières, were released and the affair was hushed up.

This assassination attempt has given rise to the most varied and fantastic hypotheses. Beauvoir of course saw it as a dramatic event in a love affair, while others have tried to present it as proof that St-George was a secret agent, either of the King or of the Duke of Chartres. But in fact we can only admit that we know absolutely nothing about the instigators or about their motives. All that is certain, according to Bachaumont's account, is that they enjoyed the protection of the court, the only "on high" that could have issued such an invitation to the first prince of the kingdom. "The complex novel that is the life of the Chevalier de Saint-George," La

---

[25] Odet Denys, *op. cit.*, p. 67.

[26] Fusil, *op. cit.*, p. 127.

[27] Bachaumont, *op. cit.*, t. XIV, 1 May 1779.

Laurencie wrote, "thus acquires a mysterious page."[28] As we shall see later, this attempt on the life of St-George was not to be the last.

---

[28] La Laurencie, *op. cit.*, p. 465.

V. WITH THE SOCIETE OLYMPIQUE - THE SYMPHONIES OF HAYDN

In 1781 the Chevalier de St-George's musical career entered a new phase. At the beginning of that year, the Concert des Amateurs ceased to exist on account of the financial difficulties of several of its most powerful supporters, especially the Farmer-General Audry and the Prince of Guéméné, the son-in-law of the Maréchal de Soubise. This was the time of Necker's fiscal reforms, the object of which was to meet the state's immense deficit. This was a chronic problem of the Ancien Régime and bankruptcy was a common occurrence.

St-George in charge of the Concert Olympique
Shortly after this collapse, the much-lamented Concert des Amateurs was replaced by the Concert de la Société Olympique, and it was St-George, who was already associated with its formation, who took over its direction.[1]
The Société Olympique was the child of the Loge Olympique de la Parfait Estime, and was at the time one of the most illustrious Masonic associations of the Grand Orient de France, whose Grand Master since 1773 had been the Duke of Chartres, son of the old Duke of Orleans and the future Philippe Égalité. The Société Olympique had over 400 initiate members, including, in addition to Chartres, senior magistrats, the highest-ranking financiers and notably various members of the Boullongne family which some people credited with St-George's paternity.[2]
Fifty-two members of the orchestra are mentioned as being among its adherents, and it is very probable that St-George himself was affiliated to the Société Olympique. In that case he would, as Gérard Jeffen[3] stresses, have been the first coloured man admitted to French Freemasonry.

---

[1] Articles on St-George by Prof. Derr in Grove's *Dictionary of Music and Musicians* and by Barry Brook in *MGG*.

[2] A. Le Bhian, *Francs-Maçons parisiens du Grand Orient de France,* collect.: "Mémoires et documents", Paris, Bibl. Nat., 1966.

[3] In *Le 5e Mousquetaire*, a broadcast by France-Musique.

A superb orchestra

According to Brenet, the Concert de la Société Olympique began its activities entirely under the auspices of the Palais-Royal, from which it took "the home, the name and the organisation of a Masonic affiliation. This method, a contemporary reports, was adopted so that the society, when it was summoned to the admission ceremony, could be vetted by ballot and then affiliated through a solemn reception into the Grand Lodge".[4]

Every subscriber, the same author tells us, paid two louis a year and received a silver lyre on a sky-blue background, which was the emblem required for entry to concerts. The orchestra comprised more than 70 players - 14 first violins, 14 second violins, 7 violas, 10 cellos, 4 double-bass, 4 horns, 3 oboes, 3 flutes, 2 bassoons, 2 clarinets, 2 trumpets and 1 timpanist -which made it entirely comparable with the orchestra of the Amateurs with its 76 players. And it included the most famous names, such as Navoigile and the Blasius brothers among the violinists, Bréval and Duport among the cellists, and Devienne and Hugo among the flautists.[5]

At the end of 1785, in consequence of alterations at the Palais-Royal, the Société Olympique obtained a room in the Tuileries Palace for its meetings. This was the prestigious Salle des Gardes, and they had it laid out for concerts too. The first performance in this new hall took place on 11 January 1786.[6]

Henceforth the concerts became brilliant social gatherings. "Since the Queen and the Princes had come to the concerts a few times without prior warning, the members got into the habit of dressing up in all their finery, and the musicians played in embroidered costume and lace cuffs, with their swords at their sides and their plumed hats placed on the benches."[7]

An orchestra such as this, Brenet adds, "was therefore very handsome to look at and, what was more important, it was no less agreeable to listen to.

---

[4] Michel Brenet, *Les Concerts en France sous l'Ancien Régime,* Paris, Librairie Fischbacher, 1900 / New York, Da Capo Press, 1970, p. 364.

[5] Jeffen in the broadcast quoted above.

[6] Thiéry, *Guide du voyageur à Paris,* 1786, t. 1, pp. 278 and 383. Quoted by Brenet.

[7] Brenet, *op. cit.,* p. 365. The author follows the description given in the *Mémorial de J. de Norvins,* published by Lanzac de Laborie, t. I., p. 158.

Just like the orchestra of the Hôtel de Soubise, it was full not only of professionals but also of the most skilful music-lovers of Paris. Viotti often conducted, and rehearsals were often held in the company of the composers. The association's prosperity made it not only possible to engage famous virtuosos, but also to acquire by special contract works that had been composed expressly by celebrated musicians."[8]

Haydn's Parisian symphonies - an unusual encounter

Thus it was that in 1784 six of Haydn's finest symphonies owed their origin to the Concert de la Loge Olympique.[9] These are the symphonies known as the Parisian, numbers 82-87, including "L'Ours" (The Bear), "La Poule" (The Hen) and "La Reine" (The Queen). According to H. Barbadette, it was St-George who went to Austria in the name of the Société Olympique to commission these symphonies from Prince Esterhazy's Kapellmeister.[10] The terms offered to Haydn were, incidentally, quite munificent: 25 louis d'or per symphony plus 5 louis for publication rights. Haydn admitted subsequently that the price seemed enormous to him because up till then his symphonies had brought him nothing.[11]

What an encounter that must have been, and what a pity that we have no written report to consult! We can only imagine this memorable scene in the annals of musical history. On the one side there was Joseph Haydn, born 1732 at Rohrau in Lower Austria, and on the other Joseph de Bologne St-George, born around 1748 on Guadeloupe. It was a meeting of two worlds. For Haydn the world from which St-George came must have seemed inconceivable, beyond the limits of his imagination. And yet, different though these two men were by origin and temperament, their musical affinity transcended the gulf that lay between them.

It was St-George too who rehearsed and conducted the first performances of these six Parisian Symphonies in the Tuileries. They took place at the end of 1787, in a series of successive concerts, and were a veritable

---

8 Brenet, *op. cit.*, pp. 365-66.

9 ibid.

10 Quoted by B. Brook in his article on St-George in *MGG*.

11 Jeffen, in the broadcast quoted above.

triumph.[12] "Every day," Le Mercure wrote, "one senses more deeply and therefore admires all the more the works of this great genius who, in each of his compositions, so well understands how to draw such rich and varied developments from a single theme.[13] Their success in France was thereafter assured, in spite of bad acoustics that St-George could do nothing to change; as Le Mercure says: "The symphonies of M. Haydn always produce the right effect but they would be even more effective if the hall's acoustics were better and if its narrow shape had allowed the director of the orchestra to position the orchestra more advantageously."

We should note in connection with St-George's activities as head of the Concert de la Société Olympique, that Barry Brook was the first biographer to mention them. Even La Laurencie did not know about them and Brenet, in his description of the Concert, says nothing on the subject. He speaks only of Viotti, and it is possible that the celebrated Italian violinist, who was also a member of the Société Olympique, deputised for Saint-George during his frequent absences from the capital.

St-George on his travels

Indeed, during the pre-revolutionary 1780s, the Chevalier de St-George seems to have travelled a good deal, perhaps to give concerts or perhaps for reasons unknown to us. On several occasions his travels took him to England - the others were not documented - and these will be the subject of the next chapter.

---

[12] Jeffen, loc. cit.

[13] "Le Mercure", end of 1787, quoted by Jeffen without the precise date.

VI. THE ANGLOMANE CHEVALIER - JOURNEYS ACROSS THE CHANNEL

The phenomenon of Anglomania

During the 1780s Anglomania was common among the French nobility. It was by no means a new phenomenon, since it had begun under Louis XV, but it reached its height during the reign of Louis XVI, and more especially after 1783 when the Peace of Versailles put an end to the War of American Independence, in which France had sided with the United States against England. After that, the English flocked to Paris in greater numbers than ever before. The Queen was infatuated with them, and so were the court and the city. English fashions were the rage.

English gardens were laid out everywhere: those of the Count of Artois at Bagatelle and of the Duke of Chartres at Monceau were among the most celebrated. English dress was adopted and so were English furnishings and even English dishes. Swords were imported from across the Channel, together with horses and carriages - especially whiskies, a kind of ultra-light cabriolet, like "birds that skimmed over the ground".[1] Jockeys and English horse races were the height of fashion, and the great ladies of the kingdom came together at Astley's, the famous English riding master. Heroes were taken over from English novels: Clarissa Harlowe became Rousseau's Julie, and Lovelace became Laclos's Valmont. Moreover England gave the French lessons in hygiene: the close-stools of Versailles soon gave way to English water-closets.

England also gave the French harmless passions such as tea, the riding-coat and whist, which displaced the game of "hombre".[2]

The purists take fright

This invasion of new ideas could hardly fail to disturb some of the more "purist" minds, some of whom even saw in it a threat to France's independence. Hence in May 1786, in the "Correspondance littéraire",

---

[1] *Souvenirs du Baron de Frénilly-Pair de France (1768-1828)*, published by A. Chuquet, Paris 1908, p. 81.

[2] P. Bluche, *La vie quotidienne au temps de Louis XVI*, Paris, Hachette, 1980, pp. 144-150.

Meister gave vent to a cry of alarm implying that here was a plot to undermine France: "Without casting suspicion on any of our present ministers, are there not grounds to believe that some enterprising genius such as M. Bertin has for some years been looking for a means of inoculating us with English ways and that he has attained some success? What is certainly true is that France has never before been invaded to this extent by this rival nation's tastes not only in fashion, but also in custom and life-style."[3]

We should recall in this connection that England was then France's main economic as well as political rival, that English competition was provoking serious crises in French industry and that France had just concluded a commercial treaty with England that was unfavourable to her economy. To convince oneself of the harmful effects of Anglomania, Meister continues, "one has only to consider our balance of trade with England over the last ten or twelve years. This demonstrates the costs that France has to bear for this passion for horses, carriages, furniture, fabrics and jewels of every kind that are shipped over here from all the ports of Great Britain." Moreover, he deplores the fact that English should be the only foreign language studied at all seriously in France, and that the only foreign books translated should be English ones.

"But that is not all. The things I have mentioned change and usually leave little trace behind, but some have a much more powerful influence on our way of life, and the very basis of our national character... Anglomania and its frightening advance also threaten the chivalry of the French, their social sense and their taste in dress."

This is serious indeed, for according to Meister these three qualities are the most characteristic expression of the nation's genius. "It is rare in society nowadays to come across people who are what one might call dressed. Women wear straight frocks and hats, and the men tails and waistcoats." He asks whether this style of dress "possesses the nobility and dignity appropriate for a nation that in this matter so long enjoyed the privilege of serving as an example and model for all other nations?"

---

[3] Grimm, *Correspondance littéraire,* May 1786.

Help - etiquette being ignored!

As for social values, how could they survive "in the midst of so many customs designed to drive us further away from them day by day, in the midst of so many new institutions that seem to have been invented simply to destroy them?" By these institutions were meant the English-style clubs that were to be seen mushrooming everywhere: political clubs, military clubs, chess clubs, clubs for Americans etc. The author blames them above all for the way they slighted social ritual, etiquette and aristocratic convention: "They are assemblies of lots of people who hardly know one another but willingly come together in the same place without taking the trouble to show one another the courtesies of wit, attention or pleasing manners. The only form of politeness that obtains in this kind of society is not to cause mutual embarrassment. People come and go at any time they like, and can turn up unwashed and ill-dressed."

Meister stresses moreover that women are not allowed in these clubs and that this undermines the spirit of gallantry: "Men and women no doubt still meet from time to time, but can one say they really see one another?" And then, because of English tea, people do not have supper as they used to, since there is not enough time before the evening entertainment. This meant that they were losing the art of conversation, the most cherished of the traditional French arts.

Faced with this "national scourge" of Anglomania, Meister sees no hope but in "the tendency we have to get tired of everything in due course".[4] But his hopes were to be disappointed, for what was at stake this time was a phenomenon that was much more than a passing fashion. It was the beginning of a revolution, or rather of The Revolution.

Political Anglomania - Philippe of Orleans

Meister's description of Anglomania leaves its political dimensions out of account. What so much appealed to the French wealthy classes was the liberal system of government established on the other side of the Channel. The "Glorious Revolution" of 1688-89 had replaced absolutism with constitutional monarchy and armed the English with guarantees against royal arbitrariness that the French could only dream of. In default of English-style freedom, France could do no more than imitate some of its

---

[4] Grimm, *Correspondance littéraire,* loc. cit.

secondary manifestations. But the closer 1789 came, the more apparent was the real motive force behind Anglomania. Anglomane circles were humming with discussion of the British constitution, the parliamentary system, Magna Carta and the law of Habeas Corpus.[5]

We have given all these details on Anglomania because they have an important bearing on the present chapter of St-George's life. The Chevalier was or became a great Anglomane. He was moreover closely linked with a man who was considered one of the main protagonists of political Anglomania - Philippe of Orleans, the Duke of Chartres, the son of Duke Louis-Philippe of Orleans.

The Prince had been converted at an early age to the liberal ideas coming from England and America, and his leaning towards the Anglo-Saxon system could only be reinforced by the repressive measures inflicted on him by the court. He was exiled three times for his opposition to the King. Queen Marie-Antoinette showed him an implacable aversion: she not only forced him, by the King's intervention, to surrender to her the castle of St-Cloud, the Duke's favourite residence and birthplace, but hardly missed an opportunity to humiliate him, as in 1779 for instance, when she made the King deprive him of his post in command of the Navy.[6]

From that time, Philippe of Orleans had drifted further and further away from the court, and his opposition to the absolutism of Versailles soon became the rallying point for all the malcontents. This went so far that some saw in him a real candidate to the throne under any future constitutional monarchy in France.

According to Madame de Staël, Necker's famous daughter,[7] there was "an idea generally rooted in the minds of publicists at the time that a deviation from the hereditary line like the one in England (when William III came to the throne) might encourage the establishment of liberty by putting at the head of the constitution a king who owed his throne to it, in place of a king who would see himself as denuded by it". And during the first years of the Revolution Philippe of Orleans was seen as such a king.

---

[5] Bluche, *op. cit.*, p. 151.

[6] Lamartine in his article on Philippe of Orleans in the *Nouvelle Biographie Générale*, 1862.

[7] Madame La Baronne de Staël, *Considérations sur les principaux événements de la Révolution françoise,* Paris, Delaunay, Bossange et Massons, 1818, t. I, p. 306.

St-George and Duke Philippe

According to his elder son, Louis-Philippe, it was in 1783, after the Peace of Versailles, that the Duke of Chartres began to make frequent visits to England.[8] Some said that he went there just to buy horses for his English stables, others that the purpose of his visits was to prepare for revolution in France.

Beauvoir affirms that St-George often accompanied the Prince on his trips across the Channel, perhaps to equip the Orleans stables with horses, perhaps for other reasons. Other writers, especially the one who wrote the article on St-George in the "Biographie Michaud", emphasise that the Chevalier played "a very active role in the political manoeuvres that had their focus in the Palais-Royal." But there is no documentary evidence for these assertions.

Perhaps St-George became an Anglomane through his connection with Philippe of Orleans, but there were doubtless deeper causes for his Anglomania. Being accustomed to change from earliest childhood, he must have been more open-minded regarding new ideas than many of his compatriots. But above all he was a man of colour without any legal status whose rights entirely depended on the good will of the King, and the wind of liberty that blew from England must have had a special attraction for him.

The Chevalier de St-George's first visit to England of which we have definite information is the one he made in 1787 and which on the surface at least had nothing to do with politics.

The death of the old Duke of Orleans

The old Duke of Orleans died on 18 November 1785, and shortly after-wards the King abolished the house of the foremost prince of the blood.[9] As a result, St-George lost his position as hunting groom at Le Raincy and also as director of Madame de Montesson's concert.[10] According to Angelo, this loss had serious financial consequences for St-George, who was "reduced again to applying himself to his favourite art", that is,

---

[8] Louis-Philippe, Mémoires 1773-1793, t. I, Paris, Librairie Plon, 1973, p. 326.

[9] Louis-Philippe, *Mémoires 1773-1793,* Paris, Libriairie Plon, 1973, t. I, p. 36.

[10] Henry Angelo, *Angelo's Picnic,* London, 1905, p. 11.

fencing.[11] In the spring of 1787 then he went to London, which at the time was an important centre for the art of the foil.

We might well ask ourselves whether the motive for this trip was really what Angelo says, for if relations between St-George and Prince Philippe, now the Duke of Orleans and one of the richest men in France, were actually as close as was said it is hard to see why the Chevalier should have felt obliged to leave France and seek funds in England, abandoning his orchestra in its hall at the Tuileries at the height of its season.

The fencing match with the Chevalier d'Eon at Carlton House

Be that as it may, it really does seem as though St-George went to London simply to fence. He undertook a whole series of contests with the most famous English and foreign masters, and these were detailed in the London newspapers.[12] Most of these encounters took place in the academy of Henry Angelo, the English fencing master of Italian origin to whom we owe so many precious, and some false, details on St-George's life. Angelo was the son of the celebrated riding and fencing master Domenico Angelo Malevolti Tremamondo.

But the most spectacular event of this visit was a contest that took place at Carlton House on 9 April 1787 in the course of which St-George took on not only the Prince of Wales, the future George IV, but also a personality who had become a legend in his lifetime - the Chevalier, or rather at that time the Chevalière, d'Eon. The painter Robineau has captured this unusual combat in a canvas showing St-George crossing swords with a lady of a certain age, in skirts and a lace bonnet, whose posture is entirely masculine and who bears the cross of St. Louis on her left breast. In the background an illustrious audience includes Lamothe, St-George's inseparable friend, the fencing masters Fabien, Béda, Rolland and Goddard, the Duke of Lausanne and, standing in the centre, the Prince of Wales.[13]

---

[11] ibid.

[12] Notably the "Morning Herald" of 9 April 1787.

[13] At the end of the 18th century this painting was in the possession of the Prince of Wales. An engraving by N.M. Picot is in the Bibliothèque Nationale in Paris. The identification of those present comes from H. Angelo's *Reminiscences,* t. II, p. 46, and *Angelo's Picnic*, pp. 36- 37.

A contest of de Saint-George with the transvestite Chevalier d'Eon,
London 9th April 1787, with the Prince of Wales in the background.
Engraving by N.M. Picot after Robineau, Cabinet des Estampes, Bibl. Nationale, Paris.

MAD.ᴸᴸᴱ LA CHEVALIERE D'EON DE BEAUMONT

Fencing at Carlton House, 9ᵗʰ April 1787

A detail from page 171

The bout ended with the victory of "Miss" d'Eon, but she "was modest enough to believe that M. de St-Georges had been kind to her".[14] However, he candidly stated that it had taken all his skill to try to parry the thrusts of his adversary.[15] The editor of the memoirs of the Chevalier d'Eon notes that "seven times, Saint-Georges was hit by his rival in spite of the encumbrance she must have suffered from wearing woman's clothing."[16]

The lady was of course a "chevalier". The story how Charles d'Eon came to adopt female clothing and present himself officially in society as a woman is too extraordinary, and too revealing about the strange twists and turns of state affairs, for us to omit a brief summary in this context.

The incredible story of the Chevalier d'Eon

Until 1774 the Chevalier d'Eon was one of Louis XV's most important secret agents. He was born on 5 October 1728 at Tonnerre in Burgundy and baptised with one of those multiple names - Charles-Geneviève-Louis-Auguste-André-Timothé d'Eon de Beaumont. His youth was marked by the delicacy of his constitution and the long blond hair that made him look like a girl. When he grew up his face remained hairless. From his early years he had a passion for swordsmanship. He studied under Mottet in Paris[17] and around 1750 attained the status of "grand prévot de salle d'armes" and at the same time became Doctor of Law and lawyer in parliament. He was presented at court thanks to the support he received from elevated personalities such as Marie d'Este, Duchess of Penthièvre (the future mother-in-law of Philippe of Orleans), the Prince of Conti, the Baron de Bezenval and the Duke of Lauzun.

---

[14] Captain Telfer, *The Strange Career of the Chevalier d'Eon de Beaumont,* 1885, pp. 308-309.

[15] Angelo, *The reminiscences of Henry Angelo, London,* 1828, t. II, p. 421.

[16] *Mémoires du Chevalier d'Eon,* published by F. Gaillardet, Paris, 1836, t.II, pp. 344 - 345.

[17] Mottet was also the instructor of Henry Angelo, who studied fencing in Paris for several years. See *Schools and Masters of Fence* by Egerton Castle, London, 1893, p. 299 ff.

D'Eon as secret agent in Russia

In 1755 Louis XV decided, together with Madame de Pompadour, to entrust d'Eon with a secret mission to Russia. France had not maintained official relations with Russia for the past twelve years because the Chancellor, Bestuchief-Riumin, was anti-French and prevented any contact between French envoys and the Empress Elisabeth.

Since his physique was eminently suitable for feminine disguise, the Chevalier d'Eon was charged in 1755 with the task of gaining admission as a tutor to the court of St. Petersburg, under the name of "Mademoiselle de Beaumont", and secretly negotiating a Franco-Russian alliance against England, for the Seven Years War was impending. D'Eon managed so well that only one year later a treaty of alliance was signed betwen Louis XV and the Tsarina, which led to an unexpected revision of the European fronts. The wily Chevalier also succeeded in obtaining the famous testament of Peter the Great and bringing it to France in 1756.

After this, d'Eon was until 1760 a secretary in the new French embassy at St. Petersburg, dressed as a man again and using the identity of the brother of "Mlle de Beaumont". His main function was to inform Louis XV of what was happening in Russia.

Louis XV's double government

"Louis XV employed different kinds of agents, spread out over the surface of the globe," writes F. Gaillardet, the editor of the *Mémoires du chevalier d'Eon*. "It was a vast network whose mesh he cast over Europe. If he wanted to extend it he only had to twitch the central line attached to his arm and reports of every kind flowed in for his attention. Within and outside it there was an abundance of confidants, spies, ministers and ministries - big and small, open and secret. It was rather the same thing as his favourites and mistresses. Nothing was straightforward or open in his strange government. It was a veritable labyrinth, an intricate maze, in which even the best-informed initiate never discovered all the turnings or all the exits."[18] It should be understood that the King had alongside his official government a second clandestine one; at this time it was headed by the Count of Broglie and the Prince of Conti. [19]

---

[18] *Mémoires du chevalier d'Eon,* t. I, p. 85.

[19] ibid.

The King's solitary battle

After spending some time in the army, the Chevalier d'Eon was sent to London in 1762 and took part in the negotiations leading to the peace of 1763.[20] To reward his services, in the same year the King conferred on him the cross of the Order of St.Louis. The King charged him with a new secret mission - informing the King of events at the English court - but he fell out of favour with Madame de Pompadour. The King was powerless against the "sultaness" and signed the official order for him to return to France. But at the same time he wrote a personal letter, signed in his own hand and dated 4 October 1763 from Versailles, where he said: " I write to advise you that today the King signed the order recalling you to France, but just with his stamp and not with his hand. In fact I order you to stay in England, with all your papers, until I convey my further instructions."

In obeying the King's secret command he was obviously in conflict with his official orders, and this led to a long, spectacular battle - a novel in itself, spiced with assassination attempts and abductions, libels and lawsuits. To stop Versailles' official representatives from seizing his secret correspondence with the King, d'Eon barricaded himself in his house and threatened to explode charges of dynamite if they tried to force their way in. He was declared mad and seditious, with both official agreement and at the same time secret support for the offender from the King, who wanted at all costs to prevent his correspondence with d'Eon falling into the hands of his favourite.

In 1765, with Madame de Pompadour in her grave, the intrigue was at last unravelled and d'Eon resumed his reconnaissance work at the Court of St. James. He had met Queen Charlotte, the wife of George III, ten years before in Mecklenburg, at the time of his first journey to Russia, and he was thought to have become her lover afterwards. Through his close relations with her, he had easy access to the news from the English court.

---

[20] In London the Chevalier d'Eon made friends among others with Henry Angelo's father, the fencing master Angelo Malevolti Tremamondo, and became, like the Maréchal de Saxe, one of the most celebrated clients of the school. See E. Castle, *op. cit.,* p. 240.

A king betrayed
But in 1771 King George III suddenly came to doubt his wife's faithfulness and, more particularly, the true paternity of his oldest son, the Prince of Wales. The Chevalier d'Eon himself[21] tells how the Queen tried to reassure her husband by claiming that the Chevalier was actually a woman. For his peace of mind, George III wrote to Louis XV requesting confirmation. Prompted by his new favourite, Madame Dubarry, who thought a lie was better than a king dishonoured and lovers parted, Louis hastened to send the wished-for response that the Chevalier d'Eon was indeed a woman. As soon as George III had received this letter he passed its contents round the whole court in confidence. In a few days all London knew the secret. But some were better informed and there was much contention and wager. The Chevalier's sex was an object of speculation and investments went up and down as if on the stock market. D'Eon was mortified by all these machinations without understanding their origin, and he fled to Ireland.

"Better to shine as a woman than be unnoticed as a man"
In the end, a letter from the Duke of Aiguillon, Louis XV's minister for foreign affairs, enlightened the poor Chevalier as to the cause of all this fuss. But what was worse, the letter gave him to understand that George III doubted the assurance given by Versailles, and that reasons of state required him to put aside his identity as a man and become a woman. D'Eon replied to the Duke on 18 October 1771: "Since it is required for the welfare of my country and an august personage, I agree to pass for a woman and promise to give no living soul evidence to the contrary. But what I cannot accept is to wear the clothing of the other sex, although for a time I did wear it in my youth out of obedience to my king. To resume this disguise permanently, or even temporarily, would be beyond me; the mere idea appals me so much that nothing could overcome my revulsion."[22] But Versailles did not want to listen. In his subsequent letters the Duke of Aiguillon urged on the Chevalier the honour, indeed the glory, in yielding to the King's request: "Better to shine as a woman than be unnoticed as a man... His Majesty has commissioned you as lieutenant and then as

---

[21] ibid., t. II, p. 98 ff.
[22] ibid., p. 124.

captain in the Dragoons. What he now wants to give you is nothing less than a commission of immortality. Can you refuse?"[23]

The intervention of Caron de Beaumarchais

This cajolery went on for more than two years, with d'Eon struggling as hard as he could to put off his sex change. However, after the death of Louis XV in 1774 and the succession of Louis XVI the demands from Versailles became more pressing, and in May 1775 the King sent a fresh negotiator to London. This was Caron de Beaumarchais, the author of "The Barber of Seville" and the future author of "The Marriage of Figaro". One may well feel surprised on finding this celebrated author involved in the story. But we must understand, first of all, that in 1775 Beaumarchais was not as famous as he was to become. His comedy "The Barber of Seville" was given its first performance in this year but was not to be set to music by Rossini until 1826, while "The Marriage of Figaro" was not written until 1781 and was set to music by Mozart in 1786. Moreover it should also be borne in mind that Beaumarchais had found admission to the court at Versailles as the King's harpist.[24] In this capacity he must have been one of the monarch's intimates, and so it is not surprising that for this mission to London Louis XVI should have employed the diverse talents of a man whose writings testify to such a predilection for both political intrigue and dramatic solutions.

A unique agreement

On 5 October 1775 Beaumarchais signed an agreement with d'Eon that must be unique in history. In it, the Chevalier d'Eon renounced his male identity for all time and undertook to wear female clothing to the end of his days. In recompense, Louis XVI granted him a pension for life and permission to return to France.

But the fulfilment of the agreement imposed a great strain on d'Eon. When he finally disembarked in France on 17 August 1777 it was in his dragoon's uniform. Ten days later, the King very formally and categorically ordered him to dress as woman, and this was done the following November. Thereafter the valiant Chevalier was never seen except cross-dressed in

---

[23] ibid., pp. 147-148.

[24] Riemann Musiklexikon, Paris, 1882.

his feminine version, and there are still some people today who believe that this was his true sex. But medical examinations and the autopsy carried out at his death in 1810 provide irrefutable proof to the contrary. He was certainly a man, in the full sense of the word. The same year, George III went mad and remained so till his death.[25]

The reader may wonder at all this detail about the intrigues of the time. Obviously we could be content simply to say that there was a lot of intrigue, but these particulars give us a clearer picture of the world in which St-George lived. They also lead us to ask how St-George could survive in such a world, fit into its ways and play the part that fate had prepared for him.

Mather Brown's portrait of St-George

At the time of his contest with St-George, the Chevalier d'Eon, in his woman's clothes, was living in London again, where Louis XVI had given him permission to withdraw in 1783. He was one of the intimates of the Prince of Wales, who was thought to be his son. The Prince liked to set him against the most accomplished fencers; and d'Eon kept his passion for the sword and the foil until a very advanced age. According to Gaillardet, it was on the initiative of the heir to the throne that the encounter at Carlton House took place between St-George and d'Eon.

These virile exertions consoled the transvestite Chevalier somewhat for the embarrassing existence to which he was condemned and about which he often complained, without success, to the ministers at Versailles.

Against this background, the seven hits to the credit of the Chevalier d'Eon seem to be attributable less to a loss of speed on the part of St-George - then aged thirty-nine, as against the transvestite's sixty years - than to his natural generosity.

Although we do not know in what other activities St-George engaged during his stay in England, we do know that it was at this time that the American painter Mather Brown did the famous portrait showing him foil in hand. In his *Reminiscences* Angelo recounts the following anecdote on the subject. After his final sitting to Brown, Saint-George came to have dinner with Angelo's parents. The mother questioned him on the portrait

---

[25] *Mémoires du Chevalier d'Eon,* p. 350 ff.

The Chevalier de Saint-George, engraving by W. Ward after a painting
from Mather Brown (1787), Cabinet des Estampes, Bibl. Nationale, Paris

and asked him if he found it like. The Chevalier replied, "Oh, Madam, it's like, all right - it's horrible!"[26]

Many whites at the time found black people hideous in appearance, and Bachaumont in describing St-George stressed "the ugliness of his face".[27] We however have neither the modesty of St-George nor the aesthetic standards of eighteenth-century Europe, and what we see is in fact a great beauty and, making due allowance for the difference in costume, an amazing resemblance to another prodigious son of the Great African Mother - the young Tutankhamen, pharaoh of Egypt three thousand years ago, whose effigy is on display in the Museum of Cairo.

As a token of friendship, St-George presented this portrait to Henry Angelo, who hung it in his fencing school. As many of his pupils asked for a copy, Angelo had it engraved by the famous artist Ward. Shortly before publishing this engraving in London on 4 April 1788, Angelo sent a copy to St-George, who was in Paris at the time. A few days later he received from him, for placing underneath the portrait, the poetical dedication by La Boëssière senior which we quoted at the beginning of this book:

> "Dans les armes, jamais on ne vit son égal,
> Musicien charmant, compositeur habile,
> A la nage, au patin, à la chasse, à cheval,
> Tout exercice enfin, pour lui semble facile,
> Et dans tous, il découvre un mode original.
> Si jcindre à ces talens autant de modestie
> Est le nec plus ultra de l'Hercule Français,
> C'est que son bon esprit exempt de jalousie
> N'a trouvé de bonheur en cette courte vie
> Que dans les vrais amis que son coeur s'étoit fait."[28]

---

[26] Angelo, *The reminiscences of Henry Angelo,* t. II, pp. 77-78, quoted by La Laurencie, *op. cit.,* p. 470.

[27] Bachaumont, *Mémoires secrets pour servir à l'hostire de la République des Lettres en France, depuis 1762 jusqu'à nos jours,* London, t. XIV, 1 May 1779.

[28] *Angelo's Picnic,* London, 1905, pp. 37 - 38.

"He has no equal in the handling of arms.
He is a charming musician and composer; expert
at swimming, skating, hunting and riding,
he takes easily to every kind of exercise,
and in all of them he finds an original style.
Like a French Hercules he manages to match
these talents with the same degree of modesty,
showing that his nature is free of jealousy
and has found no happiness in this short life
but in the true friends his heart had won."

A new comedy by St-George

The summer of 1787 saw St-George back in Paris. A new work of his for the stage was performed at the Comédie Italienne on 18 August, "La Fille-Garçon" (The Girl-Boy), a comic opera in two acts inspired no doubt by his meeting with the transvestite Chevalier d'Eon. Although the libretto by Desmaillot had no more success than that for "Ernestine" or "La Chasse", the music was "loudly applauded", as the Journal de Paris reported,[29] and the Journal Général de France emphasised that but for the music the work would have been a failure. It added that St-George's success "should serve as a flattering encouragement to give this theatre the benefit of his future productions".[30] Furthermore, two stars of the period, Mlles Renaud and Carlin, ensured that this, St-George's fifth work for the stage, had a first-class interpretation.

It is hardly surprising that the most negative critique came from the *Correspondance littéraire* again, which said: "This work is better written than anything else M. de St-Georges has produced for the stage. All the same, it seems to be just as void of originality. This calls to mind an observation that still waits to be disproved, namely that though mulattos have received as a special gift of nature their marvellous aptitude for all the arts of imitation, nature seems nevertheless to have withheld those flights of feeling and genius which give birth to new ideas and original conceptions."[31]

---

[29] Journal de Paris, 18 August 1787, p. 1009.

[30] Journal général de France, 23 August 1787, pp. 403-404.

[31] Grimm, *Correspondance littéraire, t.* XV, p. 133.

In our view, this remark tells us more about the state of mind of its author, whether Grimm or Meister, and the prejudice that informed his opinions, than it does about St-George's music.

The banishment of Philippe of Orleans

In the time between this performance of "La Fille-Garcon" in August 1787 and the summer of the following year, we have no real information on St-George's life, except for what we have already mentioned in the previous chapter from Le Mercure de France about the concerts of the Société Olympique, where the Chevalier conducted Haydn's Paris Symphonies at the end of 1787. It is possible that he followed Philippe of Orleans in his exile to Villers-Cotterets and then to Le Raincy, for he was banished from Paris for several months and did not reappear in the capital until May 1788.[32] This resulted from the royal session of Parliament on 19 November 1787, when the Duke publicly defied the King by declaring illegal the sovereign's command to ratify a loan of 125 million.

Shortly afterwards, a new two-act comedy by St-George, "Le Marchand de Marrons" (The Chestnut Seller)[33] was performed at the Palais-Royal, or to be more precise, at the Théâtre des Beaujolais. Since this theatre had been built by Philippe of Orleans a few years earlier for his youngest son, the young Count of Beaujolais, and was primarily a marionette theatre, we may suppose for lack of better information that this work was intended for children. St-George certainly loved children, and we have evidence - see Chapter VII - that he made music with them too. It is also possible that he gave lessons to the children of the Duke of Orleans, whose instructors included such celebrities as Vestris, "the god of dancing", and whose governess was a woman of letters, the Countess of Genlis.

The Palais-Royal in 1788

In the summer of 1788, St-George seems to have been a frequent visitor to the Grand Avenue of the Palais-Royal, which at the time was not only one of the wonders of Paris and the meeting-place for Parisian elegant society, but also the capital's political focus.

---

[32] Louis-Philippe, *op. cit.*, t. I, pp. 34-38.

[33] According to Gerber, *Neues historisch-biographisches Lexikon,* Leipzig, 1812.

Louis-Philippe, the eldest son of Philippe of Orleans, has this to say on the subject: "The Palais-Royal, which for good reason was known as the 'capital of Paris', had always been the place where those keen on politics used to meet together. Its garden was the spot where everyone came to bring his news and pick up the news of others. In England social life is not so active and people talk only when they really have something to say; they are happy to leave the circulation of news to the newspapers. But in France newspapers have always been able to print only what the censors allow the public to know, and so it is in public places, the gardens and cafés, that everyone tries to find out what is happening, and news is always circulated through conversation rather than in the press."[34]

In this summer of 1788, with the scarcity of wheat and the financial crisis at its height, outstanding events could be felt to be on the way and political discussions heated many a head. But on the surface Paris kept its frivolous and carefree image.

A woman painter, Madame Vigée-Lebrun has described how the regular audiences of the Opera surged out into the gardens of the Palais-Royal after the performance. There were Parisian beauties with perfumed hair and bouquets of flowers. "Sometimes," she says, "these evenings went on until two in the morning. Music was played by moonlight in the open air. Artistes and amateurs, among them Garat and Azévédo, sang on these occasions, and there were performances on the harp and guitar. The famous St-George often played the violin and the crowd gathered to listen."[35]

It was not only the Opera audiences who came. There were also those from the other great theatres, the Théâtre Français and the Théâtre Italien, for all these venues were close to the Palais-Royal. The result was that at certain hours there was regularly a terrible congestion of horsedrawn carriages. These traffic jams were known as "hindrances", and the Baron de Frénilly has left us this description: "The carriages congregated in this street from the four cardinal points of the compass when the theatres were out. When the street was jam-packed, as I have seen it some twenty times, from the Place des Victoires right up to the Place Vendôme, all the manoeuvres of the mounted watchmen went for nothing. One was stuck

---

[34] Louis-Philippe, *op. cit.*, t.I, p. 55.

[35] *Souvenirs* of Mme L.-E. Vigée-Lebrun, Paris, 1835-7, t. I, pp. 25-26.

for an hour or so, inching forward and sometimes reversing; the cry, "Look out behind!" was equivalent to "Every man for himself!". There was complete confusion, with women screaming, coachmen swearing and shafts snapping. It was like a battlefield."[36]

Besides the avenue of the Palais-Royal, St-George also frequented various salons at this time, places where music was made and no doubt politics too, notably that of the Baron de Bezenval, a lieutenant-colonel of the Swiss Guard, where he met the composer Nicolas Dalayrac.[37] The Music Calendar of 1789 mentions him simply as an "amateur", without any reference to his functions as conductor of the orchestra of the Société Olympique.

On the eve of the Revolution

In the winter of 1788-89, political debate reached its height. "There was a flood of increasingly democratic pamphlets. The famous pamphlet by the Abbé Sieyès entitled "Qu'est-ce que le Tiers?" (What is the Third Estate?) appeared at this time. As one may imagine, the answer was, 'It's the nation, and the two other social orders do not matter.' Conversation went round and round these subjects, and people's minds became more and more fermented."[38]

Following the disastrous harvest of the previous summer, destitution increased even more in the course of the winter months, and at the beginning of 1789 it was reckoned that there were 120,000 beggars out of the Paris population of 550,000. In the countryside many people had no more wheat to make bread and had to eat bread made from ferns.[39]

Finally the States General assembled at Versailles on 5 May 1789, and political events took their well-known course. The National Assembly was proclaimed on 17 June, the Bastille was stormed on 14 July, the feudal régime was abolished on 4 August, and so on.

---

[36] *Souvenirs du Baron de Frénilly-Pair de France (1768-1828)*, Paris, 1908, p. 27.

[37] According to La Laurencie, *op. cit.*, p. 470.

[38] Louis-Philippe, *op. cit.*, t. I, p. 42.

[39] O. Denys, *op. cit.*, p. 132.

The return of St-George to England

We do not know what St-George was doing during these months of growing tension, and especially during the dramatic days of mid-July.

What is certain, however, is that during the month of August 1789, the Chevalier de St-George went back to England and according to Angelo "intended to establish himself there".[40] The English fencing champion must have known what he was talking about because he followed the Chevalier to Brighton. There the Chevalier was received by the Prince of Wales. Angelo shared a house with him and they fenced together every day. (We should remind ourselves at this point that the Prince of Wales, the eldest son of King George III of England, was to succeed to the throne in 1820 as George IV after having become Regent from 1811 in replacement of his father.)

But St-George did not stay in England, "his plans having been so badly prepared that they ended in utter failure".[41] According to Angelo, St-George went to London from Brighton, and spent a highly cosmopolitan time in Grenier's, one of the capital's most elegant hotels. He was surrounded by fencers, musicians and admirers of all nationalities and he entertained them with his customary generosity. So much so, indeed, that - still according to Angelo - he ended up devoid of resources and was obliged to return to France.

In view of St-George's subsequent career, one might well conclude that this fresh stay in England had a further dimension that was either unknown to Angelo or which Angelo chose to pass over in silence.

The anti-slavery movement

There was of course in London, and had been for several years, a very active organisation for the abolition of slavery. A French branch was founded by Brissot and Condorcet at the beginning of 1789, the Society of the Friends of the Blacks. The British organisation was linked to a similar body in America, the Society for the Abolition of the Slave trade and Black Slavery, which had offices in Philadelphia and New York.

As early as 1788, Brissot had insisted "on the necessity of founding in Paris a society comparable to those in America and London for the

---

[40] Angelo, *Angelo's Picnic,* pp. 11 and 38.

[41] ibid.

abolition of the slave trade and negro slavery" in a speech delivered in Paris to a group of friends who had come together "at the request of the London committee".[42] The principal protagonists of the abolitionist movement in France, apart from Brissot and Condorcet, were the Duke of Rochefoucauld, Lafayette, the Abbé Grégoire and the Abbé Sieyès, Dupont de Nemours, Mirabeau, Clavière and Pétion, the Mayor of Paris.[43]

The French society was constituted on 3 February 1789[44] , and its links with the London organisation seem to have remained close. This might lend St-George's "mysterious" journeys to England a rather different meaning, and indeed a much more logical one than what has been usually supposed by people who do not seem to have thought about the deeper aspects of his life concealed under its brilliant surface. Beauvoir actually mentions contacts that St-George had with the Society of the Friends of the Blacks.[45]

It would certainly be hard to believe that St-George remained indifferent to the movement for the abolition of slavery. While we have no proof that the Chevalier's travels to England served to make contact with the British organisation - a purpose that would have required secrecy and disguise - it is improbable that, being in London and knowing of its existence, he should not have tried to meet its members. Clearly, and in spite of the Revolution's achievements (the Declaration of the Rights of Man being promulgated by the National Assembly on 26 August 1789), contacts of this kind were not without danger, for the proposals of the abolitionists put vast economic interests at risk, and those who defended these interests had, as is said, a long arm. And we shall see later that London was indeed the scene of another attempt on St-George's life. But from childhood he had been accustomed to a life full of danger and he had learned to live dangerously.

---

[42] From the speech published in Paris in April 1788.

[43] Schoelcher, *Vie de Toussaint Louverture,* (original edition by P. Ollendorf, Paris, 1889), éditions Karthala, Paris, 1982, pp. 23-24.

[44] Schoelcher, loc. cit. Other authors ascribe the founding to Lafayette in 1786 or Brissot in 1788. Cornevin, *Histoire de l'Afrique,* tome 2, Paris, Payot, 1976, p. 440.

[45] Beuavoir, *op. cit.,* p. 482.

What must be wrong is the assertion made by some biographers that St-George accompanied the Duke of Orleans in his British exile in the autumn of 1789. The court had imposed this exile because the Duke was held to be implicated in the events of the 5th and 6th of October of the same year, when the people forced the King and Queen to leave Versailles and come and live in Paris. Actually, the Duke did not leave for England until 14 October[46], while according to Angelo St-George had been there since the month of August.

St-George settles in Lille

According to official documents, St-George seems to have come back to France about the same time as Philippe of Orleans was leaving it. There is in the archives of Lille a list of citizens registered in the census of late 1791, and in this St-George appears with the following mention: "Joseph de Boulogne, called Saint-Georges, forty-four years old, born in Guadeloupe, returned to Lille two years ago."[47] Now, at the end of 1791 "two years ago" meant the end of 1789. It was therefore after his return from England in the autumn of 1789 that St-George settled in Lille.

Why Lille and not Paris or any other city? This is yet another question to which we have not found a satisfactory answer. All we can say is that at least one of the reasons attaching St-George to the capital, his position as conductor of the orchestra of the Société Olympique, was now removed since this Masonic lodge was dissolved in December 1789.[48] The concerts might even have come to an end earlier than this date.

---

[46] Louis-Philippe, *op. cit.*, t.I, p. 108.

[47] Quoted by La Laurencie, *op. cit.*, p. 475.

[48] According to E. Derr in his article on St-George in Grove's *Dictionary of Music and Musicians.*

The Years 1789-1799

We now enter upon the final phase of the life of the Chevalier de Saint-George, that of the years from 1789 to his death in 1799.

This phase is entirely dominated by the French Revolution as the major event in European history of that era. The last part of St-George's life would be unintelligible to us if we were to take it out of that context, and in the following chapters there will be much mention of the Revolution. Let us begin with some preliminary observations.

Reading history books is always rather like studying the plan of a city. The streets are there, and so are the areas of water, the bridges, blocks of houses and monuments, but the people are missing. This abstract nature of historiography becomes clearer when we ourselves have lived through episodes of recent history such as the Second World War. There are still many men and women alive today who lived through this war as soldiers, prisoners or inmates of the concentration camps; who saw their houses collapse under bombardment, suffered hunger and experienced all the daily drama of those years. Their experience of war has a dimension that is not to be found in history books on the war.

So far as the French Revolution is concerned, this is less obvious because there are no survivors from the period. Innumerable treatises and studies have been published in the last few years on this great political upheaval, but how many of these books enable us to share the experiences of the men and women who were part of these great events that brought about the downfall not just of a king and a system but of a world?

Their experiences must of course have varied. First there was the factor of the side on which they were placed, revolutionaries on one side and supporters of the régime on the other. Both had many subdivisions and both were united in the end - by the irony of the law dictating that revolutions devour their children - at the foot of the guillotine. Their experiences must also have varied according to their sensibilities, social standing and education. But, basically, on whatever side they were placed and regardless of personal background, all of them without exception experienced a radical change, a great upheaval, that left nothing as it was before. Habits were suddenly overturned and illusory certainties collapsed. And everyone had to learn afresh how to live - differently.

In these chapters on the Revolution we have incorporated several personal testimonies from the time, notably by Louise Fusil and Baron de Frénilly, in the hope that these may enable the reader to relive something of the effect of the Revolution on the more intimate existence of contemporaries. How did St-George himself experience the revolution? That is obviously the question that interests us most of all. The fact that he was for the revolution, that he was on the side of the Republic, fought for it and helped save it at a time when it was in grave danger, we know from his own statements and from documents in which we can place credence. But because of his status, the revolution had a further dimension for him, the emancipation of the black man.

Having been born of a slave mother deported from Africa and a white nobleman, St-George had been introduced into the world of the French nobility thanks to the goodwill of his father and not by virtue of any birth-right he could claim as his own. He had made a great name for himself in this world through his own achievements, but in spite of this he remained under a stigma. The law laid down that the posterity of black slaves should for ever be excluded from the privileges of the whites. This world could therefore never really be his world, and it brought home to him every day, beneath the outward respect and tributes, the attitude, "You may be called the Chevalier de Saint-George, but in reality you are only a moveable object".

How did St-George come to terms day by day with this strange situation that made him at one and the same time a man who was respected, admired and sought after by his most illustrious contemporaries, and a non-being, a subhuman, a primitive creature? That is a question one is bound to ask, and we hope the reader will put it to himself. Did St-George really master the situation, or did he rather bear it like a carefully concealed wound that was reopened every day?

When the revolution finally proclaimed the equality of all men, on 26 August 1789, St-George did not hesitate to embrace its cause and put its life at its service. After his brilliant career in fencing and music, he now had to face the world of the revolutionary army. In the following chapters we shall learn about St-George the officer, the commander of a regiment who had to take decisions that were not only military but also political. And this is without doubt another feature of his uniqueness in musical history, to be added to that of his origins. In the course of the following chapters it will become clear that the personality of the Chevalier de St-George was compounded of very diverse aspects, and that his life cannot be reduced to the career of a violinist and composer. Music was only one aspect of his life, and for that reason our book could not be confined to this alone.

VII. THE REVOLUTION - ST-GEORGE IN THE
NATIONAL GUARD

The events of 1789

From the assembly of the States General at the beginning of May 1789 to
the end of the same year, the revolution had accomplished much. Louis
XVI recorded the historic day of 14 July in his personal journal with the
famous word "Nothing", meaning that he had bagged nothing in the
day's hunt! But what followed was the abolition of the feudal system on
4 August, and then the Declaration of the Rights of Man on 26 August. On
5 October the people of Paris finally went to Versailles to find the
King - who was hunting again - and to take him and the Queen to the
capital, the very heart of the revolution. This symbolic act marked the end
of the era of absolutism, of which the Sun King's sumptuous palace was
the emblem.

The wind of liberty had also begun to blow over those distant islands, the
West Indies with their slave system. Soon it would take on hurricane force
and blow from four opposing directions: that of the white colonists who
aspired to independence from the control of the revolutionary metropolis,
the "little whites" who wanted to abolish the prerogatives of the former,
the so-called free coloured people who were fighting for their civil rights,
and finally the slaves, the overwhelming majority of the population of the
islands, who saw that the hour had struck at last for them to break their
chains.

Following the Declaration of the Rights of Man, a delegation of coloured
men appeared before the Constituent Assembly in Paris on 19 October to
demand their civil and political rights. Its president gave this response:
"No part of the nation shall demand in vain its rights before the assembly
of the French people's representatives!"[1] Here was a very different language
from the old one which knew nothing but "moveable objects".

---

[1] Quoted by Schoelcher, *Vie de Toussaint Louverture*, Paris, 1889, p. 6.

St-George the revolutionary - enrolment in the National Guard

Like practically all coloured men, St-George embraced the cause of the Revolution with fervour. On arriving in Lille at the end of 1789, he enrolled in the National Guard and the following year secured the rank of captain. This we learn from an archive document, "Formation du Régiment d'Hussards Américains" (Formation of the Regiment of American Hussars) which was signed by St-George and dated 15 September 1792. It includes the statement that St-George joined the Gendarmes de la Garde (the King's Guard) in 1761 and that for two years - hence from 1790 to 1792 - he was a captain of the National Guard at Lille.[2]

We should note that the National Guard was a pro-revolutionary militia founded by the Paris commune on the eve of the Fourteenth of July and commanded by Lafayette. From the end of July 1789, Mirabeau had hastened the formation of similar troops in all the provinces of France.[3]

Thus began for St-George yet another new phase, as a fighter for the great Revolution. His political and military engagement is borne out by letters he wrote some years later underlining his devotion to the Revolution, for which he says, "I have since 1789 never ceased to declare my support in the most energetic manner", and he also professes his "innate republican sentiments".[4]

Where and in what circumstances St-George made these declarations we do not know. Although we have no evidence, it is likely that he was one of a group of coloured men who, with the support of the Society of the Friends of the Blacks, were fighting in France at the time for the extension of the revolution's achievements to the colonies. This was a struggle in which they confronted the powerful Massiac Club, a body of rich colonists residing in Paris.

Back in London - a new attempt on St-George's life

Perhaps it was activities of this nature that brought St-George back to England, and we find him in London in February 1790. It was here that he became the target of a fresh assassination attempt. The "Journal Général

---

[2] Archives admin. du Min. de la Guerre, Dossier St-George, cote 91/47.

[3] Louis-Philippe, *Mémoires 1773-1793*, Librairie Plon, Paris, 1973, t. I, pp. 74 and 81.

[4] Archives admin. du Min. de la Guerre, loc. cit.

de France" of 23 February 1790 reported that the Chevalier was peacefully walking to Greenwich one night where he was going "to make music in a house where he was awaited" when he was suddenly attacked by four men armed with pistols. Nevertheless he managed to drive them off with the help of his stick.[5] As with the first attack in Paris in 1779, the assailants remain unknown.

It is interesting that Angelo makes no mention of this incident and seems indeed to have been unaware that St-George was back in England. It is also interesting that at the time two of St-George's close friends were in the British capital too - The Duke of Orleans and his secretary, Choderlos de Laclos. The Duke had been sent to London in exile, pursuing a mission invented by the King to encourage him to leave; he had been accused by the court and Lafayette - wrongly, since he could prove the contrary - of having personally incited the mob during the events of 5th and 6th October. The point of his mission was supposed to be sounding out the court in London as to its attitude over the Austrian Netherlands, which were then in revolt against Vienna, and preparing a Franco-British accord on a possible constitution for an independent republic in Brabant, of which it was vaguely implied that Philippe of Orleans would become the ruler. He left France on 14 October 1789, spent over eight months in England, and did not return to France until July 1790.[6]

Concerts at Amiens

We come across St-George again, in the company of his friend Lamothe, just before Easter 1790 at Amiens where the two musicians were to give some concerts with Louise Fusil during Holy Week.[7] The singer had made her début in the Concert Spirituel in 1789. She was only sixteen at the time while St-George was forty-two. In her *Souvenirs* she tells of a party held just before these concerts at the residence of the Viscount de Rouhaut, on the estate he owned between Abbéville and Amiens. She shows how, at the beginning of the Revolution, people still sought amusement without any thought of the bloody course it was to take.

---

[5] Quoted by B. Brook in his article on St-George in *MGG*.

[6] Louis-Philippe, *op. cit.*, t. I, pp. 107-110, where the original text of the royal instructions is also reproduced.

[7] Fusil, *op. cit.*, 1903 edition, p. 116.

Among the guests were St-George, M. de Genlis, the brother-in-law of the Countess de Genlis, and M. de Vauquelin, an officer and man of letters. These three men had together written an amusing sketch on the subject of Tipu Sahib, the Sultan of Mysore, who was then fighting against the English and whose ambassadors were an object of curiosity for the French public. Saint-George played the part of one of these ambassadors, according to Louise Fusil, and very well, she says, for he was an excellent amateur actor. One can well imagine that the part fitted St-George like a glove, not only because of his physical appearance - the inhabitants of Mysore being very dark - but also because it was a situation that St-George knew only too well, that of the natives in contest with their white colonial oppressors. The singer tells us that he embodied the part so well that when, before the performance, people thought it would be amusing to introduce St-George to her as the ambassador of Mysore, she as a young girl was completely taken in and did not recognise her friend in his disguise.[8]

We should also point out that this party was given in honour of the Marquise de Chambonas, a society lady in whose house the satyrical magazine "Acte des Apôtres" was prepared for publication, and that most of the guests belonged to the entourage of the Duke of Orleans.

After these concerts at Amiens, Louise Fusil undertook a new engagement with St-George and Lamothe at Lille in 1791.[9] Up till then, we have no further information on St-George's life except for the fact, provided by La Laurencie, that he put on another comedy, "Guillaume tout coeur", in Paris in the course of 1790.[10] This was the last dramatic work of his of which we have any knowledge.

Hostility to St-George at Tournai

So we rediscover St-George in the great city of the North giving these concerts with Louise Fusil in April 1791. This date follows from the singer's mention in her *Souvenirs* that she left Paris to give the concerts in Lille

---

[8] Fusil, *op. cit.*, pp. 23 and 116-117.

[9] ibid., p. 128.

[10] La Laurencie, *op. cit.*, p. 473. The author says he obtained this information from the Count de Marquiset.

a few days before Mirabeau's burial.[11] Mirabeau was buried at the very beginning of April 1791, having died on the second day of the month. When the performances were over, Louise Fusil says, St-George intended to repeat them in Tournai. This was a frontier town, which was then part of the Austrian Netherlands and served as an assembly point for the French emigrés who were opposed to the Revolution, especially the royalist officers who were leaving France to prepare a counter- revolutionary offensive.

Saint-George did indeed go to Tournai at the beginning of June, but because of the hostility the emigrés showed him he was unable to give the concert. And the "Moniteur universel" printed this report from Tournai dated 13 June 1791: "It is reported from this town that M. Saint-George (previously Chevalier) had arrived there with the intention of spending a few days and giving music-lovers the pleasure of hearing him in a concert, but was then secretly warned by the commandant not to show himself in public. It seems that the sentiments of M. Saint-George are well-known and they displease the French refugees who are enemies of France and liberty. These people do not, to be sure, care for music. It is said that at the hotel where this French citizen put up, someone had the impertinence to displace a seat he had reserved at table, and that M. Saint-George had the grace not to take this ill. This is a kindly act on the part of a man who excels in the art of individual revenge."[12]

These final words are clearly a reference to St-George's redoubtable reputation as a swordsman and marksman. As for the "previously Chevalier", we should note that all titles, whether noble or others, had been abolished by the Constituent Assembly's decree of 19 June 1790.[13]

It has been stated by some that St-George did not undertake this journey to Tournai for the sake of music but for politics. Thus we read in the article on St-George in the *Biographie Michaud*: "St-George went to Tournay in the month of June 1791 on the pretext of giving a concert there for music-lovers, but he was actually trying to win back to the Orleans cause some of the emigrés who were in the town at the time."[14]

---

[11] Fusil, *op.cit.*, p. 175.

[12] "Moniteur universel", no. 172 (reprint of 1841), p.709, De Tournai, 13 June 1791.

[13] Louis-Philippe, *op. cit.*, t. II, p. 212.

[14] *Biographie Michaud,* reproduced by Fétis in his *Biographie universelle des musiciens et Bibliographie générale de la musique,* Paris, 1837-44, t. 7, p. 369, both published

Odet Denys, for his part, says that the emigrés suspected St-George of wanting to spy on them.[15] But if such had indeed been his mission, the Duke of Orleans would have been very ill-advised in his choice of envoy. After all, being a coloured man was enough in itself to attract the hostility and contempt of the counter-revolutionaries without the added difficulty of working for the Duke of Orleans.

Louise Fusil was with St-George at Tournai and she brings out this aspect when says that the emigrés "would have nothing to do with a Creole".[16] Since the term "mulatto" had the force of an insult at that time, Louise Fusil honoured her friend's memory by employing the term "Creole", although it was generally reserved for whites born in the colonies.

We should add that the colonial question was a matter of great moment in France at that time. On 15 May 1791 the Constituent Assembly had voted through a decree, proposed by the deputy Rewbell, to the effect that coloured people should be admitted to all the colonial assemblies. In the debate before the vote Robespierre delivered a fiery speech in favour of the rights of coloured people, including the famous sentence, "Let the colonies perish before liberty!"

The flight of the King

On 21 June 1791, only a few days after St-George's aborted concert at Tournai, there occurred an event that changed or at least accelerated the course of the revolution, the flight of the King. During the night of the 20th to 21st of June the King, the Queen and all other members of the royal family escaped mysteriously from the Tuileries and immediately fled Paris. The whole city was in uproar. Twenty-four hours later the fugitives were recognised and arrested at Varennes, near Verdun, not far from the frontier, and brought back to Paris.

"The King's flight confirmed the suspicions that had always been cherished as to his real intentions. At one blow it destroyed the effect of all the attempts he had made to gain credibility for the sincerity of his protestations. This meant that the Jacobins had no difficulty in persuading

---

after 1840.

[15] O. Denys, *op. cit.*, p. 136.

[16] Fusil, *op. cit.*, p. 128.

the public that the King and his court were utterly incorrigible and could never be trusted to govern constitutionally and truly respect national liberty. The King's flight seemed to be proof positive of the existence of those plots and conspiracies in favour of counter-revolution of which the papers were full at the time."[17]

During these troubled days of June 1791, some talked of a republic, others of a regency that would be entrusted to the Duke of Orleans. After the flight of the King the throne was vacant, both in fact and in law, for the Constituent Assembly suspended the monarchy until the conclusion of the new constitution, and governed on its own by means of decrees. "The crown then seemed to lie at the Duke's feet, but he did not care to pick it up."[18]

All the same, he seems to have been partly responsible for the famous petition produced by the Jacobins and signed in the month of July 1791 at the Champ de Mars, which declared the King deposed on account of perfidy and perjury. The text of this was attributed to Choderlos de Laclos, Prince Philippe's secretary, and also to Brissot, the protégé of Mme de Genlis.[19]

The levy of the National Volunteers - enrolment of St-Georges

The abortive flight of Louis XVI had among its consequences the acceleration of the reorganising and purging of the army. From the spring of 1791 it had been mooted in the Assembly that the regular army should be disbanded from its feudal basis and its resources remodelled along new lines in accordance with a system of military conscription so as to eliminate counter-revolutionary elements. But the majority required for the adoption of this motion was not forthcoming at the time. In June, however, during the alarm caused by the King's flight, the first part of these reforms was approved: in its decree of 21 June 1791 the Assembly ordered the immediate levy of 91,000 volunteers into the ranks of the National Guard throughout France. In each Département registers were

---

[17] Louis-Philippe, *op. cit.*, t. I, pp. 168-69.

[18] Lamartine in his article on Philippe of Orleans in the *Nouvelle Biographie Générale,* 1862.

[19] ibid.

opened for "men of good will" to enlist for the defence of France against foreign powers hostile to the Revolution.[20]

As we learn from official documents, St-George was among the first to enlist in these troops. His entry in the Lille register, under the number 244, runs: "Joseph Bologne St-George, aged 42, born in Guadeloupe, residing Rue Notre-Dame, Parish of St-Etienne, 25 July 1791. Signed, Saint-George."[21]

In passing we might note the discrepancy between the age of 42 St-George gives here and the one he stated in the same year in the Lille census, where he figures as follows: "Joseph de Boulogne, called Saint-Georges, forty-three years, born in Guadeloupe, returned to Lille two years ago."[22] The explanation lies no doubt in the fact that the second entry was made later in the year 1791. On the basis of these two documents we have taken the date of birth as being the end of 1748.

As a first-class man of arms and horseman, a former member of the Royal Guard and for the last year captain in the National Guard, St-George must have been very welcome among the new troops. These lacked officers and instructors, and we may presume that he spent his initial time with the National Volunteers giving instruction. Louis-Philippe, the eldest son of Philippe of Orleans, gives us some interesting information on the troops of the National Volunteers. He served in the army of the line and at the age of only eighteen commanded his own regiment, that of Chartres, and so-metimes Volunteer units too; he had been the Duke of Chartres, having inherited the title from his father when he became Duke of Orleans in 1785. The Volunteers resulting from the levy of June 1791 - that is those among whom St-George was enrolled - were conceived as a popular army meant to provide a counterpoise to the army of the line. Unlike the latter, which was commanded by nobles, the officers of the Volunteers were elected by the soldiers. At the wish of the Assembly, the troops drew a pay of fifteen scls a days, twice as much as the troops of the line.

---

[20] Louis-Philippe, *op. cit.,* t. I, pp. 188-190, t. II, p. 253.

[21] Arch. adm. du Min. de la Guerre, Municip. de Lille, Dép. du Nord, "Extrait du Registre aux Inscriptions des Citoyens qui se sont offerts à marcher les premiers en Exécution du Décret de l'Assemblée Nationale du 21 juin 1791", quoted by La Laurencie, *op. cit.*, p. 449.

[22] Quoted by La Laurencie, ibid., p. 475.

Once they were formed into batallions bearing the names of their respective Départements, the National Volunteers were put at the disposal of the Minister of War, who then assigned them to the places where they were to provide garrison duty with the other corps of the army. As most of the Volunteers possessed little knowledge of the profession of arms they had to be instructed and trained. They ended up, according to Louis-Philippe, acquiring the military spirit and quite good habits of discipline. "But one had to live, as I did, in the midst of these two kinds of troops and to have them under one's command, to get an idea of the mutual annoyance caused among them by the disparity of their organisation, their structure and their pay."[23]

It was this disparate army, augmented by the far less well-prepared recruits from the hasty levies of 1792, that was to sustain the first campaigns of the revolutionary wars.

New concert at Lille

At this stage, his military obligations did not stop St-George pursuing the musical activities that remained such an important part of his life.

On All Saints' Day 1791, that is the first of November, he gave a concert at Lille that attracted much attention. The "Annonces" reports thus: "From Lille, the 3rd November (1791) - For a long time our town has not had a concert as brilliant as the one on Tuesday, All Saints Day. To confirm the point it suffices to say that M. Saint-Georges arranged and conducted it. The most distinguished talents were brought together in the kind of perfect ensemble that alone can enrapture an audience. The concert began with an overture by M.Guénin and ended with a symphony by Paesiello. M. Granville and Mlle Guérin sang in the first part and made the choir part extremely interesting. M. Lombart played a concerto by Pleyel on the cello; this was much applauded and brought the young artiste a great deal of acclaim.

But a remarkable début that attracted a lot of interest in the second part was that of M. Baillé junior, who, accompanied by M. Saint-Georges, rendered a sonata for fortepiano with a precision, facility and even a sensibility that are rarely encountered at so tender an age (he is at most ten to twelve years old). His talent is as genuine as it is precocious, and it has

---

[23] Louis-Philippe, *op. cit.*, t.I, pp.189-90 and t.II, pp.253-57.

already ranked him among the distinguished virtuosos. M. Renaut sang an arietta, and Mlle Guérin ended the concert by singing a duo with M. Granville, which earned them the most lively applause."

Unfortunately the author of this article in the "Annonces" does not detail the compositions mentioned. It would be interesting to know, particularly with regard to the sonata played by the young boy, Baillé junior, which might have been one of those composed by St-George in 1781.

"We hope," the article continues, "that M. de Saint-Georges will also conduct some of the concerts we are giving right up to next Easter, and we can promise in advance that the foremost virtuosos of France will take part."[24]

As this last sentence indicates, St-George stayed in touch with the musical world of Paris. It is moving to see how at this concert he gave a child the opportunity to demonstrate his talent before a large audience that was attracted by the still intact renown of the former director of the Concert des Amateurs and of the Société Olympique.

But it is not certain that St-George was able to finish the series of concerts arranged at Lille, for in the spring of 1792 the North of France and Lille in particular were the scene of some dramatic events.

---

[24] "Annonces", supplement of Sunday 13 November 1791, p. 4118.

VIII. THE WAR -
FOUNDATION OF THE ST-GEORGE LEGION

We have no information on St-George's movements during the confused period preceding the revolutionary wars. But if we follow the main flow of events, we can participate in the great collective spectacle of which his movements were a part.

The anti-revolutionary coalition

On 13 September 1791 France became a constitutional monarchy. Before the Assembly, the King swore fidelity to the nation and to the law. He followed the formula prescribed by the Constitutional Act, and thus acknowledged that henceforth his powers were circumscribed by the will of the people's representatives.

The King retained the right to nominate ministers and also the right of veto in the Assembly, which the day after the royal oath was taken ceased to be Constituent and became Legislative, with 745 deputies elected by the active citizens (60 per cent of the population) through the intermediary of electors (one elector per hundred voters). The principal parties making up this Assembly were the Girondins (republican) with 250 members, including the former Duke of Orleans; the Jacobins (radicals, seated on the left in the hall - whence the term "the left") with only about 30 members but very active ones, including Robespierre, St-Just and Marat; the Feuillants (royalist, seated on the right in the hall - whence the term "the right") with 20 members, and finally the Independents.

However, in his secret messages to other European courts Louis XVI let it be known that he had accepted the Constitution only because he had no choice in the matter. In fact he considered the Constitution illegal because it had not been bestowed by himself, the head of state by the will of God.[1] Moreover, during the months following 13 September 1791 foreign monarchies saw their own position under threat from the French Revolution and stepped up their preparations for an invasion of France to restore unlimited royal power. And in this they were backed up by the French princes who had emigrated.

---

[1] Louis-Philippe, *op. cit.*, t. I, pp. 268-69.

Early in 1792, the Prussian and Austrian armies began marching on the French frontiers. Under pressure from the Assembly and the public, who reminded him of his duty to defend the Constitution and the integrity of French territory, the King finally decided to declare war on Austria on 20 April 1792. But his desire to wage war against the very monarchies that might restore his position as it was before 1789, was obviously not great. Here he was supported by the royalist generals and officers, and indeed the first defensive operations ended in confusion.

The abortive invasion of Belgium

The plan of the revolutionary government was to forestall the intentions of the anti-revolutionary coalition by carrying out a rapid invasion of (Austrian) Belgium. "I really believe that this plan could have succeeded," Louis-Philippe said, "if it had been sincerely supported by the court, on the one hand, and the generals and officers who led the French armies, on the other. But for whatever reasons they agreed not to support it."[2]

The army of the North, under the command of Marshal de Rochambeau, was to invade in three main corps - one advancing on Mons from Valenciennes and Maubeuge, the second on Tournai from Lille, and the third on Furnes, Ypres and Courtrai from Dunkirk. All three were to meet up at Brussels.

The corps coming from Lille was commanded by Brigadier Théobald Dillon. As we have seen, the army now consisted of two kinds of troops, those of the line and those from the National Volunteers. According to Louis-Philippe, the army of the north by then included several batallions of National Volunteers, and these had been selected from among the best trained and disciplined. Thus it is very possible that St-George participated in these operations. But the expedition from Lille came to a bad end on the very day it set out, the 28 April 1792. Brigadier Dillon was accused of treason and massacred by his own troops. The corps retreated to Lille, where large-scale terror and agitation were the order of the day. Thereupon the whole campaign was called off and only relaunched six weeks later under the command of Marshal Luckner. On 16 June, the army of the North entered Belgium, but on the 30th Luckner received the order from Paris to return to France, and the plan of occupying Belgium was

---

[2] ibid. t. II, p. 3.

completely abandoned. The army of the North was sent to Lorraine and that of Lorraine (commanded by Lafayette) was summoned to Flanders. This gave rise to what was humorously called "the armies' musical chairs". Should we presume that St-George was involved and left for the East, or did he stay in Lille? We simply do not know.

The Duke of Brunswick's manifesto

A few weeks after this abortive campaign, the Revolution entered a crucial phase. On 18 July 1792, the Assembly declared that the country was in danger after learning of significant movements on the part of the coalition armies. This declaration was promulgated with great ceremony by mounted officers in all parts of Paris. Then on 25 and 27 July, the Duke of Brunswick, the commander-in-chief of the coalition powers, issued from Koblenz - the rallying-point of the French emigré princes - two manifestos announcing an imminent invasion to the French people. He declared that it was the purpose of the allied courts to restore their rights to the German princes with possessions in Alsace and Lorraine, to "put an end to the anarchy in France, to stop the attacks on the Throne and the Altar, to reinstate legal authority, to give the King back the security and liberty of which he is deprived, and to enable him to exercise the legitimate authority that is his due".[3]

In the first manifesto the Duke of Brunswick warned the city of Paris and all its inhabitants that they must "at once submit to the King without delay... Their Imperial and Royal Majesties[4] attribute personal responsibility for all these events, with full blame and the promise of military punishment without hope of pardon, to all members of the National Assembly, the District, the Municipality and the National Guard of Paris, the Justices of the Peace and all others concerned. Their Majesties also declare, on their imperial and kingly oath, that if the palace of the Tuileries is attacked or disgraced, or if there is the least violence or the slightest molestation of Their Majesties the King, the Queen and the royal family; if their security is not immediately safeguarded, together

---

[3] "Le Moniteur" of 3 and 8 August 1792, nos. 216 and 221, which reproduces the complete text.

[4] The Hapsburg Emperor Francis II, nephew of Marie-Antionette, and King Frederick William II of Prussia.

with their safe-keeping and liberty, the signatories will exact an exemplary revenge to be remembered for all time by delivering the city of Paris to martial law and total turmoil; the rebels guilty of outrages will receive the punishments they deserve."[5]

But the effect of this ultimatum was the opposite of what its authors expected. "It produced more enthusiasm in France for the defence of the motherland and national independence than could have been roused by the Assembly and all the popular societies together."[6] Incidentally, this was the moment when the Marseillaise, composed by Rouget Delisle a short time before for a rally of the National Guards, became the national anthem.

Fall of the monarchy - the hecatomb of the summer of 1792

At the same time, nothing could have been more dangerous for the King than the Duke of Brunswick's authoritarian declarations confirming the now general opinion that Louis XVI was in league with the foreign powers and wanted their armies to succeed. This manifesto decisively convinced a large part of the nation that the only way to prevent France from falling under foreign yoke was to change its form of government. At the very moment when the combined armies of Prussia, Austria and the German princes were invading France, together with three corps of French emigrés commanded respectively by the Counts of Provence and Artois (brothers of Louis XVI), the Prince of Condé and the Duke of Bourbon - numbering some 110,000 men - Louis XVI and his family were attacked in the Tuileries by the people during the night of 9th and 10th August 1792 and obliged to seek refuge with the Assembly.

After much debating, the deputies decided to suspend royal power until the nation had declared its will through a national convention. This organ replaced the Legislative Assembly and pronounced the definitive abolition of the monarchy six weeks later, on 21 September 1792. The fall of the King unleashed a veritable hecatomb against the enemies of the Revolution or those regarded as such. On 17 August, at the request of the Paris Commune, the Assembly decreed the institution of a revolutionary

---

[5] "Le Moniteur", *loc. cit.*

[6] Louis-Philippe, *op. cit.*, t. II, p. 98.

Tribunal. The gates of Paris were shut to prevent anyone from escaping, and a vigilante committee conducted house visits throughout the city.

We have a personal account of these days from Louise Fusil, the singer who was a friend of St-George, and who was living at the time with several other artistes in lodgings within the theatre of the Palais-Royal. She writes of 10 August: "The streets and squares were strewn with corpses, especially the square of the Palais-Royal...Nor were we spared scenes even more dire than that, for if the 10th of August saw fury on the rampage one could still surrender one's life at a cost; but on the 2nd and 3rd of September wretched, defenceless people were slaughtered in cold blood, and this went on for three days!"[7]

Massacre in the prisons

And indeed, after several thousand so-called counter-revolutionaries had been thrown into the capital's prisons after 10 August, it was decided that the procedures of the revolutionary Tribunal were going too slowly and that sentences should be speeded up. At the instigation of Danton, who was then minister of justice, and of Marat, inside every prison a popular commission with twelve members was set up to pass judgement. This is what happened:

"The prisoners were brought forward one after the other before this so-called tribunal, and its leader asked them a few questions. Then the twelve individuals making up the tribunal put their hands on the head of each prisoner and replied yes or no to the question posed by the leader in these words: 'Do you think that in all conscience we can release Monsieur So-and so?' The word 'release' was a conventional term among them instead of 'condemn', so that if the response was affirmative the miserable prisoner emerged to be instantly jabbed with pikes and killed off by the mob waiting outside the prison, who were excited by fanatical harangues. When the response was negative, the cry went up, 'Vive la Nation!' and the killers let the prisoner pass and he was given his freedom while the mob applauded. But very few were saved, at the very most perhaps a tenth of the total of the prisoners. The carnage lasted three days, from the 2nd to the 4th of September."[8]

---

[7] Fusil, *op. cit.*, p. 188.

[8] Louis-Philippe, *op. cit.*, t. II, pp. 134-35.

The mobilisation of 2 September - Creation of the St-George Légion
At the same time, Verdun was besieged by coalition forces. It was feared
that the town would fall, being in a feeble state, and that the enemy would
then march on Paris. On 2 September therefore the Paris Commune
invited all its citizens to rally round and advance against the invaders. In
a few days it had mustered 32,000 men, all armed and equipped.
St-George was in Paris at the time and, as we shall see from what follows,
he took part in the general upsurge, just as he had following the flight of
the King in 1791.
On 7 September 1792, a deputation of coloured men appeared before the
National Assembly, and their spokesman, Julien Raimond from Haiti,
presented the following petition:
"Legislators,
When your beneficient law of 24 March reminded us of our rights, we
took an oath to shed our blood for the defence of the motherland.
This sacred oath we must fulfil. Like all Frenchmen, we burn with the
desire to rush to the frontiers. Legislators, we are still few in number but
if you daign to support our zeal, the numbers will grow and we shall form
a large corps.
We therefore beg you to authorise the Minister of War to organise us as
soon as possible in a separate legion under any name you care to give it.
Nature, in its inexhaustible variety, has made us different in outward
appearance, but it has also made us just the same as the rest in causing our
hearts to burn with the desire to fight the enemies of the State. As for
myself, Gentlemen, I have been chosen by my brothers to interpret their
sentiments, but I am prevented by my age and by a personal mission from
following them in the career of honour; however, I shall contribute the
sum of 500 livres each year - and here I offer the first quarter -towards the
expenses of equipping this troop, and I shall add a similar sum as a prize
for any soldier among them who performs a deed worthy of your praise."[9]
The law of 24 March 1792 invoked by Raimond here is the decree said to
be of 4 April 1792 (the date the King sanctioned it), whereby the National
Assembly had acknowledged and declared that "coloured men and free
negroes shall, like the white colonists, enjoy equality of political rights";

---

[9] P. Descaves, *Historique du 13ᵉ Régiment de Chasseurs*, Béziers, 1891, pp. 3-4.

HISTORIQUE

DU 13ᴹᴱ RÉGIMENT DE CHASSEURS

ET DES

CHASSEURS A CHEVAL DE LA GARDE

D'après les documents officïels des Archives du Ministère de la Guerre

P. Descaves: Historique du 13me Regiment de Chasseurs,

title page and page 5

— 5 —

Le corps s'organisa rapidement ; des volontaires accoururent de toutes parts, Hommes de couleur et Français.

Dès le 15 Septembre, une grande partie des cadres étaient désignés.

Ce furent :

Chef de Brigade :	Chevalier DE ST-GEORGES.
Chefs d'Escadrons :	MM. LA ROCHE CHAMPREUX et DUMAS.
Quart.-Maître Trésor. :	M. AVENEAUX.
Capitaines :	MM. BARRIÉR, FROGER, MANCEST, MICHEL, dit Bissardon, SAINT ANGE, JOSSET et COL.
Lieutenants :	MM. POUCHIN, VERBECQ, COLIN, DUHAMEL, FOURNEAU, SERVAN, NARCISSE, DE LAVITTE et ROBERJOT,
Sous-Lieutenants :	MM. LAURIN, AUGER, GAYBLER, PRÉVOST, DANTIGNY, MUTEL, LEBLANC, ETIENNE, MARAND, MASTRICK, HELLO, BIENFAIT et JOUBERT.

La Légion Nationale du Midi fut de suite dénommée Légion Nationale des Américains et du Midi, pour ne pas la confondre avec la Légion de l'Armée du Midi créée par la loi du 27 Avril 1792, et qui plus tard devint Légion des Alpes.

Puis on la désigna ensuite plus fréquemment par les noms de :

Légion Saint-Georges.— Légion des Américains. — Légion des Hommes de Couleur.

Et sa cavalerie par ceux de :

Hussards Américains et du Midi.— Chasseurs Américains.

Le 7 Novembre, 400 hommes à pied et 150 hommes à cheval, réunis à Paris, quittent cette ville et arrivent le 16 à Amiens, où il est procédé à l'organisation définitive de la Légion.

Le 6 Décembre 1792, la Convention Nationale décrèta que la Légion ne serait composée que d'hommes à cheval :

· **DÉCRET** pour l'organisation d'une Légion franche à cheval le 6 Décembre 1792.

La Convention Nationale, après avoir entendu le rapport de ses Comités de la Guerre et des Finances, décrète ce qui suit :

ordered the re-election of colonial assemblies with the participation of mulattos and free negroes; and established without equivocation the eligibility of these persons for all offices.[10]

This decree had been a decisive victory for coloured people in their struggle with the colonists, and in this struggle Julien Raimond had since 1785 been one of the leading protagonists in France.

We do not know whether St-George was himself a member of the deputation that appeared before the Assembly on 7 September, but what is certain is that he was closely associated with it, for it was to him that the coloured men entrusted the command of their legion. In this fact we have proof that St-George was linked - and no doubt not just from that period of time - with the activities of the black revolutionaries in France. No doubt in the minds of those who initiated the legion it was also destined to participate some time in the fighting going on in Haiti, where the colonists still opposed the liberating edicts coming from Paris. And we shall see later that most of these men really were sent to the West Indies a year later. The very day when the above-quoted petition was presented, the 7 September 1792, the Assembly decreed the formation of a corps of light troops consisting of coloured men and comprising 1,000 soldiers, of whom 800 were infantry and 200 cavalry. They first received the name "Légion franche de cavalerie des Américains et du Midi". Later, it was more commonly known as the "Légion St-George", "Légion des Américains", or "Légion des Hommes de Couleur". At the beginning of 1793 it finally became the 13th Regiment of Chasseurs. Its cavalry was called "Hussards Américains et du Midi" or "Chasseurs américains".

St-George as colonel in command

The regiment rapidly took shape and volunteers flocked in from all sides. By 15 September 1792 most of the appointments had been made, with Saint-George in command holding the rank of colonel. His squadron-commanders were La Roche Champreux and a certain Dumas - who was none other than Alexandre Dumas Davy de la Pailleterie, a thirty-year old mulatto born in Haiti, and the future father and grandfather of the two authors called Alexandre Dumas. We shall have occasion to return to him later.

---

[10] Complete text in Schoelcher,. *op. cit.,* pp. 65-66.

Légion franche de Cavalerie des américains et du Midy

Formation Du Régiment

D'hussards américains et Du Midy, d'après les ordres du sept Septembre 1792.

Citoyen S.t Georges, Colonel, en Ci dans les Gendarmes d'Orgéd et 2...

Chefs D'Escadrons
d.ts colonels

Dalaume, Jean Baptiste, 18 ans dans les Dragons à S.t Domingue, Cap.ne dans la garde nationale.

Pierre Cote, Gendarme en 1775, réformé en 1788, volontaire depuis la révolution.

François Jacques La Roche Champreux, chevaux Légers en 58 où il a fait les 2 dernières campagnes, volontaire dans la garde nationale depuis la révolution.

B. Louis Barrié, Sous-dans Gustine, 12 ans dans la Colonel générale, volontaire dans la garde nationale depuis la révolution.

Capitaine

B. Jean Michel f.s Anges Jofres, dans le Reg.t d'Artillerie et Camp Dragons en 72, Surnuméraire des gardes du Corps en 81, delà dans le Reg.t de Luxembourg en qualité de Cap.ne Commandant jusqu'à la réforme, et volontaire depuis la révolution.

Capitaines

B. Henry Alexandre Srogéres, garde de la Marine 2 ans, Gendarme jusqu'à la réforme, Régiment d'Meuron dans L'Inde 9 ans, volontaire depuis la révolution.

B. Jean Louis Mait, dans les volontaires d'soutien 2 ans, et volontaire dans la garde nationale depuis la révolution.

B. Jacques Michel Bisardon, dans Bourgogne Cavalerie a fait les campagnes d'hanovre depuis 56 jusqu'en 61, et volontaire depuis la révolution.

B. x Pierre Avreneaux, Trésorier, Quartier maître, dans auvergne 5 ans dans Royal Dragon, 3 ans, dans la garde nationale volontaire depuis la révolution.

The formation of the "Légion franche" (1792). Saint-George was entrusted to command this corps (4 pages), Archives Administratives, Ministère de la Guerre, Vincennes

Lieutenants

B. (Claude antoine) Colin, Gendarme 18 mois), Commandant de la garde nationale d'Guerrea, Département d'S'allier; et en 1791 volontaire à Paris.

B. Nicolas Dubramel, depuis la révolution aide de camp du Citoyen Miaczinsky.

B. Jacques Laurent Fournier, dans le Régiment d'Denthiome cavaliers, dans le Régiment de la Gend' Dragons, volontaire depuis la révolution.

B. Jacques Michel Souchin, sur mer 7 ans, volontaire de Capitaine d'briex, au corps des Carabiniers 8 ans, volontaire depuis la révolution. Bruno, par congé à Lille. Prévost, par congé à Lille.

B. Guy de Nicolas Verber, dans Montmorency Dragons 3 ans depuis la révolution, volontaire 1er Bataillon de la halle au Bled.

Sous-Lieutenants

B. Jean Auger, dans la Colonelle Générale depuis 85 jusqu'en 91, et volontaire dans la garde nationale jusqu'à ce jour.

B. Jean Baptiste Laurin, dans le Régiment d'Angenois 4 ans et volontaire dans la garde nationale depuis la révolution.

B. Jean-Baptiste Roberjot, dans le Régiment d'Anguein, et Capit. dans la garde nationale au Département de Saône et Loire jusqu'en l'an deux.

Je Soussigné Colonel des hussards américains et du Midy, certifie le présent état véritable. Paris, ce 1er octobre, de l'an premier de l'égalité.

St-Georgs

Légion Franche des américains
Et du Midi

État-major

L., C.C.

g. 1. Colonel —— S.t George

g. 2. L.t col. —— La Roche-Champreux
Dumas

g. 1. Q.r M.e T.re — Avenel

St-George had under his command some thirty officers and non-commissioned officers; most of the professional soldiers had served in the army of the line until the revolution and then in the National Volunteers.[11] According to Angelo, a large number of the cavalry were swordsmen.[12] This certainly applies in the case of Dumas who, according to Ellwood Derr, was a former pupil of La Boëssière like St-George.[13] Odet Denys, for his part, states that there were lots of negroes from Bordeaux among the troops, former slaves serving on board slave ships who had recovered their freedom on disembarking upon French soil.[14]

---

[11] Arch. Adm. du Min. de la Guerre, St-George dossier, mark 91/47, "Formation du Régiment d'Hussards Américains et du Midi", also Descaves, *op. cit.*, p. 5, where their names and details of their military career are given.

[12] *Angelo's Picnic*, by Henry Angelo, p. 38.

[13] Article on St-George in Grove's *Dictionary of Music and Musicians*.

[14] Denys, *op. cit.*, p. 140.

IX. TO THE RESCUE OF THE REPUBLIC

The siege of Lille

In mid-September 1792 St-George rushed back to Lille, which the Austrians were besieging. This emerges from the memoirs of Louise Fusil, who says that St-George "returned to Lille at the time of the siege" and "his regiment fought against the Austrians."[1] But according to Descaves, the author of *L'historique du 13e régiment de chasseurs*, who recounts the beginnings of the St-George Legion, the corps' organisation had not been finished by that date. The question therefore arises which regiment it was with which St-George fought against the Austrians at the siege of Lille in September 1792.

It was most probably his unit of the National Guard at Lille. He still figured on its lists as captain on 1 October 1792, with the following details: "4th batallion, 2nd company, 1st platoon, 1st section, 2nd squad, no. 8. Status certified as correct, 1 October 1792. Signed, St-George."[2] As we saw at the end of the last chapter, most of St-George's officers in the new legion were like himself serving as volunteers in the National Gurad, many of them indeed at Lille, and so it is quite possible that at least some of the "Hussards américains" belonged to the unit that St-George commanded there. Be that as it may, he must have taken part in the defence of Lille, and there is no reason to doubt what Louise Fusil says in this connection since this young artiste was there herself at the time.

Before giving her concerts in the capital of the North, she had left Paris a few days after the September massacres. In a letter she wrote to a Parisian friend in October 1792 she gives a description of the siege of Lille that deserves our admiration for its eloquence and liveliness. This was no mean accomplishment in the difficult circumstances that obtained, and shows that Louise Fusil was an extraordinary peronality. One can understand that she must have been attached to St-George by a more than passing friendship. This is her account: "I had been at Lille some time when this siege suddenly hit us like a bombshell. So far as I remember, we were not in the slightest prepared for it, although we soon got used to it. At first the red-hot cannonballs rather

---

[1] Fusil, *op. cit.*, p. 128.

[2] Arch.admin. du Min. de la Guerre, quoted by La Laurencie, *op. cit.*, p. 475.

took us by surprise but afterwards people scooped them up in frying-pans or in some other metal utensil when they had twirled round a little, and thus prevented them from exploding. You can see that this was a new discovery of which I had no idea - make good use of it if you are ever in the middle of a siege, which God forbid! You can imagine that it was not I who picked them up like this - I was merely an eye-witness.

"All the same, people began to get tired of this way of living and there was a lot of muttering on the side. But General Menou issued an order that anyone who talked of surrendering would be hanged. After this friendly warning no one dared to utter his thoughts. However, I must go into a little more detail because once the danger is passed gaiety returns.

"As I have told you, we were not expecting anything when we suddenly heard that the Austrian army was advancing along the road from Tournai. Everyone started looking for horses, carriages and carts so as to get out of the town: women, children and the elderly were seen as mere mouths to feed and an added danger. But the kind of men who always exploit public misfortune for their own gain demanded such a high price for any means of transport that many of the inhabitants found it impossible to meet their extortionate demands. Those with jewellery or silver tried to sell them to get money, but things that might have been bought at a reasonable price a few days earlier had lost value to the point where one was hardly offered a quarter of what they were worth. Finally we heard that the army was drawing near and about to begin the assault. Imagine our terror! We were however told we could leave by the opposite gate but we did not have enough time. Once the first cannonballs had been fired people rushed together into the squares. Families sought refuge in cellars without having been able to collect even the basic necessities together, though some people arrived with food and clothing they had grabbed in their haste. In this situation I witnessed the kind of real equality we hear so much about: misfortune unites and breaks down barriers. The rich and the poor helped one another because they shared the same dangers, and people gave one another the things they needed... The owners of a burning house were looked after by a poor family. Children and the elderly were taken into a rich house where they would never have dreamed of receiving help a few weeks earlier. Why is the world not always like this?

"One day when things seemed more peaceful, the bombardment suddenly redoubled. No one could imagine who was responsible for this new disaster just when we were hoping that the siege was almost over. We discovered a few days later that the Archduchess of Austria had visited their headquarters for lunch and that this had revived the courage of the troops. That day came to be known as "the Archduchess's lunch"!... How could a woman fail to realise that old people and mothers with children might perish on that terrible morning? But our soldiers' courageous resistance and General Menou's determination compelled them to raise the siege."[3]

The essence of this account, with the exception of the general's name, is corroborated in the following passage from Louis-Philippe's memoirs: "General Duhoux vigorously defended Lille during the Austrian bombardment of September 1792, although the only means of defence he had was a handful of troops and the help of the inhabitants who, it must be said, gave of their utmost."[4]

At the end of September troops were mustered at Douai under the cammand of General Labourdonnaye for the relief of Lille, and the Austrians were finally obliged to raise the siege on 7 October and to withdraw to Tournai.[5]

Saint-George's participation in the battle for Lille is confirmed by yet another source. On 29 September 1792 he sent the deputy Lassource the following despatch, which was read out at the Convention in Paris and printed in the "Moniteur universel": "I announce to you, my dear fellow citizen, that I have just received the news that our troops have retaken Saint-Amand and the camp of Maulde, and that this camp will be reinstated. Your friend and fellow citizen, Saint-Georges."[6]

There is every reason to believe that this reconquest was the result of General Labourdonnaye's advance from Douai, for St-Amand and Maulde are situated between Douai and Lille. The text of St-George's despatch does not reveal whence he sent it. But the news was still fresh, so it must have come from the scene of the events, probably from Lille.

---

[3] Fusil, *op. cit.*, pp. 194-96.

[4] Louis-Philippe, *op. cit.*, t. II, p. 64.

[5] ibid., pp. 202 and 249.

[6] "Moniteur universel", July/December, no. 273, p. 1164, quoted by La Laurencie, *op. cit.*, p. 476.

St-George's and Dumouriez' campaign in Belgium

Other important events took place in the North during the following weeks. On 26 October 1792, General Dumouriez, the conqueror of the Prussians at Valmy (20 September 1792) and recently appointed commander-in-chief of the new Army of the North, launched another offensive in Belgium and, after winning the Battle of Gemmapes on 6 November, entered Brussels a few days later. Then he completed the occupation of Belgium and prepared to extend the offensive to Holland.

Most of Saint-George's biographers (particularly Angelo, the author of the article in the "Biographie Michaud", and also Fétis) affirm that the erstwhile Chevalier fought under Dumouriez in Belgium. La Laurencie for his part says that the "Hussards américains" actively participated in the Belgium campaign.

The records of the St-George legion contain no information on the subject, but it is quite possible that after the siege of Lille St-George went to fight in Flanders with his unit of volunteers in the National Guard, the members of which were probably, as we have said, at least in part identical with the hussars of the new legion. We do not know any details about the battles of 1792 in Belgium in which St-George might have taken part. Since these do not form part of the activities of the St-George legion properly speaking, they do not figure in the regiment's history.

This rather confused situation - with St-George for a certain period of time simultaneously commanding both units, whose members seem to have been partly the same - is not really surprising in the context of the period, as we shall see later on.

As for the St-George Legion in its totality as a new and separate unit, we know from what Descaves has written on the history of the regiment that it cannot have fought under Dumouriez in Belgium.[7]

The vicissitudes of the St-George Legion

Descaves tells us that the St-George Legion did not leave Paris until 7 November 1792, and arrived at Amiens on the 16th of this month with a force of 400 men on foot and 150 on horseback. Here the organisation of the corps was definitively undertaken. On 6 December the Convention decreed that it would comprise only mounted soldiers. With three

---

[7] P. Descaves, *Historique du 13ᵉ Régiment de Chasseurs*, Béziers, 1891.

squadrons, each consisting of two companies, the legion left Amiens on 9 January 1793 and on 14 January arrived at Laon, 150 kilometres south of Lille. It was here that the legion became the "13e régiment de chasseurs à cheval", which also included a certain number of whites.

On 13 February 1793 the regiment was ordered to proceed to Lille to join up with the troops of Dumouriez engaged in the Holland campaign.[8] On the same day St-George, in a letter sent from Laon to the Minister for War, complained about the poor condition of his troops - who lacked horses, clothing and equipment - and said it was impossible to follow these marching orders.[9] At the same time, the administrators of Aisne asked the Minister to keep the regiment at Laon, and praised its activity, zeal and "impressive attitude".[10]

Did St-George already foresee the disastrous turn that the campaign in Holland was to take? Or did he have information from Dumouriez's camp as to the general's state of mind? Did he see little cause for confidence in the general and therefore feel little enthusiasm in launching his regiment on an adventure damaging to the Revolution? That is absolutely possible, but the argument presented in his letter to the Minister was doubtless also well-founded.

The privations of the French armies were indeed common during this period. Louis-Philippe, who was on the staff of Dumouriez at the time, relates that the soldiers lacked everything, even food, and they were often reduced to pillaging in order to eat, with detrimental effects on discipline. Desertion spread and many units were depleted. "The administration of the armies was in such confusion and disorder that it can hardly be said to have existed. Those who saw the position at close quarters as I did could hardly imagine how we had achieved the results we had achieved."[11]

This account by Louis-Philippe of the conditions in which the first wars of the Revolution were waged may well astonish those who retain the notion from their school history lessons of a perfectly ordered plan executed according to a precise scenario. But, as we have seen, reality was somewhat different.

---

[8] La Laurencie, *op. cit.*, p. 476.

[9] Arch. admin. du Min. de la Guerre, St-George dossier, class 91/47.

[10] Arch. adnmin. du Min. de la Guerre, loc. cit.

[11] Louis-Philippe, *op. cit.*, t. II, pp. 285-87.

In spite of the difficulties, and perhaps the reluctance we mentioned above, St-George set off with his regiment on 21 February 1793 and arrived at Lille on the 28th of the month.[12]

In the meantime however the advance of Dumouriez into Holland had decided the large army of the Prince of Saxe-Cobourg, based on the Lower Rhine, to join the campaign. Dumouriez was obliged to retreat, and on 18 March 1793 he suffered a major defeat at Neerwinden in Belgium, which made him decide to pull back into France.

St-George's regiment then received counter-orders and stayed at Lille, where it was to remain over a year, until 1 April 1794, undergoing drastic reorganisation. From 17 March 1793 most of the coloured men were withdrawn from the squadrons and sent off to Brest to go and fight in the colonies as "compagnies franches". They were however detained at Nantes, where they were to stay until August 1793 and would not be sent to Brest until September; they joined the West Indian batallions in October 1793. Another detachment of coloured men was later sent to Vendée and finally incorporated in the Army of the West after refusing employment in the gendarmerie in Haiti.[13] Their refusal is understandable in view of the fact that service in this gendarmerie meant firing on their black brothers and mulatto brothers. These two groups were then fighting one another in the convulsions of a fratricidal war that sprang from the colonial policies of slavery and racism.[14]

So by the spring of 1793 the regiment commanded by St-George had ceased to be a corps of coloured men, although its staff still remained largely composed of mulatto officers. Between February 1793 and April 1794, the 13th Chasseurs were stationed in the outposts round Lille, with detachments at Marquette, Marque, Wasquehol, Flers and Fives.[15] During this period the regiment was in action several times, but Descaves does not give any details. It was not deployed in the Army of the North until April 1794, when Dumouriez had no longer been in command for over a year and St-George was no longer in charge of his regiment. It is to this time, that of the second campaign in Belgium commanded by General Jourdan,

---

[12] Descaves, *op. cit.*, p. 6.

[13] Descaves, *op. cit.*, pp. 6-7 and 39.

[14] See Chapter, "Return to the West Indies - Toussaint Louverture".

[15] Descaves, *op. cit.*, p. 39.

30 avril 1793

Citoyen.

Étant chargé en chef de faire expédier les brevets des officiers de mon corps; je vous prie de vouloir bien faire accélérer ceux des Citoyens Delobel et Duhamel Capitaines de mon régiment: d'après la demande que j'en ai faite au Ministre. —

Aussitôt les brevets remplis, je vous prie de les faire passer à Lille, où mon Régiment est dans ce mom. en garnison. —

J'ai l'honneur d'être avec considération

Votre Concitoyen

à Lille ce 16. avril 1793.
2ème de la République ... George[...]

Two letters of Colonel Saint-George to the ministry of war (April 1793),
Archives Administratives, Ministère de la Guerre, Vincennes

y son franche ... Dite Der.
nfrands americains, ft.dumidy

Au Citoyen ministre Dela guerre

Le Colonel Des hussards americains, 11 Du midy, En Vertu
Delaloi qui g e ybre qui L'autorise a la formation Dudit Corps
a L'honneur De presenter au citoyen ministre Dela guerre
Les citoyens :
     Charles Mutel,
     gaybler .,
     Elie francois Dautigny,
a trois Souslieutenaires Vacantes Dans Son Regiment, il prie
Le citoyen ministre Dela guerre De Vouloir Bien Les
Comprendre Dans Le travail Dela Dite legion En cette
qualité /
                              H George

that belong the most celebrated exploits of the regiment founded by St-George.[16] We shall not go into the detail of these exploits since they do not date from his period of command, even though the training he gave the corps must have played a part in its achievements.

The treason of Dumouriez

Nevertheless, we must relate at this point the individual action St-George took in the spring of 1793 that entered the annals of French history and contributed to saving the young republic from a conspiracy directed against it. We are referring to his intervention at the time of General Dumouriez's treason.

Like many other officers, Dumouriez had from early on been irritated by the policies of the Convention and the confusion that its decrees spread in the army. By October 1792 his criticisms had earned him Marat's public accusation of counter-revolutionary opinions. Whereas Lafayette dissociated himself from the Revolution when the King was suspended, and emigrated on 20 August 1792, Dumouriez held on until the trial of the King on 17 January 1793.

On that day Louis XVI was condemned to death by the Convention, by 361 votes to 360. The deciding vote was that of his cousin Philippe of Orleans, who had now become "Philippe-Egalité", for he had been obliged to take this name, just as Louis XVI himself had become "citizen Capet". The King was beheaded on 21 January 1793.

Louis-Philippe was taken into the confidence of Dumouriez, and he tells us how after the execution the general conceived the plan of restoring the throne to France with Louis XVI's young son on it and the Baron de Breteuil as regent, and of reviving the constitution of 1791. After the defeat of Neerwinden, the armies of the North were thrown into a disastrous situation. They were so depleted, disorganised and demoralised, Louis-Philippe says, that they were no longer in a condition to sustain any major encounter with the Austrian army. At this point, Dumouriez made secret overtures to the Prince of Saxe-Coburg, confided his plans to him and asked him for a secret armistice so that he could descend on Paris to remove the royal family imprisoned in the Temple, bring back Louis XVI's son to the North, and have him proclaimed king in the midst of his

---

[16] For these exploits of 1794 see Descaves, *op. cit.*, pp. 40-42.

camp; then he would conduct the new monarch to Paris at the head of his army. The Austrian prince accepted.[17]

Dumouriez then set about taking three towns in the North important for the execution of his plan, Lille, Douai and Péronne. On 31 March 1793 his army completed its retreat from Belgium and left Tournai to return to French territory, occupying the camp at Maulde, some thirty kilometres from Lille. Dumouriez set up his headquarters at St-Amand, about four kilometres from Maulde.

St-George intervenes

As General Dumouriez himself relates in his memoirs, he at once sent General Miaczinsky with 4,000 men to occupy Orchies, 20 kilometres south-west of Lille, and ordered him "to muster his division before Lille, enter it, and see to the arrest of the commissars of the Convention and the leading Clubbists; as soon as that was done, to proceed to Douai, drive out General Moreton, announce there, and also in Lille, the army's unanimous loyalty to the Constitution and then to proceed via Cambray to Péronne where he was to take up his position."[18]

But the plan failed, for this reason: "This wretched officer (Miaczinsky) did not fully grasp the importance of his mission and revealed it to all and sundry, including the famous mulatto St-George, colonel of a regiment of hussars. St-George betrayed him and enticed him into Lille with a very small escort; as soon as he was inside, the gate was closed on him. He was arrested and taken to Paris where he was beheaded."[19]

We should note in passing a detail that might be significant. One of St-George's lieutenants, Nicolas Duhamel, had been General Miaczinsky's aide-de-camp from 1789, before joining the regiment of American Hussars in 1792.[20]

These events at Lille occurred on April 1st or 2nd 1793. On 3 April 1793 the Convention declared Dumouriez a traitor and outlaw, promising 300,000 livres to anyone taking him alive or dead.[21]

---

[17] Louis-Philippe, *op. cit.*, t. II, pp. 375-88.

[18] *Mémoires du Général Dumouriez,* written by himself, third year of the republic, t. I, p. 101.

[19] ibid.

[20] *Formation du Régiment d'Hussards Américains,* loc. cit.

[21] Louis-Philippe, *op. cit.*, t. II, p. 406.

The end of the Orleans

The next day, 4 April, the Convention decreed the arrest of all the Bourbons, including Madame de Montesson and Philippe of Orleans. Louis-Philippe himself was then twenty years old. He was of course the eldest son of Philippe of Orleans and was to become King of France from 1830 to 1848. He escaped arrest by passing the front line with Dumouriez and joining the Austrian camp. He left there a few days later for exile in Switzerland, accompanied by his sister and Madame de Genlis.[22]

So it was that persons who had been dear to St-George vanished from the scene, some for ever and others for long months of captivity or exile. It must be seen as a particularly cruel stroke of fate that St-George was brought to play such a decisive role in the fall of Philippe of Orleans, his old friend and hunting companion; and one can appreciate his hurt and remorse when he discovered the consequences that the Convention had drawn from the frustration of Dumouriez's plans. Of course, Philippe of Orleans had long been in the sights of the fanatics among the revolutionaries, and his downfall was inevitable. But that does not alter the fact that through his intervention at Lille St-George found himself directly involved in the events that precipitated it.

In accordance with the inexorable law that our deeds rebound upon ourselves, the Revolution avenged the injustices of the Ancien Régime with its own injustices and then turned into a monster that one by one devoured all those who had furthered it and had been its instruments and defenders. The time of the Terror was at hand, and St-George like so many others fell victim to it.

---

[22] Louis-Philippe, *op. cit.*, t. II, pp. 400-427.

X. THE TERROR - SAINT-GEORGE PERSECUTED

Hunting the Bourbons
The defection of Dumouriez and the disclosure of his plans to re-establish the monarchy unleashed a veritable witch hunt for those who had been intimately or even remotely associated with the Bourbons. Like many others, Choderlos de Laclos, the former secretary of Philippe of Orleans, former adviser to Marshal Luckner and since 1792 brigadier in the army, was arrested and thrown into the prison of Picpus. As for Saint-George, he seemed to be hardly aware of the danger hovering over his head in spite of the striking proof he had just given of his loyalty to the Republic. Although he was busy at Lille reorganising his regiment after its ranks had been depleted by the withdrawal of coloured soldiers and other administrative measures, he continued to compose music. In May 1793 the "Journal de la Guitare" published an air of his composition.

Denunciation by Commissar Dufrenne - St-George before the Revolutionary Tribunal
Soon however warning signals of his downfall became apparent. Following a denunciation addressed to the Minister for War by Commissar Dufrenne on 2 May 1793, St-George was brought before the Revolutionary Tribunal in Paris on 11 May.[1] His case was serious, for he was accused of having defalcated public funds for personal profit and therefore of disloyalty to the nation. This is the text of the denunciation:
"Saint-Georges is a man to be watched. Heavily in debt, he had the idea of raising an army corps; the nation has, I believe, allocated and paid him 300,000 livres to equip his soldiers, but in spite of this they remain in desperate need! In my view not even 100,000 livres was used for the requirements of this corps, and the remainder has served to pay the debts of M. Saint-Georges, who parades an extravagant life-style and has, it is said, more than 30 horses in his stables, of which several are worth 3,000 livres each: what a disgrace!"[2]

---

[1] La Laurencie, *op. cit.*, p. 477.

[2] Letter dated from Lille and quoted by La Laurencie, *op. cit.*, p. 477, not found in the St-George dossier in the Archives of the Ministry for War.

The terms of this accusation placed St-George among those "corrupt men, grown fat on the habits, prejudices and vices of despotism" against whom colourful speeches in the National Convention uttered warnings and who were regarded as intolerable vestiges of the tyranny that had been overthrown. It was clear that if St-George did not manage to justify himself his life was done with. The Revolutionary Tribunal had been set up to wipe out every trace of monarchism and it seldom pronounced an acquittal. Death sentences were the order of the day, even during this period preceding the Terror as such.

But for the time being, the erstwhile Chevalier succeeded in clearing his name. The day after the denunciation by Commissar Dufrenne, he obtained the following statement, dated 4 May 1793, from the commune of Lille: "We, the mayor and municipal officers of the commune of Lille, certify that the citizen St.Georges, Colonel of the "13e Régiment de Chasseurs à Cheval", has demonstrated patriotic sentiments in all circumstances, especially when he came to announce the treason of Dumouriez; as for the corps he commands, we believe it to be composed of good patriots, even though we have sometimes heard complaints against certain individuals."[3] In view of this document, and in spite of an unfavourable report on the Chasseurs of the 13th Regiment addressed to the Minister for War by the Commissar Beaumé on 25 June 1793 mentioning desertions,[4] St-George was acquitted and confirmed in the rank of colonel on 1 July 1793.[5]

An ambitious squadron leader - Dumas Davy de la Pailleterie

It seems that Saint-George's second squadron leader, Dumas Davy de la Pailleterie, was not altogether foreign to the Dufrenne denunciation. We learn indeed from Alexandre Dumas's memoirs, the first two volumes of which are entirely devoted to the military career of his father, that Dumas Davy de la Pailleterie was an extremely zealous officer who enthusiastically advocated an iron discipline. His zeal was no doubt a factor in his rapid promotion in the military hierarchy. As an example we need only mention the report on the Army of the West that Dumas addressed to the Comité de Salut Public in the autumn of 1793, when he

---

[3] St-George dossier, class 91/47, Arch. adm. Min. de la Guerre.

[4] Quoted by La Laurencie, *op. cit.*, p. 477.

[5] ibid., p. 478.

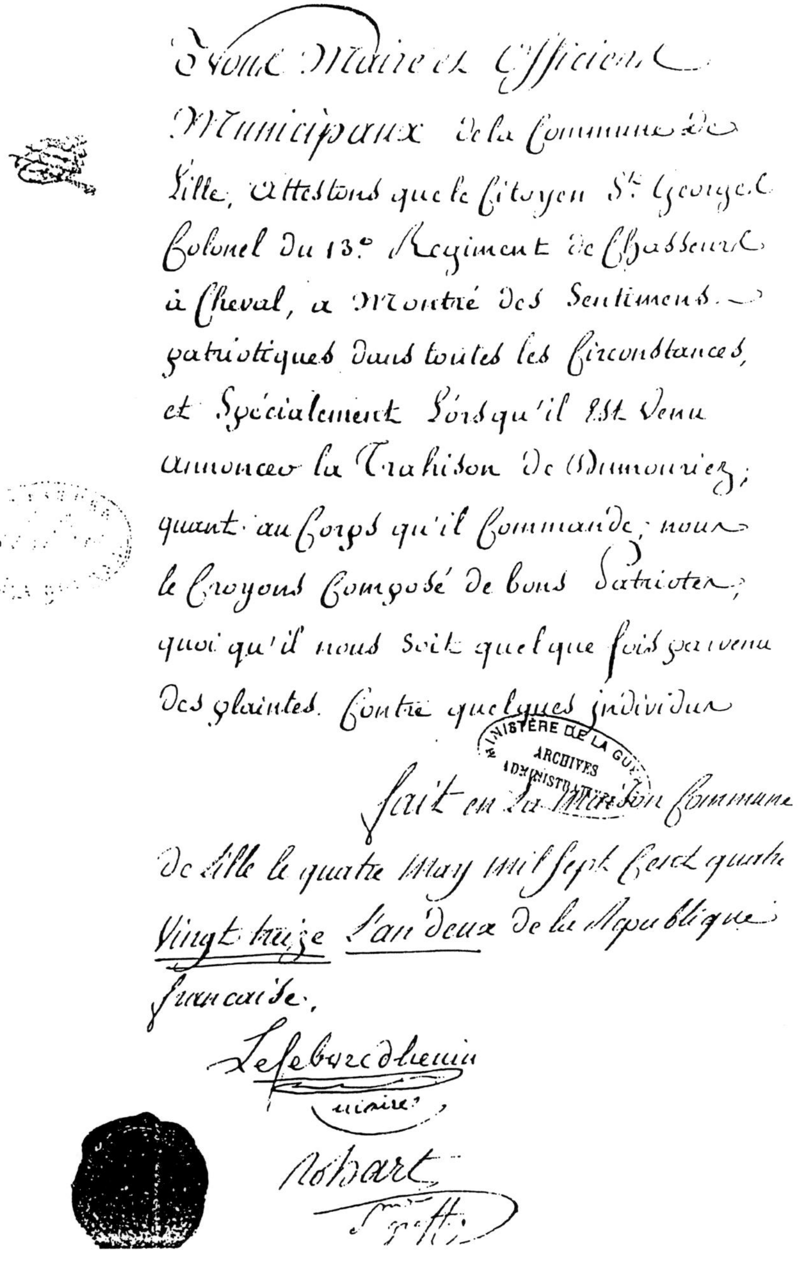

[handwritten document in French, 4 May 1793]

The commune of Lille certifies, that the citizen Saint-Georges has demonstrated
patriotic sentiments in all circumstances (4.5.1793),
Archives Administratives, Ministère de la Guerre, Vincennes

took command of this army at the age of only 31. It contains thunderous verdicts such as: "In the Army of the West there is hardly any part, military or administrative, that does not call for the firm hand of reform... In the last analysis, I have found few general officers capable of doing well." In consequence, he demanded of this Committee purely and simply the replacement of the general staff in its entirety.[6]

In the first volume of his memoirs, Alexandre Dumas devotes several pages to relations between his father and St-George, and to the story of the horses that was the subject of the Dufrenne denunciation. His account is partial and defamatory, clearly inspired by his desire to glorify his father and moreover contradicted by numerous contemporary observations on the character of St-George. The novelist was born in 1802 and did not know St-George personally - indeed he hardly knew his own father since he died when Dumas was only four years old. We shall therefore pick out only one incident from the memoirs, which is not only amusing but also indicative of St-George's generosity of spirit.

A duel declined

Alexandre Dumas states that when St-George was summoned before the Revolutionary Tribunal to justify himself against the accusation levelled at him and to explain the affair of the horses for the 13th Chasseurs, he "saw fit to blame my father for everything, saying that it was he who was charged with equipping the regiment with horses. The Minister for War then wrote to my father, who immediately proved that he had never ordered a single requisition, nor bought or sold a single horse. The Minister's ruling completely exonerated my father."[7]

For his part, St-George had been exculpated by the Revolutionary Tribunal and so the affair was officially closed. After all, if the accusations against him had had the slightest foundation he would not have been confirmed in the exercise of his functions; for the tribunal was not soft-hearted or inspired by the idea of giving the benefit of the doubt. But for Dumas it was not closed at all. Bearing a grudge towards his colonel, he pressed for transfer from the 13th Chasseurs and at the end of July 1793 secured his promotion to the post of brigardier in the Army of the North.

[6] Alexandre Dumas, *Mes Mémoires,* t. I, pp. 102 and 104, Brussels, 1852.
[7] ibid. p. 129.

Then, thirsting for vengeance, as his son tells us, he decided to go and find
St-George and kill him. Alexandre Dumas places this incident in the summer
of 1794, but it is more likely that it happened before November 1793 since
St-George was in prison after that.

Alexandre Dumas tells how his father went to St-George's home six times
to cut his throat but he was never there. According to Dumas, "St-George,
brave though he was with a pistol or sword in his hand, liked to choose his
own duels", and this is true in the sense the Chevalier had always refused
to fight a duel with those he liked - we recall the incident with the
violinist Jarnowics -and also with those whom he was sure of defeating.
In spite of everything, St-George was fond of the young Dumas Davy de
la Pailleterie, and Alexandre Dumas himself confirms this in relating what
followed.

Seeing that Dumas would not calm down, St-George finally went to his
former squadron leader to make him see reason. He said to him: "So you
really wanted to kill me? Dumas kill Saint-Georges? Is it possible? But
aren't you my son? When Saint-Georges is dead can anyone but you take
his place? Come on, get up! (Dumas was in bed.) Get them to serve me
a chop and let's have an end to all this nonsense."[8]

The two men sat down at table and their reconciliation was apparently
achieved.

We do not know whether the unkind words Alexandre Dumas employs
regarding Saint-George reflect his father's real opinion. It may also be that
they reflect his own state of mind, for the celebrated novelist is known to
have possessed the weakness of trying to conceal his African origins. His
father was, like St-George, the son of a black slave and a white aristocrat,
but he tried to invent a white family tree for himself, like many other
half-castes who had "jumped over the barrier", that is, who had acquired
a rather fair skin by generations of cross-breeding. These "new whites"
were often the worst enemies of coloured people and hated anything that
might recall their own African origin. This was an inevitable consequence
of the racist ideology that had been planted in people's minds.

We should also realise that it must have been natural for Alexandre Dumas
in his memoirs to try to exalt the father whom he had hardly known and
who must have taken on the stature of an almost mythical personage in his

---

[8] Alexandre Dumas, *Mes Mémoires,* t. I, p. 131.

childhood memories. It was natural too for Dumas Davy de la Pailleterie to feel jealous of St-George, who was then much more famous than he was. He had cherished high ambitions in fencing - as we have said he was, like St-George, a former pupil of La Boëssière - and must have envied St-George his title of "god of arms" and probably his position as commandant too.

Finally we should mention that Alexandre Dumas was a close friend of Roger de Beauvoir, the author of the novel, "Le Chevalier de St-Georges", and that he probably inspired the biased picture that this book paints of St-George.

The law on suspects

Let us now return to the events of the second half of the year 1793. The rehabilitation of St-George after the business of the horses was not to be of long duration. With the collective arrest of the Girondins at the end of May 1973 and the establishment of Jacobin dictatorship under the direction of Robespierre and Danton in July, the Revolution had entered its most radical phase. On 5 September 1793 a new law was promulgated on suspects, and this effectively wiped out the Revolution's greatest achievement, the Declaration of the Rights of Man. On the strength of this law, in Paris alone thousands of citizens were sent to the scaffold in the following eleven months - 1,400 during the two months of June and July 1794. Tens of thousands of others found themselves behind prison bars. This was the beginning of the period of the Terror. Every commune obediently drew up lists of suspects and, as Louise Fusil tells us, when there were none to hand they simply had to be fabricated.

The young actress was at Boulogne at the time and the revolutionary committee there had omitted to draw up a list of this sort. This provoked the anger of the proconsul Joseph Le Bon, who had been sent from Paris to see to the arrests. "What, no list of suspects! he exclaimed. One of the members of the committee, a Gascon wig-maker, was so frightened of the possible consequences for them that he assured the citizen representative there had been a mistake, that he had had a list in his hands and would go and get it from the town council and bring it to the place where the proconsul was staying... The wig-maker then closeted himself with another member of the committee and they hurriedly prepared a list comprising all the names they could remember, preferably people from outside the Département, English and those who were most prominent in the town, either for their wealth or for their position. Meanwhile guards had been placed at the town gates and with the aid of this list three-quarters of the inhabitants were arrested."9 Louise Fusil herself was among those arrested, although she subsequently managed to clear herself and get released.

Even if procedures were not always so totally arbitrary, the very definition of "suspect" opened the way to every kind of abuse. Indeed, the definition embraced as potential counter-revolutionaries "all those who by reason of their birth, interests, attitudes, relationships or situation might wish for the restoration of the monarchy".10 Clearly this definition could include any citizen, even the most humble peasant who, seeing his existence threatened by the galloping inflation and famine of the time, harked back with nostalgia to the Ancien Régime and perhaps saw it as the lesser evil. How much more vulnerable then was a man who had been attached to the house of Orleans for many years and who had already been accused of corruption and "parading an extravagant life-style".

St-George dismissed

On 25 September 1793 St-George was relieved of his command on the orders of the Minister for War, Bouchotte, who at the same time suspended eight other officers of the regiment, La Roche Champreux, 1st squadron leader, Captain Puchin, lieutenants Lemerre, Augustin and Dantigny, as well as the second-lieutenants Génégé, Lavaillère and Palotte.11 No justification was given for this action.

We note that a few days earlier, on 11 September 1793, the same Minister Bouchotte had notified the former second squadron leader in St-George's regiment, Alexandre Dumas Davy de la Pailleterie, of his promotion to the post of general in command of the Army of the Eastern Pyrenees, and that he did so in the most flattering terms: "This appointment will provide you with yet another occasion to show your devotion to the public cause and to overthrow its enemies. The republicanism you have

---

9 Fusil, *op. cit.*, pp. 200-201.

10 Report to the Convention quoted by Louis-Philippe, II, p.393.

11 La Laurencie, *op. cit.*, p. 478.

shown so far is a sure guarantee that you will spare none of them."[12] But the people's representatives in this army refused to recognise him as the new commander and Dumas was then appointed to the Army of the West.[13]

Petition of St-George's officers

It was probably on the day after St-George's dismissal that some ten officers of the regiment addressed to the authorities this undated declaration in favour of their colonel: "The undersigned officers of the 13th Regiment of Light Cavalry, always respectfully obedient to the orders of the constituted authorities, believe that it is just and their duty as true republicans to express their regret at losing a citizen as brave as St-Georges, in whom they have seen only a good commander perfectly fulfilling his duties as a patriot inspired by the purest of motives and carrying to the highest degree his love for his comrades of the 13th Regiment. We fervently wish that the suspicions that have been raised against his motives should be dispelled on examination of his conduct, and that such a brave man, who can have no enemies except by some mistake, should be reinstated in office for the defence of the Republic for which we are fighting and for which we take pleasure in shedding our blood."[14]

A second denunciation

But this petition did not have the desired effect. St-George, who was then at Chateau-Thierry, the main town of a district on the River Marne in L'Aisne (40 km to the south of Soissons), remained suspended. To make his position even worse, the commandant of this place, Latuellière, presented a denunciation of him to the Chateau-Thierry watch-committee on 24 October 1793.

Unfortunately, the text of this denunciation is no longer to be found in the St-George dossier; but the document totally withdrawing it two days later is there. It says the following: "Extract from the minutes of the Watch-Committee of Chateau-Thierry. Session of the fourth day of the first decade of the second month of Year Two of the French Republic[15], nine

---

[12] Dumas, *op. cit.*, t. I, pp. 78-79.

[13] ibid., pp. 86-100.

[14] St-George dossier, loc. cit.

[15] In the revolutionary calendar (see Index) 26 October 1793.

n°. 4.

Petition of Saint-Georges' officers: "...such a brave man...should
be reinstated in office for the defence of theRepublic..." (26.9.1793?)
Archives Administratives, Ministère de la Guerre, Vincennes

o'clock in the morning - Citizen Latuellière, commanding the detachment of the Revolutionary Army stationed in this town, appeared before the Watch-Committee. He stated that, inspired by love for the public good, he had received from the lips of several citizens of this town whom he did not know the charges in the denunciation of citizen St-Georges, which he had conveyed to the committee the day before yesterday. But having informed himself in more detail on the case, he was completely convinced that there was no reliable basis to these charges and he had been misled in the matter. As a result, he withdrew this denunciation in its entirety and asked for this to be minuted and signed. Signed in the records, Latuellière, Captain."[16]

A letter from St-George to Bouchotte

Like the petition of the officers of the 13th Chasseurs, this declaration remained ineffectual. On 31 October 1793, therefore, St-George decided to write to Minister Bouchotte himself and enquire as to the real reasons for his dismissal:

"At Chateau-Thierry, the ninth day of the first decade of the second month of Year Two of the French Revolution.

Citizen Minister,

I have been waiting in obedience in the hope that you would be so good as to inform me of the causes of my suspension. I can remain no longer in this cruel uncertainty. I have nothing in the world to reproach myself with. I have always given every proof of my civic sense and the republican sentiments that are deeply rooted in me. Be so gracious, Citizen Minister, as to allow me to rebut the false accusations that have been levelled at me, and to prove that your faith has been abused. I demand this justice in the name of humanity, which is due to every French republican. I am, with the most patriotic sentiments,

Yours fellow citizen,

St-George, Brigadier."[17]

---

[16] St-George dossier, loc. cit.

[17] Quoted by La Laurencie, *op. cit.*, p. 478. The letter is no longer in the St-George dossier.

A "measure necessary in the circumstances"

But St-George did not receive the graciousness he was requesting. A few days later, in a letter addressed to "citizen St-Georges, formerly brigadier of the 13th Regiment of Chasseurs", Bouchotte merely replied: "You may send me all the documentation you think might induce the Executive Council to change its decision, and I shall submit it to them."[18] In another version that La Laurencie found in due course in the St-George dossier in the Administrative Archives of the Ministry for War, the only explanation that Bouchotte gave for St-George's suspension was that "the Executive Council has judged this measure necessary in the circumstances".[19]

Philippe of Orleans dies on the guillotine

We have no means of knowing to which circumstances exactly the Minister for War was referring, since his letter contains no further details. We should however remember that at this very moment the trial of Philippe of Orleans was proceeding before the Revolutionary Tribunal in Paris. He was formally arraigned with some forty Girondins on 3 October 1793 and brought back from the Fort of St. John at Marseilles to Paris, where he was imprisoned in the Conciergerie. He defended himself with all the adroitness and composure he could muster against the charge of high treason and collusion with Dumouriez. But he was doomed. "He received the news of his sentence with the greatest possible calm and asked to be executed as soon as possible. The same day, 6 November 1793, about four o'clock in the afternoon, he was led to the place of execution... Passing along the Rue St-Honoré, he gave his old home a wry glance and replied to the boos of the crowd with a gesture of contempt. He said, 'Once they used to applaud me!'... He climbed down from the tumbril and ascended the platform of the guillotine. The executioner's assistants wanted to pull his tightly-fitting boots off. 'No, no, he said to them indifferently, you can pull them off more easily afterwards - hurry up, hurry up!' Those were his last words."[20]

---

[18] ibid., p. 479. Bouchotte's reply has also disappeared from the dossier.

[19] ibid.

[20] Lamartine in his article on Philippe of Orleans in the *Nouvelle Biographie Générale*, 1862.

It is probable that during the trial of Philippe of Orleans the question came up of Dumouriez's attempt to seize Lille and of how this plan was frustrated thanks to St-George's intervention. And it is quite possible that Philippe of Orleans mentioned, as part of his defence, that St-George was his friend. Might not these have been "the circumstances" which made St-George's dismissal necessary in the eyes of the Executive Committee? What is more, they seemed to make it necessary to imprison the erstwhile Chevalier, whose brilliant past in the high society of the Ancien Régime suddenly rose up over his head like a menacing shadow.

St-George in prison
The imprisonment took place in the first days of November 1793, at the same time as the execution of Philippe-Egalité or a few days after. By order of the representative Lejeune, St-George was transferred to the house of detention at Houdainville, near Clermont-sur-Oise, where he was to stay for 18 months.
On 4 November 1793 his successor in the post of brigadier of the 13th Chasseurs was named as Jean-François Target, a former dragoon of the erstwhile Regiment Colonel Général, corporal in the National Guard and then sergeant in the Gendarmerie. It was under his command that St-George's regiment, now more than twice the size following several reorganisations, and comprising 6 squadrons with a complement of 1,275 men, distinguished itself with the Army of the North under General Jourdan during the renewed campaign of Belgium in 1794.[21]
Like so many others during the Terror, St-George thus disappeared from the scene, and it is a miracle that he escaped the scaffold. No doubt he owed his survival only to the undeniable services he had rendered the Republic, even though at this time many others died who had done as much. This, then, is another miracle in the life of this man who was born under the sign of turmoil and seemed destined for a life in which danger was never absent but was always in the end overcome.
For St-George incarceration must have been a very peculiar experience, plunging him back into his childhood world of Guadeloupe. It must have recalled forgotten images, memories of slaves at the mercy of some all-powerful master, prisoners of an arbitrary system based on an ephemeral

---

[21] Descaves, *op. cit.*, pp. 9, 40-42 and 185.

ideology and interest. Was he aware of the striking resemblance between their situation and his own?

At the age of 45, after a dazzling career that had lifted him into the society of the most illustrious personages in the Kingdom of France and to an honourable position in the Army of the Republic, St-George found himself thrown back to his point of departure. In the house of detention at Houdainville what was he but an anonymous prisoner, a number? Strange are the ways of destiny, one might say, and the destiny of St-George had certainly not concluded its surprises.

XI. UNDER THE SWAY OF THE GUILLOTINE

House visits

While St-George was languishing in prison, where he seems to have started composing music again, those of his old friends that destiny had spared for the moment led a life of constant anguish and fear in Paris. Louise Fusil gives this account:

"This was the time when house visits were being made...These visits were made at night and of course we took great care to burn any papers that might seem in the slightest suspicious. I had some verses written at a time when no one could have foreseen that they would become a death warrant. They had been given to me when I was at Tournai, and were in the spirit of that time. I thought I had burned them long ago but, as my whole life I have been absent-minded and scatter-brained, I forgot about them.

"I had gone to bed when these gentlemen came to pay their visit. I got out of bed and opened up my writing-desk. They read the letters from my husband, who was in the army then. Then they closely examined every piece of paper and poked little pointed iron probes into the armchairs and even the mattresses. Finding nothing suspicious, they wished me good-night. The next morning when I was trying to tidy up all the scattered papers, the first thing I found was a parody of the "Pauvre Jacques" song. Everyone had been singing it three years before but now the parodied lines could have sent me to the Revolutionary Tribunal. The original words are:

> Pauvre Jacques, quand j'étais près de toi.
> Je ne sentais pas la misère,
> Mais à présent que je vis loin de toi,
> Je manque de tout sur la terre.

(Poor Jack, when we were together, I was not aware of our poverty, But now that I live far away from you, I lack everything in this world.)

And the lines of the parody:

> Pauvre peuple, quand tu n'avais qu'un roi,
> Tu ne sentais pas la misère,
> Mais à présent, sans monarque, sans loi,
> Tu manques de tout sur la terre.

(Poor people, when you still had a king, You were not aware of your poverty, But now, without a monarch, without laws, You lack everything in this world.)
I do not know by what miracle this piece of paper escaped their notice."[1]

The battle against fear

At this time of tension and perpetual fear, friendship assumed a special significance, and in this connection we have further valuable and moving testimony from Louise Fusil:

"We felt the need to communicate to one another the fears that pursued us and which, alas, only too often came true. Friends who parted the evening before were never sure of seeing one another the next day. We felt that if we all kept close together we had more courage in facing any blow that might fall. We resigned ourselves to not having long to live, and this was a complete denial of our own existence. We did not say when we took leave of one another, 'See you soon' but 'This may be the last time' or 'In a better world'!

"The whole of our society was living a new kind of life, but moments of gaiety broke through, all the same. That French sense of humour that never abandons us sometimes showed itself when friends came together who ran the same dangers. We played at Revolutionary Tribunal so as to get used to the sight of it without trembling. The roles for the rehearsal were shared out at Talma's. The chairman was played by Bonhomme, a big Newfoundland dog. It was very unfair to give a role like that to this poor animal, because he had the sweetest temper of any creature I've ever known but he played the part to perfection. When the verdict had to be pronounced, someone pinched his ear or tail to make him bark. And that meant, Off with his head."[2]

The avenue of death - Baron de Frénilly's account

It was in the spring of 1794 that the Terror entered its cruellist phase. The guillotine worked without intermission. It is hardly possible today, two hundred years later, to imagine what those times were like. But eyewitnesses from the period have left us their accounts. This is how Baron

---

[1] Fusil, *op. cit.*, pp. 211-213.

[2] ibid.

de Frénilly depicts the Paris of the time and particularly the day when Danton was executed, 5 April 1794:

"I wanted to get a glimpse of the daily slaughter. In the Rue Saint-Honoré, three tumbrils painted red and drawn by two horses, escorted by five or six gendarmes, came at a walking pace through an immense and silent crowd that showed no joy and did not dare to show abhorrence.

Each cart contained five or six victims. The only one I remember clearly is the first because two faces struck me with surprise and horror. One was that of Danton, Robespierre's Pompey, the great victim of the day... A few days later, the whole of the Grand Chamber of Parliament passed along this funereal road. I did not myself see this terrible procession; the first had been too much for me. When it passed by I was with a paint-seller who lived in the Rue du Coq. At the sound of the tumbrils everyone rushed to the windows and I retreated to the back of the room. The Farmers-General were still waiting their turn. They had been imprisoned for a year in their former Hôtel des Fermes in the Rue de Grenelle-Saint-Honoré...

"The prisons, convents and hotels in Paris - anywhere that could be shut off - overflowed with prisoners; and among them we should not forget the actors of the Comédie Française, for whom incarceration came to be like a title of nobility. The Comédie Française was the theatrical aristocracy, and it kept its status during the Revolution. Except for Dugazon and Molé, they all made it a point of honour not to demean themselves and preferred to be imprisoned as dukes and peers than free as actors..."

The desolation of Paris

"Not a single carriage was to be seen in Paris. Life entirely contracted to within the family, and even here little was said, and that in a low voice, with the doors well shut. No one felt sure of the morrow. Women did not go out at all, and the men seldom. People you met in the street were dressed in the 'carmagnole' style, that is in a short jacket and trousers of grey-brown cloth, with a coloured tie, their hair short and smoothed-down, and wearing a cap, iron-tipped shoes and with a club in their hands. That was the fashion... Every wall displayed in large letters, 'Liberty, Fraternity, Equality or Death'. The door of every house carried a notice with the names and ages of the inhabitants. Masterpieces of the stage were banned from the theatres, or if anyone dared put them on they had to go through a revolutionary expurgation to remove all reminiscences, allusions and titles...

"So there was nothing to see but silent streets and locked doors. The only acquaintances I came across were my neighbours d'Aucour and Saint-Just, the man of letters... All the others were either in prison or scattered far and wide to their country estates, if they had not already fallen under the revolutionary axe."[3]

Famine and cold

The evils of the Terror were matched by those of the famine and an extremely severe winter that seemed as though it would never end.

"The war at the height of its ferocity," Frénilly continues, "had driven out of France all the money that was still to be found there. There was literally not a minted coin to be seen, and with fall after fall in the currency eventually assignats for thirty sols were issued which were worth only two. Food had risen to a prodigious price... The value of paper changed from day to day, and anyone who made a deal payable in a week often received one third less than the value of the sum agreed... It was because of these conditions that the Convention invented the law of the maximum price, and this put the cap on the general misery. Before this law people could keep alive by ruining themselves... but after the publication of the maximum price law all goods disappeared from the market as if by magic. Buying and selling were done in secret. Every purchase was a conspiracy, and suddenly, in the city of Paris alone, there was a complete lack not just of bread, and not just of fuel, but of all the necessities...

"No one who has not lived through them can imagine what those times were like. It was tactless, indeed incredibly inconsiderate, to go to a friend's for dinner without taking your bread along. People came together in secret to eat the white bread that certain suspect bakers dared to make, for bakers baked by order, using only flour made from peas, vetches and chestnuts that was delivered to them by the government. Long queues of hungry people formed outside every baker's shop to get a bit of black, gooey bread; they waited from early dawn, or even all night, and thus wasted a third of their day. And everyone had to join the queue, or send

---

[3] *Souvenirs du Baron de Frénilly-Pair de France (1768-1828),* ed. by A. Chuquet, Paris, 1908, pp. 180-183.

someone to do it, because otherwise you came under suspicion of having bread at home. This was a crime that the government punished with fines and the mob with looting."[4] In the intense cold, even basic fuel was lacking, and it was at this time that the Convention had the Bois de Boulogne cut down.

The Festivity of the Supreme Being

In the month of May 1794 Robespierre, who had attained the height of his power by eliminating all those who opposed his madness, had a decree voted abolishing Christianity and instituting the cult of reason, the "Supreme Being", in its place. This new cult was to be consecrated by a grand act of celebration. One may well ask how an event of this kind could be organised at a time when people lacked even bread, but dictatorship makes such contradictions possible. Let us turn again to the account by Louise Fusil, who lived through it:

"The time preceding the Festivity of the Supreme Being witnessed the most monstrous extravagances. It really seems as though people are sometimes overcome by an access of intoxication. Deprived of religion, they were on the point of deifying Lepelletier and Marat. The Marseillaise anthem had become the evening prayer. At the last verse, 'Amour sacré de la Patrie' (Holy love of country), the cry went up, 'Down on your knees!', and it would have been perilous not to obey this command...

"It was not possible to be gainfully employed by any theatrical administration without belonging to the Institute of Music, which was the Conservatoire of the time. It was financed by the government and was therefore always available for national festivities. The only one I escaped from was that for Marat, because I was fortunately ill at the time.

"Chénier, David, Méhul and Gossec, artists and men of letters, were in charge of this administration. David worked out the plan, laid down costumes and programmes, and designed the course of the festivities. Lesueur et Méhul in particular composed the hymns we had to sing, the Chant du Départ', the 'Ronde de Grandpré' and the hymns in celebration of the Supreme Being.

"This festivity was undeniably the finest of the period. On the terrace of the Tuileries palace they had erected a rotunda, the front of which formed

---

[4] ibid. pp. 188-189.

an amphitheatre. The performers descended stairs on both sides and there was a banister to support the women, who stood in twos from top to bottom and sang hymns. They wore white tunics and a sash over their breasts, a crown of roses on their heads, and they bore a basket full of rose petals in their hands.

"This harmony of costumes was delightful to behold. A large orchestra, consisting of all the musical celebrities left in the capital and conducted by Lesueur, occupied the front part of the rotunda. The Deputies of the Convention, finely dressed, were on the balcony. Opposite, near the flower-beds, was the statue of Atheism. Robespierre came forward, torch in hand, to set this on fire and a kind of firework shot out. This effigy was replaced by an effigy of Reason, which was revealed blackened by the flames of Atheism and Fanaticism.

"The ceremony finished very late. We were dying of hunger and thirst. Talma and David had great difficulty finding anything for us to eat. Yet again we were forced to hide because eating might have seemed too prosaic to Robespierre; he was situated on top of the Mountain and no doubt thought we should make do with incense for nourishment. It was there, as was reported later, that Bourdon (from l'Oise) said to him, 'Robespierre, the Tarpeian Rock is close to the Capitol!' "[5]

Robespierre on the scaffold

Robespierre's fall was indeed not far off. On 27 July 1794 (9 thermidor) he was overthrown and guillotined the next day, with 21 of his companions including St-Just. Thus ended the period of Jacobin rule. "The prisons opened and hope of a better future was reborn", Louise Fusil wrote, but the Revolution had not finished devouring its children. Only a few weeks after the end of the Jacobin Terror, another terror, known as the "white" one, began. This was conducted by the royalists, who undertook to purge the country of those who had wanted to purge it of royalists.

---

[5] Fusil, *op. cit.,* pp. 214-15. The Tarpeian Rock was a peak in ancient Rome from which traitors were cast down. It formed the western slope of the Capitoline Hill where the Temple of Jupiter, the Romans' supreme god, was situated.

For the time being, at least, there was a breathing-space during which people dared to make enquiries about their relations and friends who had disappeared.

XII. ST-GEORGE'S LAST CAMPAIGN - A BUREAUCRATIC EPIC

Attempts at release

St-George seems to have started taking steps to secure his release and rehabilitation in August 1794. On 18 August, at Houdainville, he signed as a true copy a deposition in his favour, which had been delivered the same day by several municipal officials of Egalité-sur-Marne - the revolutionary name for Chateau-Thierry.

They wrote: "We, citizens living in the commune of Egalité-sur-Marne, certify that on every occasion we have been with General (sic) St-Georges, who has been suspended from his duties for reasons of public security, we have never detected anything anti-social in his words or deeds; we certify on the contrary that during his stay in this commune he has shown himself to be a good and courageous republican who has openly complained of the waste of his valour, and has shown the most fervent desire to confront our oppressors and their lackeys. Egalité-sur-Marne, 1st Fructidor 2nd republican year, one and indivisible." (18 August 1794)[1]

But, for the moment, St-George had to be patient. His requests seem to have gone astray in the maze of administrative channels, and it was not until the beginning of the autumn of 1794 that a Parisian correspondent of unknown identity enquired as to the reasons for St-George's suspension in a letter to the Ninth Commission for the Organisation and Movement of the Land Armies. Replying to his question, Commissar L. A. Pille said on 6 October 1794 (15 Vendémiaire Year III) that in issuing the order of suspension the former Executive Council had not "made known the reasons for its decision".[2]

---

[1] St-George dossier, loc. cit.

[2] Quoted by La Laurencie, *op. cit.*, p. 481. This letter is no longer in the St-George dossier, nor is the one to which it is a reply.

Départ. de l'aisne

District d'Egalité sur marne

Municipalité d'Egalité sur marne

Nous citoyens, habitans la commune d'Egalité sur marne certifions que toutes les fois que nous nous sommes trouvés avec le général St georges, suspendu de ses fonctions par mesure de sûreté générale, nous n'avons jamais reconnu en lui des discours et actes inciviques, certifions au contraire que pendant son séjour en cette commune il s'y est montré en bon et courageux républicain, qu'il s'est plaint avec franchise devoir son courage dans l'inaction et a témoigné le plus vif désir de se mesurer avec nos oppresseurs et leurs esclaves. Egalité sur marne le 1er fructidor 2e année républicaine une et indivisible ont signé

minguet   vandeuil gendarme

off. mic. p.   grino. capt. national

naud et command.   Dorm — bretoy

           collard, povet.

P. copie conforme a l'original, a houdainville ce 1er fructidor 2e année républicaine
St George. ch. J. O. aux et indivisible.

To secure his release and rehabilitation St-George signed on 18 August 1794,
at Houdainville, as a true copy a deposition in his favour, which had been delivered
the same day by several municipal officials of Egalité-sur-Marne - the revolutionary
name of Château-Thierry. Archives Administratives, Ministère de la Guerre, Vincennes

Decree of release postponed

Finally, on 24 October 1794, the National Convention's Committee of Public Security ordered the immediate release of St-George in the following terms: "2 Brumaire of Year Three of the French Republic one and indivisible. The Committee has decided that Colonel Joseph Bologne-St-Georges, detained in the house of detention of Houdainville near Clermont-sur-Oise, will immediately be released and that the seals will be removed from all the places where they have been applied, on condition that he conforms to the laws of 20 August and 9 September (old style). The People's Representatives comprising the Committee of Public Security. Signed Goupilleau de Fontenay, A. Dumont, Merlin de Thionville, Bentaboll, Reverchon, Rewbell."[3]

But this decision does not seem to have been carried out until several months later, for St-George states in a letter to the Committee of Public Safety - which we shall quote later - that he had been incarcerated for 18 months. This means that he was not actually released until the spring of 1795, having been arrested in the autumn of 1793. We have not found any document explaining this delay in the St-George dossier of the Administrative Archives of the Ministry for War, which are in any case extremely incomplete by now.

St-George requests his rehabilitation

Be that as it may, at the beginning of April 1795 St-George asked the Committee of Public Safety for his rehabilitation as commander of his regiment, writing as follows:

"St-Georges, Brigadier of the 13th Regiment of Light Cavalry, suspended from his duties, to the citizen representatives of the people comprising the Committee of Public Safety.

Trusting in your justice, I claim a redress to which I am entitled after the persecution I have suffered. My devotion to the Revolution is well-known throughout the Republic. I have not ceased since 1789 to declare my support with the greatest possible commitment. Our country would perhaps have had difficulty in avoiding the most disastrous reverses but for the zeal with which I intervened in preventing the loss of the important position of Lille to the forces of Coburg and Dumouriez.

---

[3] St-George dossier, loc. cit.

CONVENTION NATIONALE.

COMITÉ

DE SURETÉ GÉNÉRALE ET DE SURVEILLANCE
DE LA CONVENTION NATIONALE.

Du *Deux Brumaire* l'an trois de la République
Francaise une et indivisible.

[handwritten text of the decree]

The decree of the Committee of Public Security (24.10.1794), that Saint-George
should be released from the house of detention in Houdainville,
Archives Administratives, Ministère de la Guerre, Vincennes

The latter's memoirs show you, citizen representatives, the extent of the service that I rendered my country at that disastrous time. I was nevertheless suspended some time afterwards by Bouchotte and imprisoned by order of Representative Lejeune for 18 months. Relieved at last of all these undeserved persecutions, I find myself in a situation where I cannot be refused the most obvious justice. The most fervent of all my wishes is to continue to serve my country and to sacrifice my last drop of blood. Be so good therefore, citizen representatives, as to order my restitution to the regiment I commanded and which is without a comm ander at present. I am sending you the supporting papers to back my request. You will surely entertain this because you are just, and someone who is innocent, oppressed and persecuted is sure to find support and justice at your hands.

Greetings and fraternity,

Saint-Georges."[4]

On 4 April 1795 this letter was sent to the competent authorities, accompanied by the report of someone named Eloy[5] who repeats the gist of the text and enumerates the written evidence attached: the release mandate of 24 October (2 Brumaire Year III) from the Committee of Security; an extract from the enrolment register of Lille proving that St-George was among the first to enlist as a volunteer in the levy of 1791; the certified statement from the municipality of Lille that he had come to report the treason of Dumouriez; the declaration by the officers of the 13th Chasseurs asking for his restoration to command, and the confirmation of good conduct from the municipality of Egalité-sur-Marne (all documents contained in the St-George dossier and reproduced in the preceding pages), as well as "a few other documents relating to his suspension and incarceration" which are no longer included in the dossier.

This request for rehabilitation came at a moment when St-George's old regiment was without a proper commander.

---

[4] Typed copy in the St-George dossier, loc. cit. The original is lost. The date must be 4 April 1795 or a few days earlier.

[5] St-George dossier, loc. cit.

On 15 January 1795 the 13th Chasseurs had been abolished on the orders of the People's Representatives with the Armies of the North and Sambre-et-Meuse.[6] Colonel Target, who had been in command since St-George's dismissal, was also suspended and imprisoned. As we learn from a report by Commissar Pille, member of the 9th Commission in the Committee of Public Safety, of 12 May 1795,[7] Target was eventually rehabilitated, after being released and reimprisoned several times, but only as a supernumerary with the rank of acting brigadier. The regiment itself was, as we have said, officially abolished on 15 January 1795 and survived only provisionally, with the result that a general uncertainty prevailed in St-George's old corps when he requested his reappointment in early April 1795.

A problematical reorganisation - three colonels at the ready

A few days later, on 11 April 1795, a new 13th Chasseurs was formed by amalgamating the previous one with its second version, a regiment of light cavalry that was initially assigned to the Army of the West and then to the Army of the North, and was commanded by Colonel Bouquet.[8]

Without regard to St-George's request, the general staff charged with carrying out the merger appointed Colonel Bouquet, the commander of the second version of the 13th, to take over the new regiment. This appointment was only provisional however since it had to be approved by the Representatives of the People, who were now in the position of having to make a definitive choice between the three aspirants to the command of the 13th Chasseurs.

In his report of 12 May 1795 quoted above, Commissar Pille of the 9th Commission recommended the Committee of Public Safety to opt for St-George: "The Committee will no doubt decide to announce the reappointment of Colonel St-Georges, against whom there is no evidence

---

[6] Descaves, *op. cit.*, pp. 9 and 15-16.

[7] St-George dossier, loc. cit.

[8] For the history of the second version of the 13th see Descaves, *op. cit.*, pp. 11-14. The exploits of this regiment have sometimes been confused with those of St-George's regiment. The only connection between the two, before their merger, was the incorporation of a detachment of 73 coloured men from St-George's Legion in the second version in the summer of 1793. See Descaves, pp. 7 and 12.

on file, and who seems to have been suspended without reason. On the contrary, the Commission (for the Organisation and Movement of Land Armies) has flattering testimonies to his gallantry and public-spiritedness provided by his companions in arms. These attest to having seen Colonel St-Georges confront the enemy and lead not only his Chasseurs but also an entire column in his delight at serving the Republic - and in an action where by virtue of his rank he did not need to take part at all, since only 50 men of his corps were present. "[9]

A friendly gesture - Target withdraws

St-George's honour was restored in yet another document, the letter from Colonel Target of 18 March 1795 (28 Ventôse Year III) in which he surrendered to his predecessor his claim to the post of the regiment's command, and in the following terms of cordiality: "Soissons, 28 Ventôse Third Year of the Republic. Target, acting brigadier of the 13th Regiment of Light Cavalry, to the republican St-Georges, 1st commander of the brigade and founder of the Regiment.

My friend,

Since I have had the misfortune to be the passive and involuntary instrument of the injustice done to you, it falls to my honour and duty to make this good once and for all. I did not know you when I took over command of the regiment you had formed. But since I owed this honour only to your disgrace, I believe I cannot make myself more worthy of the post I have occupied in your absence than by having it restored to the man to whom it ought always to have belonged.

I therefore assure you on my word as a man of honour that it is my most fervent wish to restore to you a command of which you should never have been deprived; and, if I have rendered some slight service to the regiment and my country, the only reward I ask is the honour of serving under your orders in whatever rank it might be.

I shall consider it the happiest circumstance of my life if you consent to regard Target as the best and sincerest of your friends. Target."[10]

---

[9] Pille's report in the St-George dossier, loc. cit.

[10] Letter in the St-George dossier, loc. cit.

Pontoise le 28 ventôse 3me année
Républicaine.

Paget Chef de Brigade provisoir
du 13e Regt de Chasseurs à Cheval
au Républicain St Georges
1er Chef de Brigade et fondateur
du Régiment.

Mon ami,

Puisque j'ai eu le Malheur
d'être l'instrument passif et involontaire
de l'injustice qui t'a été faite il
est de mon honneur et de mon devoir
de la réparer authentiquement.

Si j'ai commandé après toi le
Régiment que tu as formé; Je ne
te l'aurais jamais soit; Mais n'ayant de
cet honneur que tu Dirigeas, Je ne
crois pas pouvoir me rendre plus digne
du poste que j'ai occupé en ton absence
qu'en faisant le remettre à Celui
à qui il eut toujours du appartenir

Je te Déclare donc par une
parole d'honnête homme que j'aime

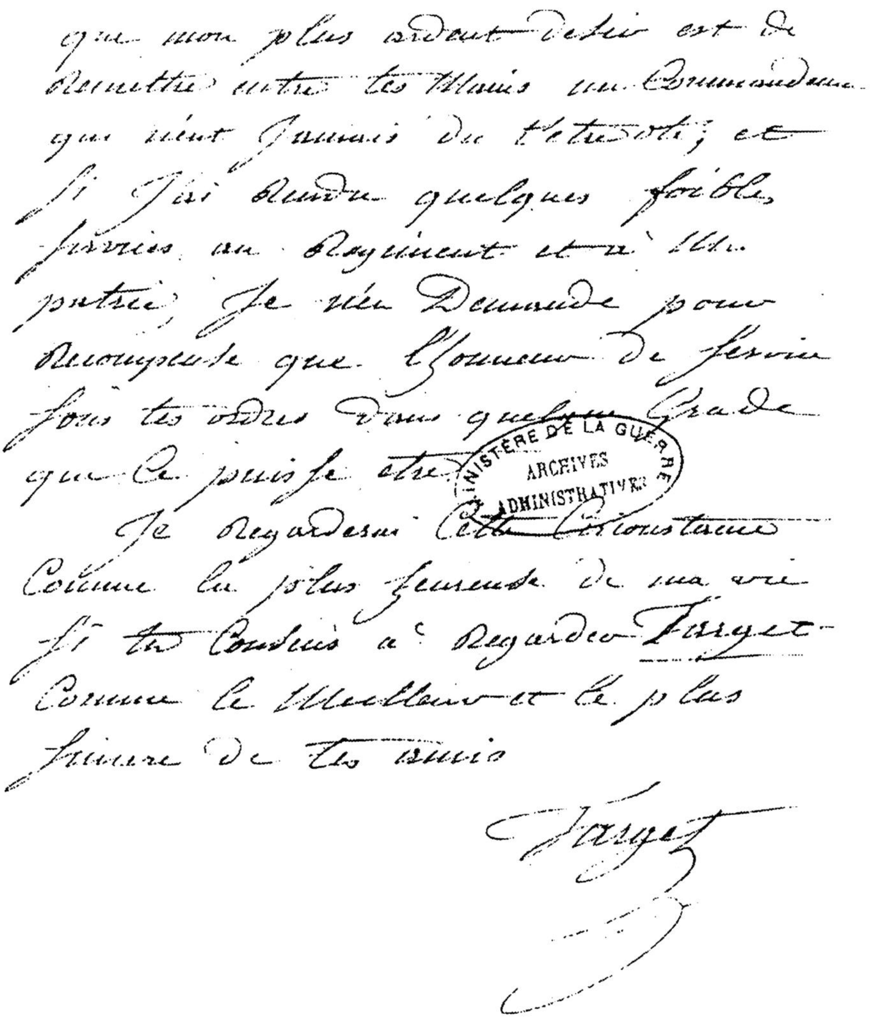
que mon plus ardent desir est de
remettre entre tes mains un commandement
qui n'eut jamais du t'être ôté; et
si j'ai rendu quelques foibles
services au Regiment et à ma
patrie, je n'en demande pour
recompense que l'honneur de servir
sous tes ordres dans quelque grade
que ce puisse être.

Je regarderai cette circonstance
comme la plus heureuse de ma vie
si tu consens à regarder Target
comme le meilleur et le plus
sincere de tes amis

Target

MINISTÈRE DE LA GUERRE
ARCHIVES
ADMINISTRATIVES

The letter of apology from Colonel Target to Saint-George (18.3.1795) - 2 pages,
Archives Administratives, Ministère de la Guerre, Vincennes

Target's withdrawal in favour of St-Georges, dated 18 March 1795, was duly acknowledged in Commissar Pille's report of 12 May, so that only St-George and Bouquet remained as candidates. Regarding the latter, Commissar Pille noted in his report that "this officer appears to merit the Committee's attention, but he is far from having as strong a claim as Colonel St-Georges".

St-George reinstated - Colonel Bouquet's opposition

The day after the Pille report, 13 May 1795 (24 Floréal Year III), the Committee of Public Safety decreed that: "St-George will be reinstated in his rank as Brigadier of the 13th Regiment of Chasseurs. The 9th Commission will suggest to the Committee a possible transfer for Bouquet."[11] By this was meant finding him another post in the army. At the same time, the 9th Commission (for the Organisation and Movement of the Land Armies) was charged with the execution of this decree.

However, this reinstatement and rehabilitation did not mean that St-George was free of his troubles. Colonel Bouquet quite simply refused to leave his post. Maintaining that "it has often happened and still happens every day that an order is contermanded by someone else's order", he demanded in his letter of 28 July 1795 "a further, definite order" from the 9th Commission before yielding his post to St-George. And he accused St-George of having "sometimes considered himself in command of the regiment" and of having "given orders as a result".[12] In his letter he complained specifically that St-George had movement orders issued to several men of the old 13th Chasseurs who had not been incorporated in the new regiment, and that he, Bouquet, had been obliged to send them back to where they had come from, which caused the Republic nugatory expense and confusion among the troops.

The situation was complicated by the fact that on 28 July 1795 St-George had not yet rejoined his corps but was still at Paris. He must have explained his reasons for this to the Commission, but we do not know what they were since the relevant papers are missing from the dossier.

---

[11] Written at the bottom of the Pille report with the date. St-George dossier, loc. cit.

[12] Bouquet's letter to the 9th Commission of 9 Thermidor Year III (28 July 1795), St-George dossier, loc. cit.

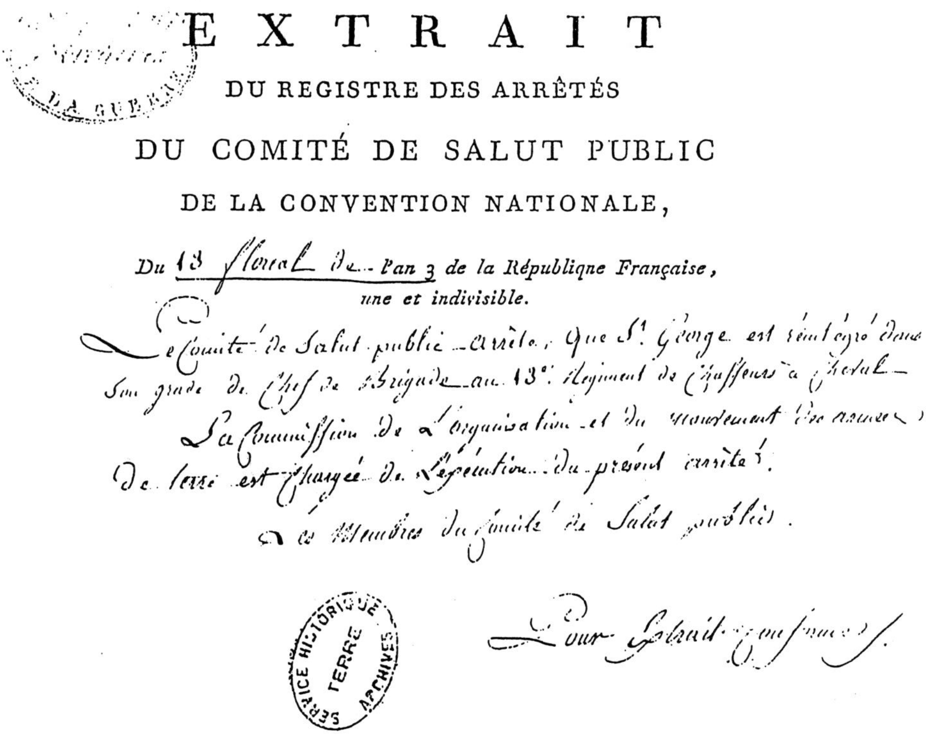

EXTRAIT

DU REGISTRE DES ARRÊTÉS

DU COMITÉ DE SALUT PUBLIC

DE LA CONVENTION NATIONALE,

Du 13 floréal de *l'an* 3 *de la République Française, une et indivisible.*

Le Comité de Salut public arrête, que St. George est réintégré dans son grade de Chef de Brigade au 13e Régiment de Chasseurs à cheval.

La Commission de l'organisation et du mouvement des armées de terre est chargée de l'exécution du présent arrêté.

Les Membres du Comité de Salut public.

Pour Extrait conforme.

(Extrait...) The decree of the Committee of Public Security from 13th May 1795: "St. George will be reinstated in his rank of Chef de Brigade of the 13th Regiment". Archives Administratives, Ministère de la Guerre, Vincennes

St-Georgeists versus Bouquetistes - a regiment divided

When St-George finally arrived at his regiment's depot at Valenciennes on 25 August 1795 he found it divided in two camps. His own squadrons of the old 13th Chasseurs remained loyal to him whereas those of the former new version of the 13th commanded by Bouquet were fiercely hostile. The latter, like Bouquet himself, immediately directed several communications[13] to the authorities asking for St-George's formal recall. They based this request on a law of 13 Prairial (1 June 1795) which laid down that reinstated officers must rejoin their units within a month. All the evidence indicates that, for whatever reason, St-George had not observed this.

In spite of these petitions, General Kermovan, the commanding officer at Valenciennes, had St-George recognised as in command of the brigade of the 13th Chasseurs at a muster of them on 1 September 1795.

Bouquet was furious and wrote to the 9th Commission the same day to complain of "this abuse of authority", which according to him was "contrary to law, contrary to the army order of 2 Fructidor, contrary to the public interest and that of the regiment in particular, and undermined discipline..."[14]

St-George dismissed again

With the skilful and prolific use of his pen, Bouquet finally managed to convince the Representatives of the People that retaining himself in command of the 13th Chasseurs was the only solution in conformity with the law and in the interest of the Republic. On 10 October 1795, Goupilleau de Fontenay, the People's Representative with the Army of the Interior, wrote to his colleague Merlin of Douai: "The Committee (of Public Safety) has done justice to the brigade commander Bouquet by rendering him the command of the 13th Regiment of Light Cavalry that had been taken from him in favour of St-Georges. It is important that the Committee should immediately take steps to transfer St-Georges elsewhere and that he should no longer remain with the corps. That would have the worst effect."[15]

---

[13] St-George dossier, loc. cit.

[14] Letter of 13 Fructidor Year III = 1 September 1795, St-George dossier, loc. cit.

[15] St-George dossier, loc. cit.

ARMÉE
DE
L'INTÉRIEUR,
&
FORCE ARMÉE
DE PARIS.

ÉGALITÉ LIBERTÉ.

Paris, *Ce ... vendémiaire* l'an *... de* la République française une et indivisible.

DES REPRÉSENTANS DU PEUPLE,

Chargés de la direction et de la surveillance de la Force armée de Paris, et de l'Armée de l'Intérieur,

The letter of Goupilleau de Fontenay, the People's Representative
with the Army of the Interior (10.10.1795):
"...St.George should no longer remain with the corps".
Archives Administratives, Ministère de la Guerre, Vincennes

This communication was sent to the 9th Commission the next day, with the order to recommend "another destination for the citizen St-Georges" within twenty-four hours.[16] On 19 October 1795, Commissar L. A. Pille proposed the appointment of St-George as brigade commander with the 11th Regiment of Dragoons, in succession to Colonel Neuilly.[17]

St-George's eventual defeat - by a paragraph!

But the Committee of Public Safety decided otherwise. It decided on 30 October 1795 (8 Brumaire Year IV) that "In view of Article 15 of the law of the 3rd of this month (25 October) which dismisses the citizen St-George, there is no room for further deliberation."[18] This was a completely new law inspired by reaction to the royalist riots of 13 Vendémiaire (4 October 1795), and it stipulated in Article 15 that all officers who were not serving on 5 April 1795 (15 Germinal) and who had been appointed to their posts between this date and 2 August 1795 should be suspended. This was a pretty arbitary dispensation and was designed to exclude from the army any royalist elements who had infiltrated their way into the military hierarchy during the period in question.[19] The fact is that after 4 October 1795 the wind had changed again in France and it was now on the threshold of the Napoleonic era. On 26 October 1795 a new government was appointed, the Directory, under which the country was to become a bourgeois republic before becoming Bonaparte's Empire.

The law of 25 October became the instrument of our colonel's final downfall. Contrary to the proposal of Commissar Pille, he was not transferred elsewhere but permanently suspended.

What a blow for St-George! Of course it was by no means the first in his troubled life, but to us it seems particularly painful. After all his conflicts,

---

[16] Note on the previous document

[17] Report to the Committee of Public Safety of 28 Vendémiaire Year 4, St-George dossier, loc. cit.

[18] Written at the bottom of this report.

[19] O. Denys, *op. cit.*, pp. 154-56.

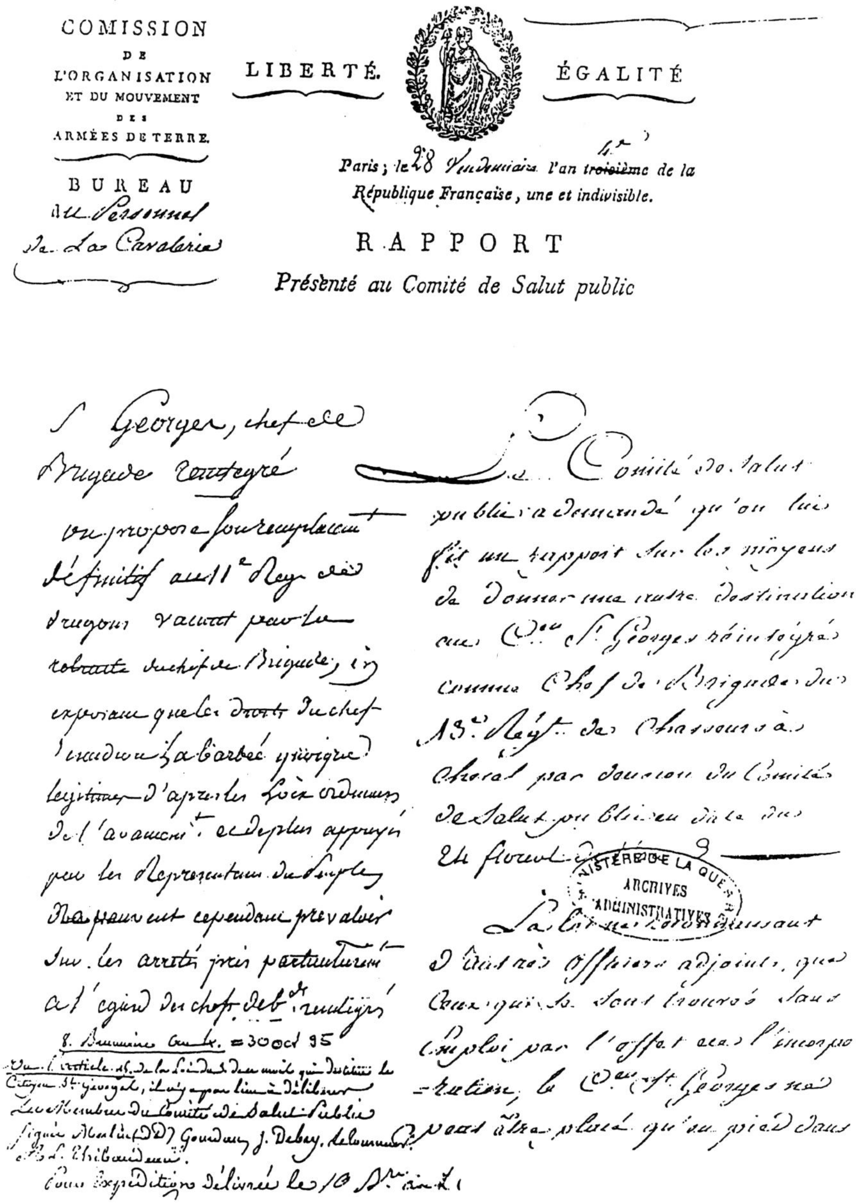

COMISSION DE L'ORGANISATION ET DU MOUVEMENT DES ARMÉES DE TERRE.

BUREAU du Personnel de la Cavalerie

LIBERTÉ. ÉGALITÉ

Paris; le 28 Vendémiaire l'an ~~troisième~~ 4e de la République Française, une et indivisible.

RAPPORT

Présènté au Comité de Salut public

St Georges, chef de Brigade réintégré

On propose son remplacement définitif au 11e Regt de dragons vacant par la retraite du chef de Brigade, en exposant que les droits du chef d'escadron Labarbée quoique légitimes d'après les loix ordinaires de l'avancement et de plus appuyés par les Représentans du peuple, ne peuvent cependant prévaloir sur les arrêtés pris particulièrement à l'égard des chefs de bde réintégrés.

8 Brumaire an 4e = 30 oct 95

Vu l'article 16 de la Loi du 3 de ce mois qui destitue le Citoyen St-George, il n'y a pas lieu à délibérer. Les Membres du Comité de Salut Public signé Merlin (DD) Gourdan J. Debry, Letourneur, A. C. Thibaudeau.

Pour expédition délivrée le 10 Bre an 4.

Le Comité de Salut public a demandé qu'on lui fît un rapport sur les moyens de donner une autre destination au Cen St Georges réintégré comme Chef de Brigade du 13e Regt de Chasseurs à cheval par décision du Comité de Salut public en date du 24 floréal an 3.

La Con ne connaissant d'autres Officiers adjoints que ceux qui se sont trouvés sans emploi par l'effet de l'incorporation, le Cen St Georges ne peut être placé qu'au pied dans

MINISTÈRE DE LA GUERRE ARCHIVES ADMINISTRATIVES

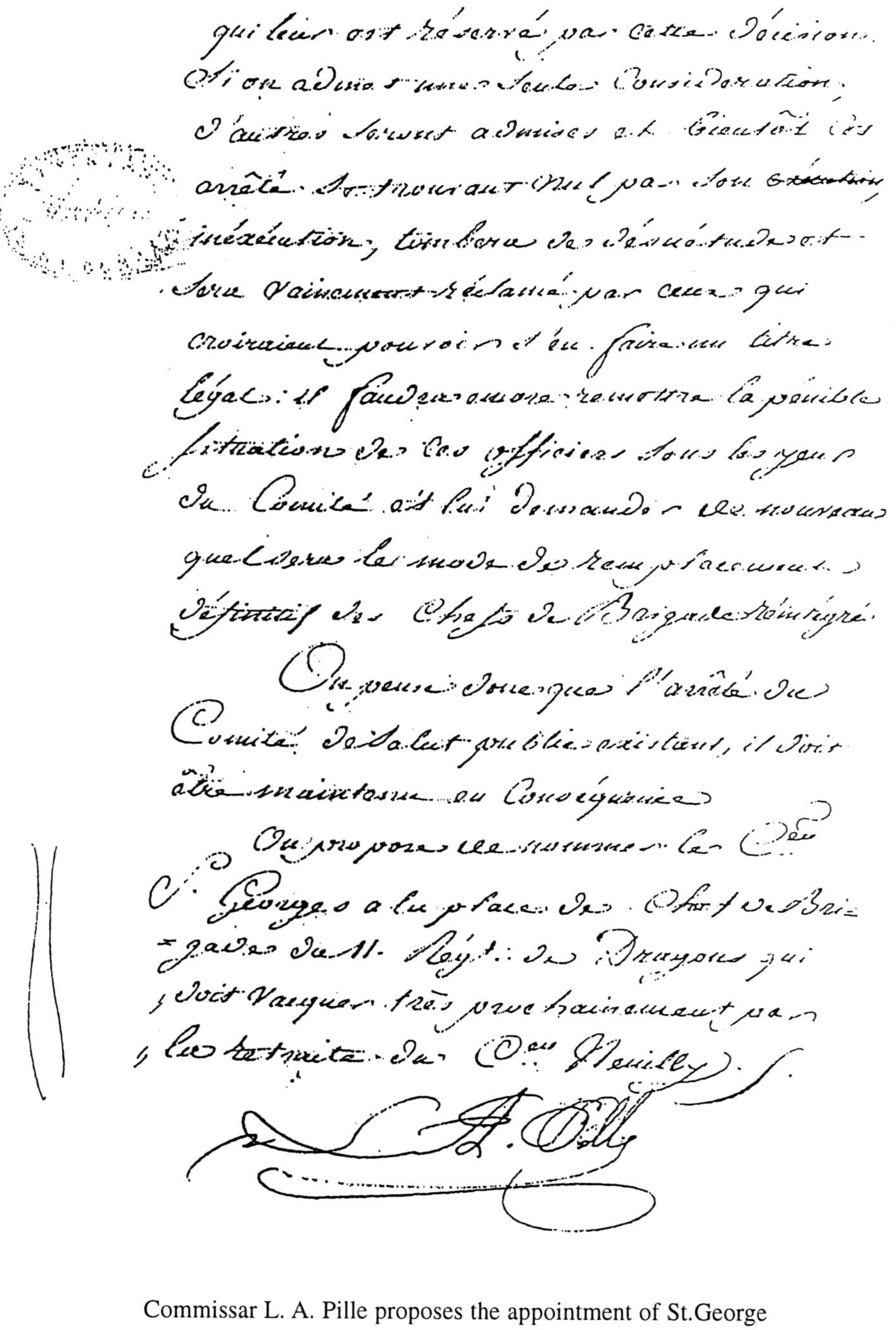
qui leur ont réservé par cette décision.
Si on admet une seule considération
d'autres seront admises et bientôt cet
arrêté demeurant nul par son ~~exécution~~
inexécution, tombera en désuétude et
sera vainement réclamé par ceux qui
croiraient pouvoir en faire un titre
légal: il faudrait alors remettre la pénible
situation de ces officiers sous les yeux
du Comité et lui demander de nouveau
quel serait le mode de remplacement
définitif des Chefs de Brigade réintégrés.

On pense donc que l'arrêté du
Comité de Salut public existant, il doit
être maintenu en conséquence.

On propose de nommer le Cen
St. Georges à la place de Chef de Bri-
=gade du 11. Régt. de Dragons qui
doit vaquer très prochainement par
la retraite du Cen Fleuilly.

L. A. Pille

Commissar L. A. Pille proposes the appointment of St.George
as brigade commander with the 11th Regiment of Dragoons (19.10.1795),
Archives Administratives, Ministère de la Guerre, Vincennes

St-George -the celebrated St-George - was beaten by bureaucracy! Not by the enemy, not by an adversary worthy of him, but by a stupid little point of drafting. We leave it to the reader to imagine St-George's feelings in the circumstances.

In these last chapters we have made the acquaintance of a different St-George - the officer and commander. And perhaps the reader will have asked himself if he is really dealing with the same man whom he met at the beginning. There is such a change in the setting, tone and role of the character. That is precisely what is special about St-George - this diversity in the aspects of his personality that allowed him to feel equally at ease in a concert hall, on the conductor's stand, in the salons of high society, among fencing champions and in a revolutionary army. Whereas it would be unthinkable, for instance, to say "Colonel Mozart" or "Colonel Haydn", this multiplicity of roles was perfectly natural for St-George.

XIII. RETURN TO THE WEST INDIES - TOUSSAINT LOUVERTURE

St-George in St-Domingue

According to the decree of 30 October 1795 by the Committee of Public Safety, St-George had to leave the 13th Regiment and "withdraw to any other commune but the one where the regiment is stationed at present."[1] But return to civilian life seems to have been difficult for him, especially as in the islands of his childhood, the French West Indies, the fight for the Republic and for liberty was at its height.

St-George therefore embarked for Haiti (then the French colony of St-Domingue) in the company of his old friend Lamothe. Louise Fusil tells us about this voyage[2] but does not mention the date. According to Odet Denys[3], the two men of arms left some five months after St-George's second dismissal, with the official mission that the Directory sent to the island in the spring of 1796. This mission comprised the Commissars Sonthonax, Giraud, Leblanc, Roume and Raimond - the last being none other than the mulatto Julien Raimond whom we have already met at the time when the St-George Legion was founded. The Commissars landed at Le Cap on 11 May 1796. They took with them 30,000 muskets to rearm the troops of Haiti and enable them to fight more effectively against the British, who were blockading the Dominican coasts.[4]

We possess no precise details as to St-George's stay in Haiti, which seems to have lasted about a year, from the spring of 1796 to the spring of 1797. But we can at least place it in its historical context by briefly recapitulating the events in the colony of St-Domingue before and during this period. These events were marked by the emergence of that other black hero of the eighteenth century, Toussaint Louverture. This also gives us the opportunity to recount the life of this extraordinary personage, whom St-George must have met.

---

[1] Extract from the records of the Committee of Public Safety, 8 Brumaire Year IV, quoted by La Laurencie, *op. cit.*, p. 483.

[2] Fusil, *op. cit.*, p. 128.

[3] O. Denys, *op. cit.*, p. 161.

[4] Schoelcher, *Vie de Toussaint Louverture,* original edition by P. Ollendorf, Paris, 1889, éditions Karthala, Paris, 1982, pp. 178-79.

Retrospective - the liberation of the slaves in 1793

On 20 August 1793 the civil commissar Sonthonax, who had been sent to St-Domingue by the revolutionary government of France, proclaimed the liberty of the slaves throughout the territory of this colony. This historic event took place in the course of a solemn ceremony in the town of Le Cap and it was greeted by the slaves with delirious joy.

The action of Sonthonax was motivated above all by the disastrous situation prevailing in the "pearl of the French West Indies" at the time. A civil war had been raging for two years between the colonists opposed to the Revolution on the one hand and the mulattos and enfranchised negroes on the other; the latter were fighting for the introduction of the civil rights that the revolutionary régime had granted them. The economic ruin brought about by the civil war was exacerbated by constant Spanish incursions on French territory and the threat of a British invasion.

Landing of the British

The anti-revolutionary colonists had indeed made contact with Britain to obtain her support against the Revolution, and had promised her that they would surrender the Dominican ports that they controlled. Confronted with this state of affairs, Sonthonax judged that the liberation of the slaves was the only way to defeat the reactionaries, for the slaves comprised the overwhelming majority of the population of St-Domingue - 700,000 as against 40,000 whites in 1789.[5] (The Convention in Paris was to declare the general abolition of slavery in all French colonies some months later, on 4 February 1794.)

Only three weeks after Sonthonax's action, the British landed on St-Domingue, with the stated intention of restoring the conditions existing before the Revolution, in other words, of abolishing the Republic and reintroducing slavery. With Britain in command of the seas and most of the island's ports, the republican troops' attempts to repulse this invasion were doomed to failure, for all supplies from outside were cut off.

In the spring of 1794 a British victory seemed inevitable, bringing with it the fall of the Republic in the colony and the return of slavery.

---

[5] Schoelcher, *op. cit.*, p. 1.

Toussaint Louverture (portrait), Schoelcher, Vie de Toussaint Louverture,
original edition by P. Ollendorf, Paris, 1889, Editions Karthala, Paris, 1982

Toussaint Louverture appears on the scene
It was at this point that Toussaint appeared on the scene. He was to be called "L'ouverture" later because he opened the way to a new future and the rehabilitation of the negroes. On 6 May 1794 he came forward at the head of four thousand well-armed and disciplined black soldiers to offer his services for the salvation of the Republic and the freedom it had brought to the slaves. Who was this man?

In appearance "nothing but an old nigger", a former slave, rather weak in health, with a face that contemporaries found ugly. But the outward appearance concealed a burning endeavour, a lively intelligence and the soul of a great man entirely devoted to the cause of raising his people from the degradation into which slavery had plunged them. He was so much to epitomise this cause that Lamartine later said of him, "This man is a nation."

Like St-George, Toussaint was chosen by destiny to demonstrate to the world of the whites the vanity of its prejudices against black humanity. What the former accomplished by his artistic genius the latter was to accomplish by his military and political genius. Both of them were distinguished by the moral quality of a heart that is strong, simple and without guile; and it was this quality that enabled them to bear the contempt shown to their colour - the one with dignity, the other with grace.

Biographical sketch
Toussaint was born on 20 May 1743 on the Bréda estate at Haut-du-Cap. According to tradition, he was descended from an African prince named Giaou-Guinou. But prince or no, he was born into slavery. When he was old enough to work he first served as a stable boy. His master, Bayon de Libertat, was the manager of the estate and he singled out Toussaint and appointed him coachman, one of the highest jobs in the slave hierarchy.[6] According to recent research, Toussaint was enfranchised by his master around 1769, at the age of twenty-six. He would then have cultivated some land in his own right, enjoyed certain advantages and employed a few slaves himself.[7] He married a negress, Suzanne Simon, and adopted

---

[6] D. Bellegarde, *Histoire du Peuple Haïtien,* Port-au-Prince, 1953, p. 71.

[7] Schoelcher, *op. cit.,* introduction by J.Adelaide-Merlande to the edition of 1982, p. XVIII.

her son, a mulatto named Placide. His wife also bore him a legitimate son, Isaac, who was black like himself.

After he had passed forty, he conceived a burning desire to educate himself. He studied with an old negro, his godfather Pierre Baptiste. Toussaint had been christened and remained loyal to his religion throughout his life. After learning to read and write, he is said to have become an assiduous reader of the philosophical and humanitarian works of Abbé Raynal, as well as several classical authors such as Herodotus and Caesar.[8]

Toussaint seems to have taken no part in the bloody slave uprising led by the negro Boukman in August 1791; he even protected his former master's family from the rebels.[9] This revolt was provoked by an excess of violence shown to the slaves by some of the colonists, and turned into a terrible and indiscriminate massacre of white settlers.

But in November of the same year, at the age of forty-eight, he joined a band of runaway slaves that had unleashed a long guerilla war against the white colonists of the North, using hidden bases in the mountains of the Spanish portion of the island. Toussaint soon achieved dominance over these fierce men and turned them into disciplined soldiers who were well-armed and devoted to him unto death. In 1793 he entered the service of the Spanish army, which gave him arms and munitions, and he swiftly became one of its ablest commanders.

When the new governor of French and Republican St-Domingue, General Lavaux, found himself face to face with the disastrous situation of spring 1794, he decided to write to Toussaint secretly and ask for his help. So it was that on 6 May of that year the black warrior rallied to the French flag, on which were henceforth inscribed the principles of liberty, equality and fraternity.

The reconquest of St-Domingue for the Republic

This flag Toussaint raised first in all the communes of the North-East where, thanks to the support of the black troops, the Spanish had established themselves. After that, he energetically set about the task of recovering the places seized by the British in the Artibonite and the North.

---

[8] Bellegarde, *op. cit.*, p. 71.

[9] Schoelcher, *op. cit.*, p. 89.

His success amazed Lavaux, who put him in command of all the recaptured territory. He amazed the governor even more with his organising ability and the wisdom of his advice.

To reward his services, on 23 July 1795 the National Convention promoted Toussaint, now 53 years old, to the rank of brigadier-general. This was the first time for France so to honour someone who was not a half-caste but pure black. On the eve of the nomination, the Convention had heard a very eulogistic report on Toussaint, in which Commissar Defermont said among other things: "He is an intrepid and obedient soldier. He is an enterprising commander. Nothing is more fitting than his conduct to obviate the prejudices levelled at men of his colour."[10]

Governor Lavaux himself, who soon formed a close friendship with Toussaint, leaves us the following account. On a tour of inspection in the West of the island, he writes in November 1794, "I wanted to visit this brave man's posts. When I arrived at La Marmelade, an important district of St-Domingue, all the inhabitants but particularly the whites never tired in their praise of Toussaint's virtues because he rendered his services to all, regardless of persuasion or colour...I asked him to meet me at Dondon and I had cause to praise his intelligence in the disposition of his posts, the discipline of his troops and the selection of his senior officers he presented to me... The parish of Petite-Rivière afforded us the gratifying sight of more than 15,000 farmers, who had returned full of gratitude towards the Republic. Blacks, whites, mulattos, military, farmers, land-owners - all blessed the virtuous leader whose good offices kept order and peace among them.[11]

Blacks and mulattos - alliance and discord

Toussaint was not alone in preventing St-Domingue becoming a British colony and returning to the slave system. Generals Rigaud, Beauvais and Villatte played an important part too.

All the battles were fought in the most difficult conditions, and the troops suffered widespread privations. The British blockade stopped any supplies coming from France, and the soldiers lacked muskets, munitions and often even clothing and food. In spite of these hardships, negroes and mulattos were united as the sole defenders of St-Domingue and they kept up their

---

[10] Quoted by Schoelcher, *op. cit.*, p. 120.

[11] ibid., p. 109.

resistance with great courage. Their courage was duly honoured by the Convention when it was apprised by Commissar Defermont in these terms: "These negroes and mulattos have gloriously lived up to the title of Frenchmen. Reduced to their own resources, deprived of all assistance and almost without ammunition, they fought courageously and were never beaten in spite of all their tribulations. They battled with energy, honour, perseverance and success against the Spanish and the English." In recognition of this the Convention decreed on 25 July 1795 that "the men armed for the defence of the Republic in the colony of St-Domingue have deserved well of their country".[12]

But while the struggle against the common enemy united mulattos and negroes, the conflict between them remained below the surface as the heritage of racism and slavery. By imposing a differentiation of value between white and black, the racist ideology had inevitably managed to attribute higher value to individuals containing some "white blood" than to those containing none. The ideology even traced learned distinctions in this privileged class, depending on whether their "white blood" amounted to 25, 50 or 75 per cent. This hierarchy of skin colour was almost like a veterinary assessment, and it was reinforced by law and social convention so that in the end it made a deep imprint on the consciousness of the non-whites themselves. The half-castes had come to consider themselves superior to the blacks, and this feeling was confirmed in their legal status. This was in many cases initially that of enfranchised slave with certain property rights - including ownership of slaves -but it later became that of French citizen in the course of the Revolution. The category of the emancipated did of course also include blacks but, as enfranchisement occurred much more often with those of mixed blood, racially pure blacks were a minority.

In the second half of the eighteenth century the mulattos on St-Domingue had become a fairly powerful social class; despised and without civil rights though they were, they owned land and slaves. When the Revolution broke out, this class of owners fought for its rights and used the blacks as auxiliaries in the struggle. The abolition of slavery did not in the beginning strike them as at all desirable because it removed one of their property rights. Though they were victims of the slave system they ended

---

[12] Schoelcher, *op. cit.*, p. 119.

Toussaint Louverture, Bibliothèque Nationale, Paris

up defending it, and that was the Machiavellian intention of earlier white legislators, who wanted to make a bulwark against the mass of black slaves out of the intermediate category of half-castes. Some of these went so far as to ally themselves with the white colonists to defend the old order of things. Even though acts of betrayal of this kind were the exception, there were nevertheless many half-castes who took a hostile view of the liberation of the slaves proclaimed by Sonthonax in August 1793 and of black access to jobs in the administration and the army.

Mulatto uprising at Le Cap - Toussaint's intervention
The latent conflict erupted on 20 March 1796 when the mulattos of Le Cap, angry at Governor Lavaux's "negrophilia" and accusing him of too often preferring blacks to half-castes, seized him and carried him off to prison. They proclaimed the mulatto general Villatte the new governor of St-Domingue.

But the black officers loyal to the governor sent news of the arrest to Toussaint at Gonaïves, about 130 kilometres from Le Cap. Shortly before, the black general, on being informed about the spirit of revolt that reigned among the mulattos of Le Cap, had written them a letter appealing to their good sense: "What is this!" he wrote, "You are surrounded by enemies on all sides and have been weighed down with every kind of evil for the last four years, and yet you want to stir up new troubles and cause a civil war?...Ah, brothers, have the strength to shield yourselves from the poison of those with evil intentions, distrust the wicked...Would it not be infinitely better to live together like brothers in mutual love, and to concentrate on destroying and driving off our enemies?"[13]

When he saw that his appeal for conciliation had not been heeded, Toussaint decided on sterner measures. He at once dispatched two batallions and 800 horsemen towards Le Cap, but sent an ultimatum in advance. This at least had the effect of freeing the governor, but the rebellion went on. Villatte's supporters spread the rumour that Lavaux had ordered in two ships loaded with chains to put the negroes back in irons. The black soldiers who had run to help the governor immediately rushed to his residence crying out for his head. Lavaux was about to be slaughtered when Toussaint arrived and confronted the mob. He conducted them to the

---

[13] Quoted by Schoelcher, *op. cit.*, pp. 159-160.

port entrepot, opened the gates and let them convince themselves there were no chains. Thereupon things calmed down. Villatte, realising that he did not have the strength to take on Toussaint's troops, left the island and sought refuge in France.

"A black Spartacus - the negro foreseen by Raynal"

As for the liberated governor, who owed his life simply to Toussaint's intervention, he expressed his gratitude by appointing him major-general and Lieutenant-Governor of Saint-Domingue, and he declared that henceforth he would act only in concert with him. This appointment was announced with great ceremony on 1 April 1796 on the Le Cap parade-ground before an assemblage of the people and the army. Lavaux there proclaimed Toussaint "saviour of the legal authorities, a black Spartacus, the negro foreseen by Raynal who would avenge the outrages committed against his race."[14]

Raynal's prediction to which Lavaux was referring was couched in the following terms: "Nations of Europe, your slaves will break the sacrilegious yoke that oppresses them... All the negroes need is a leader... Where is this great man? He will emerge, without any doubt, and raise the sacred standard of liberty. This hallowed signal will gather round him his companions in misfortune. Fiercer than a mighty river, they will leave behind them on all sides the indelible traces of their just resentment...The old world will add its acclaim to that of the new, and all will bless the name of the hero who has restored the rights of the human race!"[15]

However, for the present, before he could gather all his companions in misfortune round the standard of liberty Toussaint had to quell the divisive forces raging between negroes and mulattos. To achieve this, he always started by employing the means of persuasion, and it was only when they failed that he resorted to disciplinary measures.

On 14 April 1796 he wrote to Lavaux: "Since yesterday I been back at Gros-Morne. Together with the municipal officials, I held a review of the volunteer troops and the National Guard. I have also mustered most of the planters and estate managers. I read them your proclamations, and they were satisfied. I preached Christian teaching to them. I gave them a glim-

---

[14] Quoted by Schoelcher, *op. cit.*, p. 172.

[15] Quoted by Schoelcher, *op. cit.*, p. 173.

pse of the evil being prepared for them by the enemies of freedom in their attempts to mislead them. They digested the truths I told them, and we need have no more fear that they will be deceived."[16]

Appeal for responsibility

In a proclamation a few weeks later, when there were disturbances in the parishes of St-Louis-du-Nord, he said: "O, my African brothers! You who have caused me so much weariness, work and misery, you whose freedom is sealed with half of your purest blood! How long must I suffer the pain of seeing my lost children shun the advice of a father who adores them?" Referring to excesses perpetrated against the settlers, he said in the same speech: "But, brothers and sisters, you are not capable of these atrocities on your own, I know. Monsters soaked in crime are trying to drag you after them to their precipice so that they will not be alone in the wild." And he concluded with this appeal for responsibility: "Never forget, my brothers, that there are more blacks in the colony than there are coloured folk and white men together, and that if disturbances arise the Republic will blame us, the blacks, because we are the strongest and it is up to us to keep law and order by setting a good example. I am responsible for everything that happens because I am in charge, and what account could I render to France, which has showered its benefits on us, if you cease to listen to the voice of reason?"[17]

This reminder of duty was to be a constant theme of Toussaint's public speeches. For the black population of the colonies, so long accustomed to being at the mercy of their white masters' cruel abuse of power, it was a hard lesson to learn. So their leader had to repeat it often. And as the country's economic ruin demanded hard work and an efficient administration, he often had to remind the people that liberty did not mean licence and idleness; but his orders forcing citizens to work in the fields gave his adversaries of all colours the pretext to bring the most absurd accusations against him, such as that he wanted to reintroduce slavery. "All the hatred of the wicked," he wrote to Governor Lavaux on 11 May 1796, "is

---

[16] ibid., p. 174.

[17] Schoelcher, *op. cit.*, p. 175.

directed against me. Let them attack me as often as they will. I don't care, I'm not afraid of them."[18]

The arrival of the new commissars from Paris

On the same 11 May 1796 the commissars from Paris landed at Le Cap, among them - if Odet Denys is right - St-George. Though we do not have precise information on his stay in St-Domingue, we do have the testimony of Louise Fusil's pen as to certain rumours going round Paris to the effect that he and Lamothe had been caught up in a riot in the colony.[19] Now, the main event during the period of his stay on the island was indeed a riot in the South, and we may assume that in one way or another St-George was involved in these events, especially as they had a direct connection with the business of the commissars from Paris.

Rigaud's mulatto dictatorship in the South

For some time the province of the South had enjoyed a kind of independence from the authorities of the colony. The mulatto general Rigaud held sway there over a population consisting for the most part of citizens of his own colour. As we have said, after the uprising at Le Cap in March 1796 many mulattos had come and taken their stand under the orders of Rigaud. He, according to Schoelcher, pursued the idea of caste like a passion. Almost all public offices were in the hands of half-castes, while the negroes were relegated to the work- place.

In order to remedy this state of affairs and restore the government's authority in the South, the new civil commissars dispatched a delegation to this province in June 1796. The report it produced on its visit was a veritable act of indictment against Rigaud. Having arrogated the title of governor-general to himself, he administered the country through the army, in which the blacks occupied only subordinate posts. What was even worse, the report said, was that slavery actually still existed there, and the blacks had shown the delegates "the prisons, the irons and the

---

[18] ibid., p. 177. All these quotations come from the voluminous correspondence between Toussaint and Lavaux in the several-volume dossier "Papiers de St-Domingue", kept in the Paris National Library and used by Schoelcher.

[19] Fusil, *op. cit.*, p. 128.

suffering that were their lot."[20] In a confidential message to Julien Raimond, Rigaud justified the prisons as "houses of correction for the punishment of farmers who left their work to become brigands".[21] In fact, the whites of the South were deprived of all civil rights.

Liberty was certainly no easy matter, and coloured people like Raimond and St-George, trained in the idealistic revolutionary school of France, far from the racial hatreds of the colonies, must have been horrified at the way their confrères treated the lofty principle of the equality of all citizens.

The delegates broke the farmers' chains, abolished the prisons and set up a commission of enquiry to determine the reasons for the detention of some 900 black and white citizens.

Rebellion against the commissars at Les Cayes

These measures provoked the mulattos to rebellion, and on 31 August they surrounded the delegates' house at Les Cayes. There were massacres in the streets and white people were executed at the Fort of Islet. The delegates were powerless to stop the revolt and in the end surrendered all their authority into the hands of Rigaud. He was to stay the undisputed master of the South until 1799. Altogether, some 300 people died at this terrible time.

It is possible that St-George accompanied these delegates. That would explain the rumours mentioned by Louise Fusil, but there is no evidence of this. On 17 August 1796 the Directory confirmed the appointment of Toussaint Louverture to the rank of major-general. In the same decree it gave its agreement that Toussaint's two sons should be sent to France in order to "undergo instruction and education at government expense".[22] At the beginning of 1797, these children - one a mulatto and the other black - left St-Domingue on board the "Watigny", a vessel capable of slipping through the British blockade. They arrived in Paris in February 1797, and about the same time we find St-George there too.

Did he make the voyage with them? We do not know, but what seems certain is that he returned to France distraught, broken and perhaps already ill. We shall relate the last two years of his life in the next chapter. For the

---

[20] Page 27 of the report, quoted by Schoelcher, *op. cit.*, p.204. The complete report is among the Papers of St-Domingue.

[21] Quoted by Schoelcher, *op. cit.*, p. 205.

[22] Schoelcher, *op. cit.*, p. 178.

moment, let us return to St-Domingue and resume the story of Toussaint Louverture's life.

A Bonapartist governor - intrigues against Toussaint

In the spring of 1797 Toussaint finally succeeded in driving the British from Le Mirebalais and recovering the Artibonite line from them. As a reward he was appointed general in command of the army. He was then 54 years old. A few months later, however, following the coup d'état of 4 September (18 Fructidor), the Directory in Paris came under the control of Napoleon Bonaparte. Napoleon detested the egalitarian principles of the Revolution, and the fame of the black general was intolerable to him because it was a blemish on his own. At the Council of the Five Hundred disturbing speeches were heard, and there was even talk of restoring slavery in the colonies. In April 1798 General Hédouville was sent to St-Domingue as the new governor, with the secret mission of destroying Toussaint's paramount authority. To accomplish this, Hédouville decided to use the mulatto general Rigaud, who was still completely in command in the South.

Remorselessly the governor schemed to set the two men against one another so as to weaken the position of both. Toussaint was the more perceptive and guessed Hédouville's game. He tried to alert Rigaud to the Machiavellian wiles of the Bonapartist governor; but the governor had the last word. When a riot forced him to leave the colony precipitately in October 1798, he cunningly tossed behind him the apple of discord that would unleash on St-Domingue the most terrible of its civil wars - he wrote to Rigaud releasing him from all obedience to Toussaint.[23]

Toussaint's entry to Port-au-Prince

But the storm did not break out until the British had finally left the island. In May 1798 Toussaint took the important town of Port-au-Prince from them, and his entry there, after the capitulation of the British troops, deserves to be narrated.

In order to avoid reprisals and to spare the inhabitants, Toussaint had allowed the foreign occupiers to withdraw before his own army entered the city. He entered on 15 May to the acclamations of the entire population,

---

[23] Bellegarde, *op. cit.*, p. 73 ff.

who had erected triumphal arches along his route. The settlers went to receive him with crosses, flags and censers.

They asked him to sit under a canopy carried by the four most important of the island's planters. But old Toussaint, with his handkerchief over his head under a three-cornered hat and in his blue uniform without epaulettes, refused these honours, saying: "God is the only one who should walk under a canopy, and it is only to the master of the universe that incense should be offered." When he was informed that it was customary for governors to be received in this style, he replied that it was customary for him to be on horseback and it was thus that he had made his entry into the city.[24]

On 31 August 1798 Toussaint signed an agreement with the British whereby they withdrew completely from the island and were conceded certain commercial advantages for Great Britain. A month later not a single foreign soldier was left on the soil of French St-Domingue, and this was an exploit of which Toussaint had every reason to be proud, for he had achieved it without any help from mainland France.[25]

Toussaint master of the whole island

The problem still had to be solved of the South, which no longer recognised any authority except that of Rigaud. Toussaint launched his campaign to subdue this province in June 1799. This time, however, his habitual wisdom seems to have abandoned him. He underestimated the strength of the hatred between the negro and mulatto "castes " and gave his officers too much freedom of action. Hostilities were conducted brutally and Rigaud's lieutenants were defeated on all sides. The reprisals that followed Toussaint's victory seemed excessive even to the victor. "I gave the order to prune the tree, not to pull it up," he said.[26] Rigaud withdrew to France, where he was subsequently imprisoned by Napoleon. Now that he had control of all the French part of St-Domingue, Toussaint judged the time ripe for the take-over of the Spanish part of the island. This had fallen to France in 1795 by the Treaty of Bâle, the terms of which had not however been executed as yet. On 27 January 1801 he entered

---

[24] Account by Colonel Malenfant, quoted by Schoelcher, *op. cit.*, pp. 228-29.

[25] Schoelcher, *op. cit.*, pp. 230-33.

[26] Quoted by Bellegarde, *op. cit.*, p. 73.

Santo Domingo at the head of an army of 25,000 men and thus unified the whole island under his command.

A constitution for St-Domingue

Toussaint now used the power his position gave him to organise the country, set up schools and promulgate the constitution of 8 July 1801 which included the following provision: "Slavery is banned from this territory and servitude is abolished for ever. All men are born, live and die as free Frenchmen." Article 4 stated: "Every man, whatever his colour, is eligible for every employment." And Article 5: "No other distinction exists but that of merit and ability." The terms of the Constititional Act nominated Toussaint governor-general of St-Domingue for life.[27]

The Napoleonic expedition against Toussaint

Napoleon saw in the promulgation of this constitution a derogation of the authority of metropolitan government, and basically a personal insult, for it was diametrically opposed to his colonial policy. As soon as he had his hands free in Europe, the First Consul equipped a powerful expedition designed to topple Toussaint and get the blacks back to work for the colonists. On 1 February 1802 a fleet of 79 ships with 22,000 men under the command of General Leclerc sailed into the roads of Le Cap.

When he was ordered to surrender, the commander of Le Cap, Henry Christophe, one of Toussaint's most loyal generals, reacted by setting the town on fire, so that when they landed the Napoleonic army found nothing but ruins. This same Henry Christophe was so traumatised by the sudden appearance of the immense enemy fleet on the horizon that he subsequently built the huge fortress of Laferrière 1,000 metres above the plain of Le Cap. This imposing site was intended to ward off any return of the invaders but they never materialised.

Two sons

General Leclerc brought choice hostages with him - Toussaint's two sons. But Toussaint refused to weaken. On 9 February 1802 a memorable event occurred at Ennery, at the foot of the Puylboreau. Toussaint confronted his sons with the choice between taking his side or that of France. Isaac, flesh

---

[27] Bellegarde, *op. cit.*, p. 78.

of his flesh and black like himself, chose France and cried, "I cannot fight the country that has made me a man by giving me the dignity of thought!" Placide, the mulatto, threw himself into Toussaint's arms and said, "I cannot abandon the one who has made me a man by giving me liberty." Their old father embraced them both and praised them, the one for following the urging of his mind and the other for following the urging of his heart. But it was Placide who was the chosen one. Toussaint took him by the hand, presented him to his guard of honour on the parade ground and said to his grenadiers, "This is my son Placide. I appoint him commander. He is ready to die for our cause."[28]

The battle against Napoleon
This was the moment when the war of independence began. By rejecting Leclerc's ultimatum and ordering his troops to fight to uphold the constitution, Toussaint Louverture set himself up on equal terms with Napoleon Bonaparte and cut the knot that had tied St-Domingue to France for 260 years.

Leclerc's troops were better equipped than Toussaint's army and they won several important victories in the first phase of the war. Toussaint well understood that time and the climate were on his side, and he judged it too costly to prolong the fighting there and then. On 5 May 1802 he ordered a halt to operations and withdrew to his residence at Ennery. But this seeming submission was merely a manouevre and while he gave the appearance of being busy with the cultivation of his land he continued to follow events with close attention. The spread of yellow fever in the ranks of Leclerc's army bore out his strategy. But Leclerc for his part had his suspicions of the black general and had him closely watched.

Capture and death of Toussaint
On 7 June 1802 he drew Toussaint into a trap, seized him and put him with his family on a ship with the significant name of "Le Héros". When he set foot on the deck of the ship the old warrior uttered these prophetic words: "By my overthrow all they have achieved in St-Domingue is to cut down

---

[28] Bellegarde, *op. cit.*, p. 79.

the trunk of the tree of black liberty. But it will grow again from the roots, for they are many and go deep."[29]

On landing in France, Toussaint was imprisoned, on Napoleon's orders, in the dungeon of the Fort de Joux in the Jura. There he died on 7 April 1803 and his body was cast in a communal grave.

The final victory

But as he had prophesied, the tree put forth new shoots and by a combination of all their forces the negroes and mulattos went on to gather the fruits of their heroism on the heights of Vertières. The glorious Napoleonic army and its generals Leclerc, Rochambeau and Noailles were defeated by the "coastal people" in November 1803. So, eight months after Toussaint's death, independence was won, and on 1 January 1804 the first black State of the New World was proclaimed under the ancient name of Haiti.

Posterity has placed Toussaint Louverture among the ranks of legendary heroes. Auguste Comte inscribed Toussaint's name in his Positivist calendar, among those like Plato, Charlemagne and Washington whom he considered worthy of replacing the saints of the Gregorian calendar. Lamartine devoted a long dramatic poem to him, Wordsworth honoured him with a sonnet and Chateaubriand in his *Mémoires d'Outre-Tombe* accused Napoleon not only of causing Toussaint's death but also of imitating him in his own life.

Elsewhere the struggle goes on

The black man's victory in Haiti did not mean that the struggle against slavery was concluded, far from it. Toussaint's inspiring strength and the determination of his successors enabled Haiti to affirm and maintain its independence, but this was an exceptional case. In the other French colonies the Revolution's achievements were annulled by Napoleon, who by 1802 had reimposed slavery elsewhere in the French West Indies, Guiana and La Réunion. It was not to be finally abolished here until 27 April 1848, as a result of the energetic and dedicated campaign by the deputy Victor Schoelcher.

---

[29] Bellegarde, *op. cit.*, p. 82.

The first colonial power to abolish slavery in all her possessions was Britain. Thanks to the efforts of William Wilberforce in parliament and to the British abolitionist movement, the slave trade was forbidden to the British from 1808 and slavery itself was abolished in 1833. In the United States slaves were not to be freed until 1865.

We should remember that even if slavery has disappeared from the earth in its most virulent form it still survives in racist feelings, segregation and exploitation. Nor should we forget that in various parts of the world the black man is still fighting for the fundamental rights that belong to him as much as any other human being.

XIV. ST-GEORGE'S DEATH

A meeting in the gardens of the Palais-Royal

By the spring of 1797 Saint-George was back in Paris again. He returned, Odet Denys says, disappointed, mortified and saddened. "He had not found new strength on the soil of his infancy in the Caribbean, nor the zest for life he hoped for. The myth of Antaeus* had not been re-enacted for his benefit. On the contrary, the bloody conflicts he witnessed had left him wounded."[1]

He wandered like a stranger through this Paris of the turn of the century which, after the massacres of the Terror, had turned into a society of fops and belles in their Greek and Roman tunics. Then one day he chanced upon an old acquaintance - Louise Fusil. In her *Souvenirs* the singer gives this account of their reunion:

"I had heard that Saint-Georges and Lamothe had left for St-Domingue when it was in the throes of revolution; the rumour was even put about that they had been hanged during a riot. For quite a time I thought they were dead and I mourned for them. Then one day I was sitting in the gardens of the Palais-Royal with one of my friends and we were both busy reading a newspaper, so that I did not at first notice two persons who were standing in front of me. On raising my eyes I recognised them and let out a cry as if I had seen a couple of ghosts. It was Lamothe and St-Georges! He sang the words:

> I thought you were hanged but here you are at last.
> Where were you these two years that have passed?

'No', I said, 'I did not exactly think you were hanged but certainly dead, and I took you for ghosts.'

'In a way we are because we've come back to this world', they told me."[2]

---

* In Greek mythology Antaeus was a giant who regained his strength every time he touched the earth from which he was born. He was invincible until Hercules killed him by lifting him off the ground

[1] Denys, *op. cit.*, p. 175.

[2] Fusil, *op. cit.*, pp. 128-29.

Pangs of heartbreak

And according to Odet Denys, St-George added, "They didn't hang me but they put an end to me. Since my stay over there I've been looking for myself everywhere but without finding myself."[3]

This sentence is a good illustration of the state of mind in which St-George must have found himself after his return to France. A disorientation seemed to have taken possession of him, a fundamental uncertainty as to his real roots and loyalties. St-George had been born between two worlds and he contained two identities that had been forged by different historical experiences and rendered irreconcilable by colour prejudice. He had always been face to face with the question of identity posed by every human society, but this question had never been so acute and intractable as it was on his return to the West Indies. During his life in Europe, art and the ideal of liberty had been a substitute for roots, and they did not grow out of the soil of one nation or out of one particular colour but were nourished by the aspirations common to all mankind.

Through music and fencing St-George had attained an equilibrium, an integration of opposites, which kept him above any specific sense of belonging, without in any way excluding him from the society in which he lived. Now this equilibrium had been smashed by the experience of St-Domingue: he had been obliged to choose between the opposing interests erected by colonial racialism while at the same time being himself a contributor through force of circumstances. He belonged to the blacks through his mother, the whites through his father and the mulattos through his own personal condition.

St-George seems not to have foreseen this choice, at least not in the agonising form in which it confronted him in the Dominican inferno. However much he fought against it there must have been a kind of rupture within him, and the premature physical disintegration that followed was only the external symptom. In the end, the malignant tumour of racism with all its metastases was too strong for him.

Attempt to return to the army

Having come back to France in this bewildered state of inner deracination, Saint-George turned to the army yet again, hoping to find there a

---

[3] Denys, *op. cit.,* p. 175.

meaningful task that would give his life some purpose again. During his absence the article that had led to his suspension in October 1795 had been rescinded, and this fact encouraged him to claim the restoration of his post in command of the 13th regiment. In April 1797 he wrote this letter to Rewbell, now a member of the Directory, who stamped it with the date of 4 Floréal (24 April 1797):

"George, Commander of the 13th Regiment of Light Cavalry, to citizen Rewbell, one of the members of the Executive Directory:

Citizen,

I commanded the 13th Regiment of Light Cavalry from the time of its inception. Deprived of this position on 29 September '93 (old style) by Minister Bouchot, I was reinstated on 24 Floréal of Year III. But a decree of the following 8 Brumaire ruled that since I was affected by Article 15 of the law of the 3rd of the said month of Brumaire I was obliged to leave the 13th Regiment of Light Cavalry and withdraw to any other commune but the one where the regiment might be at the time.

Article 15 quoted above is one of those rescinded by the law of 14 Frimaire of Year V* of which I attach a copy.

I have constantly demonstrated my loyalty to the Revolution. I have served it since the beginning of the war with a tireless zeal that is undiminished by the persecutions I have suffered. I have no other resource but that of being reinstated in my rank. I address myself to you with confidence, Citizen Director, and I claim from your sense of justice the post of Brigade commander of which I have been deprived on the strength of an article that no longer applies since it has been repealed by a subsequent law.

Greetings and respects,

George."[4]

Let us pick out two points from this letter. The first is that "I have no other resource". At the time St-George wrote his letter he was in a situation from which there seemed to be no escape except through the army to which he had devoted over seven years of his life. The Revolution for which he had fought with "a tireless zeal" had taken all he had, his possessions, his position and - what was even worse for him - his muse. He had not

---

* 14 Frimaire Year V = 4 December 1796.

[4] St-George dossier, loc. cit.

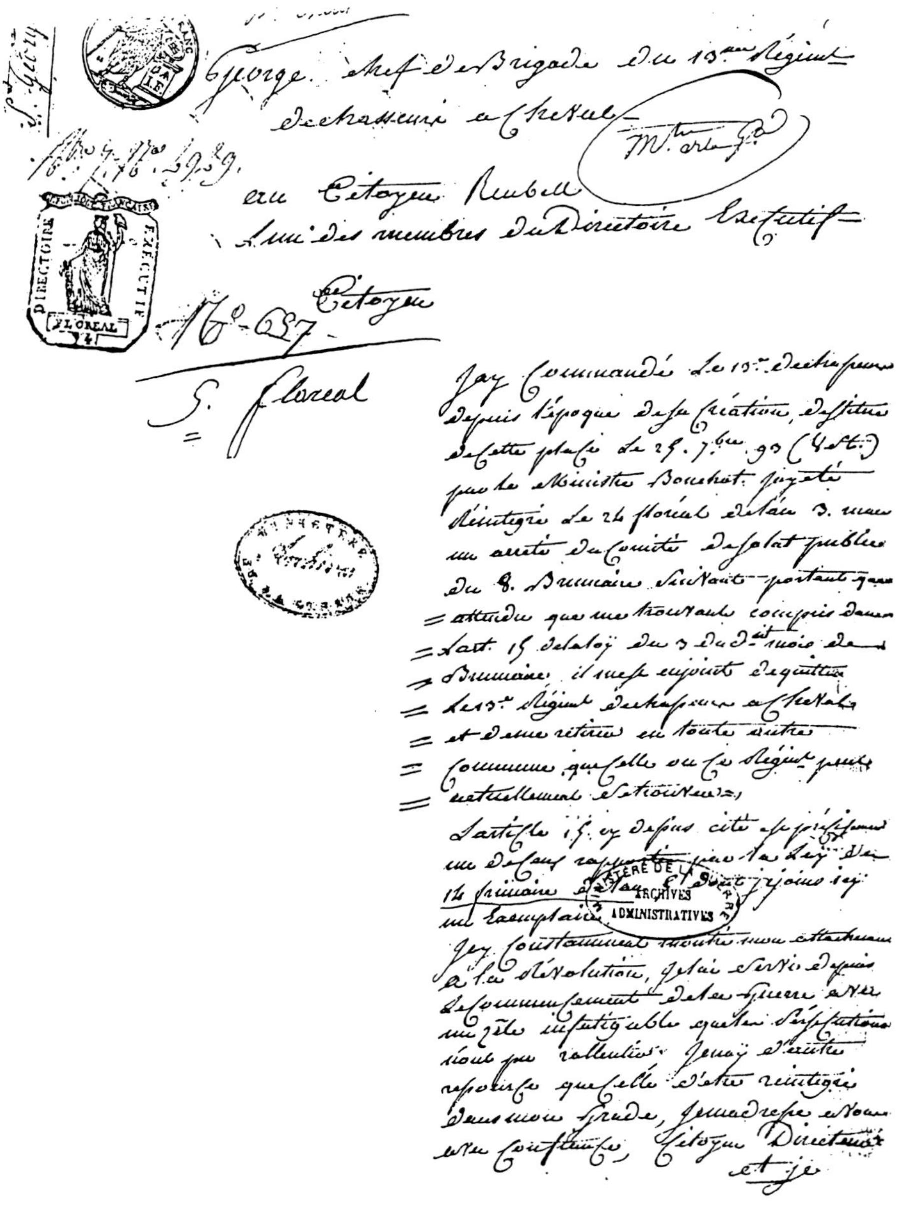

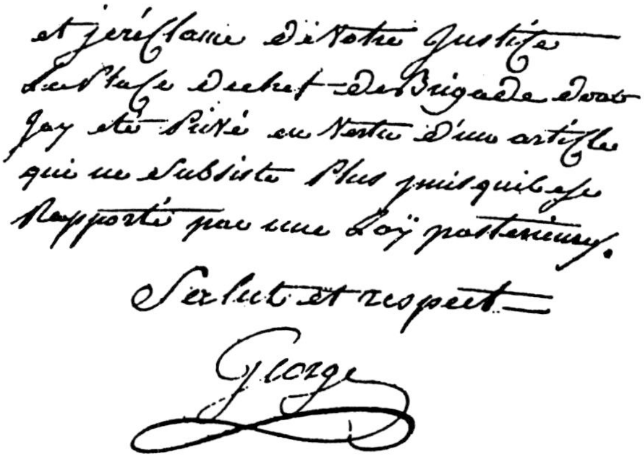
et je reclame de votre Justice
ma place de chef de Brigade dont
Jay été privé en vertu d'un article
qui ne subsiste plus puisqu'il a été
Rapporté par une Loy posterieure.
Salut et respect
George

St.George claims the restoration of his post
in command of the 13th regiment (April 1797),
Archives Administratives, Ministère de la Guerre, Vincennes

composed anything for years, and the spring of his inspiration seemed to
have run dry or been blocked.

The second point is the name he gives himself - George, just that. What is
meant by this reduction? Saint-George no longer exists; the famous Saint-
George, the brilliant violinist, the god of arms, has disappeared - carried
off by the revolutionary whirlwind and destroyed by the fratricidal
hurricane of colonial warfare.

We do not know what reply this letter received. It is possible that it
received none. What is certain is that St-George was not reinstated.

Swan-song

Some of the early biographers of the Chevalier de St-George, notably
Gerber, the author of the article in the *Biographie Michaud*, and Fétis,
wrote that he ended his life in obscurity and poverty. After the research
conducted by La Laurencie, however, we know that at least for a certain
time St-George tried to make a recovery, to fight against the disintegrating
forces that had overcome him and to find his feet again through the art that
was closest to his heart - music.

In the spring of 1797 a society called the "Cercle de l'Harmonie" was
founded at the Palais-Egalité, formerly the Palais-Royal, in the old
apartments of the Duke of Orleans, which brought together "in a
magnificent setting all that talent, games and the arts can offer to make life
agreeable".[5] No one was admitted to this Cercle before going through a
selection procedure. The society also organised concerts, and it was St-
George who took on the direction. He seemed not to have lost his former
gifts, for these concerts, "Le Mercure" assures us, left "nothing to be
desired in the selection of the items and the quality of execution".[6] Perhaps
he began composing again, for in 1799 Pleyel published his last series of
sonatas and airs for the violin.[7] But it is possible that these works were
composed earlier, perhaps at the time of his imprisonment.

---

[5] Mercure français No. 20, 6 February 1797, quoted by La Laurencie, *op. cit.*, p. 485.

[6] ibid.

[7] According to Gerber, *Neues Tonkünstler-Lexikon,* 1812, p. 290

The death of St-George

Be that as it may, these activities, far from being a new beginning, were merely St-George's swan-song, a final blaze of glory. He soon became conscious that he was suffering from a disease of the bladder and, as the author of the *Notice Historique* tells us, "because of his habitual neglect he took little notice; he even concealed an ulcer that was the source of his sickness; gangrene set in and he died on 12 June 1799. He went to his grave accompanied by the regrets of all those who had enjoyed the privilege of his acquaintance."[8]

The register of deaths of the "Archives de la Seine" contains the following entry on St-George's decease: "Saint-Georges Bologne Joseph, sixty years old, 13 Rue Boucherat, unmarried, 22 Prairial Year VII (10 June 1799 - date of death). Nicolas Duhamel, ex-officer, same address (witness). Domicile, Rue de Chartres."[9]

In his book Odet Denys quotes Lamothe as saying: "At his death, there was no knowledge of any family. His father had had a legitimate daughter who figures in 1775 in the register of the 'Bénéfices d'inventaires' of Paris under the name of Elizabeth Bénédictine de Bologne Saint-Georges, but I searched for her in vain. Perhaps she had emigrated, or perhaps she had died. So far as I know she never had anything to do with her half-brother. The beautiful Nanon had long ago taken her silent leave of this world. This man who was once so much sought after and whose numerous letters, which he scrupulously preserved, testify how much he was loved, ended with only Duhamel and myself for companions."[10]

St-George's final place of residence had been in the Rue de Chartres but he died in the Rue Boucherat, the residence of his old companion in arms Nicolas Duhamel, lieutenant in the St-George Legion from its creation and then captain in the 13th Regiment of Chasseurs.[11]

---

[8] La Boëssière, *op. cit.*, p. xxii.

[9] Arch. de la Seine, Fonds des Insinuations (3rd and 6th arrondissments), table no. 39, quoted by La Laurencie, *op. cit.*, p. 487.

[10] O. Denys, *op. cit.*, p. 195. The author indicates as the source of his official information the Archives of the Dép. de la Seine, Registre D 98 39 and DC 6 19, Folio 260, verso.

[11] Descaves, *op. cit.*, pp. 5, 8, 17-19.

The official notice is based on information provided by Duhamel and it gives St-George's age at death as sixty. However, according to his own frequently-quoted statements as to the date of his birth, he was only fifty at the time of his death.

Epilogue

So passed away the man whom La Laurencie called "one of the most unusual and attractive figures from the end of the eighteenth century"[12], a man who was extraordinarily gifted and whose multifarious talents made him like a hero in the classical mode, an embodiment of the ideal "mens sana in corpore sano", a modern Heracles who received his own Shirt of Nessus.*

From another point of view, one may say that thus ended one of the most moving dramas that the world of music has ever known. A composer may be seen simply in relation to his work, and this strictly musicological approach will produce learned analyses, identify influences and establish what in his work is new or is not new. But the man himself, the living reality from which the music sprang and of which it is only a reflection, eludes an approach of this kind.

In eighteenth century Europe there were greater musicians than St-George from a musicological point of view. But were there any greater from the human point of view? None of these composers had to struggle for recognition as a human being. The human condition and human dignity belonged to them from their cradle. None of them bore on his shoulders the burden of a continent abused and a race despised, degraded and treated like cattle. Between them and him the difference is like that existing between a garden flower and a flower on lonely mountain-tops swept by the winds.

At the conclusion of this book we might ask ourselves the question - to whom does Saint-George really belong? To Africa, black America or Europe? We will not perpetuate the conflict that tore Saint-George apart at the end of his life by giving one response rather than another. Rather will we give the answer - to each of them and to all peoples, for the great human epic of which his life was part knows no national or racial frontiers.

* * *

---

[12] La Laurencie, *op. cit.*, p. 487.

* The Shirt of Nessus - Nessus was a centaur whom Heracles shot with a poisoned arrow. The centaur revenged himself by getting Heracles to put on his poisoned tunic. In agony the hero threw himself on a funeral pyre.

The Republican Calendar of the French Revolution

This calendar was introduced by the National Convention on 24 November 1793, and actually took its beginning from 22 September 1792, which was the first day of Year One. The year began with the autumn equinox (22 September) and was divided into 12 months of 30 days each, plus 5 or 6 supplementary days consecrated to the celebration of the republican festivals. Moreover, each month was subdivided into 3 sections of 10 days.

The months of the republican calendar were as follows:
1st month - Vendemiaire   (22 September - 21 October)

2nd month - Brumaire   (22 October 21 November)

3rd month - Frimaire   (21 or 22 November - 20, 21 or 22 December)

4th month - Nivôse   (21, 22 or 23 December - 19, 20 or 21 January)

5th month - Pluviôse   (20, 21 or 22 January - 19, 20 or 21 February)

6th month - Ventôse   (19 February - 20 March)

7th month - Germinal   (21 or 22 March - 18 or 19 April)

8th month - Floréal   (20 or 21 April - 19May)

9th month - Prairial   (20May - 19 June)

10th month - Messidor   (20 June - 19 July)

11th month - Thermidor   (20 July - 18 August)

12th month - Fructidor   (18 or 19 August - 21 September)

(according to Larousse)

BIBLIOGRAPHY

Adams Charles Francis — *The Works of John Adams, Second President of the United States*, Vol. III.,Boston, Charles C. Little and James Brown, 1851.

Angelo Henry — *Angelo's Picnic,* London, 1905. (The biographical abstract of St-George in this book was originally published in H. Angelo, *A treatise on the utility and advantages of fencing,* London, 1817.)

Angelo Henry — *The reminiscences of Henry Angelo,* London, 1828.

Babeau J.F. — *La vie militaire sous l'Ancien Régime,* Paris, Firmin-Didot, 1889-90.

Bachaumont Louis Petit de — *Mémoires secrets pour servir à l'histoire de la République des Lettres en France, depuis 1762 jusqu' à nos jours,* vol. XIV, London, 1779.

Beauvoir Roger de — *Le Chevalier de St-Georges,* Paris, edition Dumont, 1840.

Bellegarde Dante — *Histoire du Peuple Haïtien (1492-1952),* Port-au-Prince, 1953.

Biographie Michaud, Paris, 1811-62

Bluche P. — *La vie quotidienne au temps de Louis XVI,* Paris, Hachette, 1980.

Blume F. — *Musik in Geschichte und Gegenwart,* Leipzig, 1949.

Brenet Michel — *Les Concerts en France sous l'Ancien Régime,* Paris, Librairie Fischbacher, 1900, reprinted New York, Da Capo Press, 1970.

Brook Barry S. — *The Symphonie Concertante* in Musical Quarterly, vol. 47, 1961.

Caix de St-Aymour — *Une famille d'artistes et de financiers aux XVIIe et XVIIIe siècle - Les Boullongne,* Paris, Henris Laurens, editor, 1919.

Castle Egerton	*Schools and Masters of Fence,* London, 1893.
Césaire Aimé	*Cahier d'un retour au pays natal,* Paris, Présence Africaine, 1983.
Cornevin Robert	*Histoire de l'Afrique,* vol. 2, L'Afrique précoloniale, 2nd edition, Payot, Paris, 1976.
Denys Odet	*Qui était le chevalier de St-Georges?,* Paris, Le Pavillon, Roger Maria, editor, 1972.
Descaves P.	*Historique du 13e Régiment de Chasseurs,* Béziers, 1891.
Dumas Alexandre	*Mes Mémoires,* vol. 1, Bruxelles, 1852.
Dumouriez	*Mémoires du Général Dumouriez écrits par lui-même,* Paris, An III de la République (1794/95).
Eon, Charles de	*Mémoires du Chevalier d'Eon,* publ. by F. Gaillardet, Paris, 1836.
Fétis	*Biographie universelle des Musiciens et Bibliographie générale de la musique,* Paris, 1837-44.
Frénilly, Baron de	*Souvenirs du Baron de Frénilly,* Pair de France (1768-1828), publ. by A. Chuquet, Paris, 1908.
Fusil Louise	*Souvenirs d'une actrice,* abridged edition, Paris, Librairie de "l'Art du Théâtre", Charles Schmid, editor, 1903.
Gerber	*Neues historisch-biographisches Tonkünstler Lexikon,* Leipzig, 1812.
Grimm, Meister et al.	*Correspondance littéraire,* 1776-1779.

Grove's Dictionary of Music and Musicians.

Ki-Zerbo Joseph	*Histoire de l'Afrique Noire,* D'hier à demain, Paris, Editions Hatier, 1978.
La Boëssière	*Traité de l'Art des Armes,* 2nd edition, Paris, L'imprimerie de Didot, L'Aîné, 1818. (Original edition was published without historical notes around 1766.)
La Laurencie	*L'Ecole française de violon,* 3 vol., Paris, 1922-24.

Le Bihan A.   *Francs-Maçons parisiens du Grand Orient de France,* collect.: "Mémoires et documents", Paris, ed. of the Bibliothèque Nationale, 1966.

Louis-Philippe   *Mémoires 1773-1793,* 2 vol., Paris, Plon, 1973.

Massin Jean and Brigitte *Wolfgang Amadeus Mozart,* Paris, 1970.

Nouvelle Biographie Générale, 1862.

Pluchon P.   *Histoire des Antilles.*

Riemann Musiklexikon, Paris, 1882.

Robaglia A.   *L'escrime et le duel,* Paris, 1884.

Schoelcher Victor   *Vie de Toussaint Louverture,* original edition by Paul Ollendorf, Paris, 1889, reedition, Editions Karthala, Paris, 1982.

Staël, Mme la Baronne de *Considérations sur les principaux événements de la Révolution Françoise,* Paris, Delaunay, Bossange et Masson, 1818.

St-John Perse   *Eloges,* Paris, Editions Gallimard, 1960.

Archives des DOM-TOM, Paris, dossier Bologne St-George (Series E 37 Archives Nationales); Etat-Civil de Basse-Terre/Guadeloupe.
Archives Administratives du Ministère de la Défense, Paris, dossiers St-George (cote 91/47) et Légion des Américains et du Midi (cote Xkg).
Bibliothèque Nationale, Paris, Département de la Musique.
Goethe-Museum, Düsseldorf - Anton-und-Katharina-Kippenberg-Stiftung, Musikalien.

CATALOGUE OF COMPOSITIONS

SAINT-GEORGES Joseph Boulogne Chevalier de

Source: Répertoire Internationale des Sources
Musicales (RISM), A/1/7, p. 306/307

L'autre jour à l'ombrage. Romance nouvelle ... avec accomp^t de guitare. -
Paris, Imbault.

Il n'est point, disoit mon père (Air de
l'opéra: Ernestine) (in: Journal de Paris,
1777). - *[Paris] s.n., (1777)*

A symphony (D) and six Italian canzonets
for one voice, with an accompanyment for
a piano forte, harpsychord or harp. -
London, author. - P.

(Zuweisung fraglich:) The Mona melodies,
a collection of ancient & original airs of
the Isle of Man, arranged for the voice
with a piano-forte accompaniment. -
London, Mitchell

Op. 1a. Six quators (C,Es, g, c, g, D) à
deux violons, alto et basse ... oeuvre
Ier (1^r livre de quatuor). - *Paris, Sieber;
Lyon, Castaud, (1773).*-St.

Op. 1b. Trois sonates pour le clavecin ou
forte-piano avec accompagnement de violon obligé ... Ier oeuvre de clavecin. -
Paris, Le Duc, (1781).-St.

Op. 2. Deux concerto à violon principal,
premier et second dessus, alto et basse,
hautbois ou flûtes et deux cors ad libitum
...oeuvre IIe. *- Paris, Bailleux (gravés*
par Mme. Annereau, (1773).-St.

- Paris, Bailleux; Lyon; Bordeaux;
Toulouse.

Op.3. Deux concerto (D,C) à violon principal, premier et second (dessus), alto
(premier et second) et basse, hautbois,
flûtes et deux cors ad libitum...oeuvre
IIIe. *- Paris, Bailleux; Lyon, Castaud;*
Bruxelles, Godfroy, (c. 1774).-St.

Op. 4. Concerto (D) à violon principal,
premier et second dessus, alto et basse,
hautbois ou flûtes et deux cors ad libitum
...oeuvre IV. *- Paris, Bailleux; Lyon,*
Castaud; Toulouse, Brunet; Bordeaux;
¨Bruxelles; Lille (gravé par Mme Annereau),
(c. 1775).-St.

Op. 5. Deux concerto à violon principal,
premier et second dessus, alto et basse,
hautbois ou flûtes et deux cors ad libitum
... oeuvre V. *- Paris, Bailleux; Lyon,*
Castaud; Toulouse, Brunet; Bordeaux;
Lille (gravé par Mme. Annereau), (1775).
- St.

Op. 6. Deux simphonies concertantes (C, B) pour deux violons principaux, deux violons ripieno, deux hautbois obligés, deux cors ad libitum, alto et basse, avec un violoncello obligé en suprimant le second violon principal ... oeuvre VI. - *Paris, Bailleux; Lyon, Castaud; Toulouse, Brunet; Bordeaux; Bruxelles; Lille, (1775).* - St.

Op. 7. Deux concerto pour un violon principale, premier et second dessus, alto et basse, deux cors ad libitum...oeuvre VII. - *Paris, Bailleux, Lyon, Castaud; Toulouse, Brunet; Bordeaux; Bruxelles; Lille (gravés par Mme. Annereau), (c. 1777).* - St.

Op. 8. (12 Concertos...). Concerto (Nr. I) à violon principal, premier et second violon, alto et basse, deux hautbois, deux cors. - *Paris, Sieber, (1775).*-St.

- Concerto (C) à violon principal...- *ib., Sieber.*

- Concerto (G) à violon principal...- *ib., Sieber.*

- IXe Concerto pour le violon...oeuvre VIII. - *Paris, Le Duc; Lyon; Bordeaux; Toulouse; Bruxelles (gravé par Mlle Ollivier).*

- Paris, Henry; Lyon; Bordeaux; Toulouse; Bruxelles; Rouen; Caen; Lille (gravé par Mme Lobry).

- Concerto (X) à violon principal, premier et second violon, alto et basse, deux hautbois, deux cors. - *Paris, Sieber.*

- Concerto (XI) à violon principal, premiet et second violon, alto et basse, deux hautbois, deux cors. - *ib., Sieber (1777).*

Op. 9. Second oeuvre de deux symphonies concertantes (C, A) pour deux violons principaux, deux violons ripieno, alto et basse, deux hautbois et deux cors, ad libitum...oeuvre IX. - *Paris, Le Duc (gravées par Mme Lobry).*-St.

- ib., Le Duc (gravées par Mlle Ollivier).

Op. 10. Deux sinfonies concertantes (F, A) à plusieurs instruments. - *Paris, de La Chevardière; Lyon, Castaud; en province, chez tous les marchands de musique (gravées par Huguet), (c. 1778)*-St.

Op. 11. Deux sinfonies (G, D) à plusieurs instruments. - *Paris, de La Chevardière; Lyon, Castaud; Bruxelles, Godefroy; Bordeaux, Bouillon & Saulnier.*-St.

Op. 12. Symphonies concertantes à deux violons principales, premier et second violon, alto et basse ... (N° 12: Es). - *Paris, Sieber. -* St.

Op. 12/13. Deux simphonies concertantes
(Es, G)... - *Paris, Sieber.*

Op. 13. Simphonies concertantes...
(N⁰ 13: G). - *Paris, Sieber.*-St.

Op. 14. Six quatuor concertans (D, B, f,
G, ES, g) pour deux violons, alto et vio-
loncelle...3ᵉ livre de quatuor...oeuvre
XIVᵉ. - *Paris, Boyer, (1785).* St.

(Op.post.1). Six sonates pour le violon
...oeuvre postume, l livre (B, Es, A).-
*Paris, Pleyel (gravées par Richomme),
No. 258*. - P.

- ... oeuvre postume, 2 livre. - ib.,
Pleyel (gravées par Richomme), No. 259.

(Op.post. 2). Concerto (D) à violon principal, deux violons, oboe, cor, alto et
basse... 2ᵉ oeuvre postume. - *Paris,
Pleyel, No, 262, (1799).*-St.

(ohne Opuszahlen:)
Concerto à violon principal, premier et
second violon, oboé, cor, alto et basse. -
*Genève, Henry Scherer; Paris, aux adres-
ses ordinaires de musique.* - St.

Six quartetto concertans (B, G, C, F, G,
B) pour deux violons, alto et basse...
(2ᵉ livre de quatuor). - *Paris, Durieu
(gravés par Mlle. Fleury), (1777).* - St.

Publications of Avenira Foundation

BOOKS:

"Pater Noster" from E. F. Smidak
The book is dedicated to all mothers, who, ever since life has begun on this earth, have to bear the burden of life. In a sense the book is an image of life in its timelessness. - 69 illustrations of artists from all over the world.
English/German/French/Italian   ISBN 3-905112-01-9

"Isaak Ignaz Moscheles 1794-1870 - The life of the Composer and his Encounters with Beethoven, Liszt, Chopin and Mendelssohn"
from E. F. Smidak
English edition   *ISBN 0-85967-821-0*
German edition   *ISBN 3-905112-05-1*

"Smidak Principles" from E. F. Smidak
Action and Re-Action, Power and Responsibility,
Metus - Positive Fear, Ignotum - The Unknown
English edition   *ISBN 3-905112-03-5*

"J'accuse - Environment and Smidak Principles"
from E. F. Smidak
English edition   *ISBN 3-905112-06-X*

"Joseph Boulogne Chevalier de Saint-Georges"
from E. F. Smidak
English edition   *ISBN 3-905112-07-8*
French edition   *ISBN 3-905112-08-6*

"Juan Crisostomo Arriaga 1806-1826" from E. F., Smidak
Czech edition

COMPACT DISCS:

"Isaak-Ignaz Moscheles 1794-1870"
Concerto No. 3 in G minor for Piano and Orchestra, Op. 58
Bonbonnière musicale
Concerto for Flute, Oboe and Orchestra

"Juan Crisostomo Arriaga 1806-1826"
String Quartets No. 1, 2, 3

"Joseph Boulogne Chevalier de Saint-Georges ca 1739-1799"
We are now producing compact discs with the compositions of
Chevalier de Saint-Georges.

FILM:

"Isaak Ignaz Moscheles 1794-1870"
Symphonie Concertante for Flute and Oboe

Avenira Foundation
Haldenstrasse 22
CH-6006 Luzern - Switzerland
Tel: ++41 41 410 95 80
Fax: ++41 41 410 95 81

1312